International Labour Office
Central and Eastern European Team

Pension Reform in Central and Eastern Europe
Volume 1

Restructuring with Privatization:
Case Studies of Hungary and Poland

Edited by Elaine Fultz

Elaine Fultz (editor)
Pension reform in Central and Eastern Europe - Volume 1
Restructuring with Privatization: Case Studies of Hungary and Poland
Budapest, International Labour Office, 2002

ISBN 92-2-112980-2

ILO publications can be obtained through major booksellers or ILO local offices in many countries, or direct from ILO Publications, International Labour Office, CH-1211 Geneva 22, Switzerland. Catalogues or lists of new publications are available free of charge from the above address, or by email: pubvente@ilo.org
Visit our website: www.ilo.org/publns

Printed in Hungary

Table of Contents

TABLES

The Hungarian Pension System Before and After the 1998 Reform

The Polish Pension Reform of 1999

CHARTS

The Hungarian Pension System Before and After the 1998 Reform

The Polish Pension Reform of 1999

FRAMEWORKS

Foreword

This is one of two volumes devoted to pension reform that are appearing as part of a series of studies of social security issues prepared by the ILO project, *Strengthening Social Security in Central and Eastern Europe through Research and Technical Cooperation*, sponsored by the French government. The research component of this project seeks to analyze the restructuring of social security schemes in selected countries of Central and Eastern Europe that has taken place since the political and economic transformation begun in 1989. The studies examine both social policy formation in the region's new multi-party democracies and their early experience in implementing reforms. The broad objective of the research is to provide countries still deliberating reforms with pertinent information on the recent experience and policy results of neighbors addressing similar issues. It is intended as well to empower the government's social partners in their role as participants in making social policy.

The research component of the project focuses predominantly on old age pensions. Other topics are also examined, however, and further volumes will address disability pension reform, the impact of social security reforms on gender equality, and the efficacy of social security reforms in combating social exclusion arising in the wake of the economic transformation. These studies will appear in the spring and summer of 2002.

The two pension volumes (of which this is the first) examine approaches to reform taken by four advanced EU-applicant countries, the Czech Republic, Hungary, Poland, and Slovenia. Hungary and Poland, on the one hand, have enacted major pension reforms that involve privatization of their national pension schemes, replacing them in part with systems of individual savings accounts managed commercially. In the Czech Republic and Slovenia, by contrast, governments have decided to reform their existing public pay-as-you-go systems without privatization. At the same time, they enacted laws that encourage citizens to save for retirement in private pension funds on a voluntary basis. Thus, the two volumes examine distinct policy choices made in a similar regional context.

The questions of key interest in this volume bear on the early challenges of implementing the new privatization laws together with their impact on the pre-existing public pension system and on the adequacy of future pension benefits. Since Hungary and Poland are the most advanced CEE countries in pension privatization, their early experience in this regard is of considerable relevance to neighboring countries and provides an important opportunity for sharing knowledge within the region.

The analysis is provided in three parts: following this section, a Comparative Overview highlights the similarities and differences in the two countries' efforts and experiences. Chapter 1 then provides a detailed case study of the 1998 Hungarian reform, and Chapter 2 provides a similar analysis of the pension restructuring undertaken in Poland in 1999.

Chapter 1 is the work of a team of Hungarian researchers led by Mária Augusztinovics (Institute of Economics, Hungarian Academy of Sciences) and including Róbert I. Gál (TÁRKI Social Research Centre), Ágnes Matits (independent actuary), Levente Máté (Computer and Automation Research Institute, Hungarian Academy of Sciences), András Simonovits (Institute of Economics, Hungarian Academy of Sciences), and János Stahl (State Financial Supervisory Authority). Professor Augusztinovics gave both studies their essential shape in an early outline, as well as integrating the work of the team into a unified whole. Their research effort benefited greatly from expert consultation and data made available by the National Pension Insurance Administration and the State Financial Supervisory Authority of Hungary. The Polish study (Chapter 2) is the work of a single author, Agnieszka Chłoń-Domińczak, of the Gdansk Institute of Market Economics. Ms. Chłoń is also a policy advisor to the Polish Ministry of Labour and participated directly in the formulation of the Polish reform. In making financial projections for the study, she relied on the Institute's Social Budget Model, developed in cooperation with the ILO and the Polish Ministry of Labour and Social Policy. Markus Ruck of ILO CEET gave the studies a final critical review and Mercedes Birck executed the final changes and oversaw the printing process. We acknowledge all these contributions and thank the authors for their excellent research.

In addition, ILO CEET gratefully acknowledges the financial support of the Ministry of Employment and Solidarity of the Government of France. We appreciate its support for strengthening social security in Central and Eastern Europe and particularly value its understanding of the significance of social security for social cohesion.

We at ILO CEET hope that, by casting light on the issues, problems, and challenges encountered in pension restructuring that involves privatization, these studies will help to strengthen pension policy deliberations in all CEE countries and to improve planning and implementation in those which are pursuing reforms along similar lines.

Jean-Pierre Laviec
Director
ILO Budapest

Elaine Fultz
Senior Specialist in Social Security
ILO Budapest

Pension Reform in Hungary and Poland: A Comparative Overview

Elaine Fultz

In the transforming countries of Central and Eastern Europe, pension privatization is often seen as a way of infusing existing pension schemes with positive features. Reliance on private funds managers and markets moved by profit motives would increase efficiency and investment yields, thereby improving workers' well being in retirement. Individualized accounts with private pension funds would increase the transparency of financing and benefit computation. The shift from pay-as-you-go financing to prefunding of pensions would provide needed capital for investment and help to develop national financial markets. Shifting a part of the costs and risks of retirement provision to the private sector would relieve the financial burden on the public pay-as-you-go scheme and, as populations age, help to avoid the need for increases in contribution rates or cuts in benefits.

Throughout the region, those interested in achieving these outcomes in their own countries have been eager to know how reforms are faring in the countries that have moved most swiftly to innovate. The interested parties include not only governments but also workers and their trade unions, entrepreneurs and their associations, bankers, insurance companies, fund managers, and experts in academic and research institutions. To this audience, we address these case studies of pension restructuring in Hungary and Poland initiated in 1998 and 1999 respectively. As the most advanced countries of CEE in pension privatization, Hungary and Poland have moved beyond policy deliberations, planning, and legislative action to implement major reforms. At the time of these studies, Hungary had three full years of implementation experience and Poland, nearly three.[1] While too short for judging many aspects of these efforts, these periods do reveal the early challenges of getting the new schemes up and running, as well as

---

[1] Both studies were initiated early in 2001 and completed in December.

11

providing a basis for evaluating some of the predictions and assumptions made in drafting the laws in light of actual experience.

In profiling the reforms, the case studies give particular attention to the financial and administrative issues raised by the partial privatization of pensions, its effect on the preexisting public pension systems, and its likely impact on future benefits. At the same time, the studies identify early issues and problems encountered in establishing mandatory private pension funds in the transforming economies of Hungary and Poland. To facilitate comparison, the studies are organized and presented in a similar manner. Such comparison reveals a number of striking convergences, as well as some significant areas of divergence. Drawing on the studies, this section will highlight these patterns.

The major difference between the Hungarian and Polish reforms lies in the extent to which they restructured their *public* pension schemes in parallel with privatization. The studies show that in both countries the inherited schemes were targets of widespread dissatisfaction. Moreover, *ad hoc* changes made during the early years of transformation further eroded public confidence and reinforced the perception that the schemes were arbitrary and unfair. (See Augusztinovics *et al*, sec. 4.2 and Chłoń, sec. 1.3.b, this volume). These common sentiments did not, however, lead to similar reforms. In Hungary, the 1998 reform left the public defined benefit (DB) structure largely intact and, where making changes, delayed effective dates for more than a decade.[2] Thus, the public scheme operates today ‧much as it did before the 1998 reform was implemented and, in the view of the case study authors, continues to exhibit many of its earlier flaws.[3] The Polish reform, by contrast, revamps the public pension system substantially, replacing it with a new notional defined contribution (NDC) system in which benefits will reflect each individual's own contributions in a more nearly linear way.[4] This

---

[2] Digression (redistribution) in the benefit formula, although gradually decreasing, will continue until 2009; and the pension scale (valuation of countable years of service) will not become linear before 2013.

[3] The authors describe these flaws as an opaque and excessively redistributive benefit formula; a method of valorizing earnings which disadvantages those who retire in periods of high inflation; the absence of ceiling on earnings subject to the employer contribution; and the absence of individual contribution records. In addition, long-term financial difficulties facing the system due to demographic aging of the population (after 2020) were unaddressed by the reform.

[4] Benefits will be paid under the old formula until 2009, but establishment of the individual accounts needed for the new system has begun.

arrangement will give future pensioners the benefit they have 'paid for,' eliminate redistribution toward low-income earners, and automatically diminish benefits in response to increases in average life expectancy.[5] However, the reform will also cause wage replacement rates to fall in future years to levels below the minimum standards stipulated in ILO Conventions.[6] Should the reform be left unchanged, it will raise the prospect of increased poverty among pensioners. Thus, in marked contrast with Hungary where little changed in the public system, Poland is moving toward a substantially reformed public system with new problems and challenges.

Alongside this major difference, the two reforms exhibit a number of noteworthy similarities. These relate to: (1) early difficulties in implementation, especially with respect to the requirement for new automated information systems; (2) the lack of coordination between benefits under the new retirement pension schemes and benefits under the unreformed public disability schemes; (3) the deferral of decisions setting important parameters of the new private benefits; (4) participation, market structure, and performance of the new pension funds; and (5) the allocation of the burden for paying the transition costs of privatization.

Early difficulties in implementation

The studies show that reforms in both countries were formulated, debated, and enacted in considerable haste in the wake of long periods of stalemate (See secs. 1.3 in both Augusztinovics *et al* and Chłoń, this volume). During the stalemate two ministries in each country – the finance and welfare ministries in Hungary,

---

[5] Benefits will be reduced unless workers delay retirement and make additional contributions.

[6] Wage replacement rates are projected to decline from 65 percent for men and 50 percent for women born in 1949 and retiring under the old system to 40 percent for men and 30 percent for women born in 1974 and retiring under the reformed system. Benefits from both the first and second tiers are included in these replacement rates. As will be subsequently discussed, part of this decline results from cuts in public benefits aimed at covering the transitional financing costs of privatization. ILO Convention 102 generally calls for a minimum benefit standard of 40 percent of the wages after 30 years of contributions, with provision for an upper limit and floor.

and finance and labor ministries in Poland – promoted competing blueprints for restructuring pensions. The welfare and labor ministries prepared proposals designed to restructure existing public pensions while both finance ministries called for partial privatization of the pension scheme, as advocated and promoted by the World Bank.[7] Both governments ultimately chose the privatization proposals and then established tight timetables for drafting and approval of authorizing legislation.[8] The Hungarian government allowed only a few months to work out the details of the new law, and *ad hoc* changes were made by Parliament throughout its deliberations. Some amendments were adopted with limited attention to their workability and consequences. In Poland, where the time crunch was more severe, reform legislation was enacted just a few days before its effective date.[9]

Symptomatic of this haste is the fact that neither government had put in place the required information systems at the time implementation of the reforms began. Given that both reforms called for greater individualization in pension record keeping, this omission had multiple consequences for policy and practice.

In Hungary, it prevented the Pension Insurance Fund (PIF) from establishing the legislatively-mandated public individualized accounting of contributions by and on behalf of workers.[10] This did not create a barrier to the launching of private pension funds since, in Hungary, employers rather than the PIF must transfer contributions to these funds. Rather the effect was to reduce the transparency of this area of pension administration since, in the absence of public records against which to track employer transfers to the private funds, there was

---

[7] In Hungary, the reform was prepared in the Ministry of Finance with direct participation by World Bank officials. In Poland, the Office of the Plenipotentiary was headed by a World Bank official on leave. Compared to Hungary, the Office worked more closely with the labour ministry.

[8] In Poland, this sense of urgency was fueled by coming Parliamentary elections. In Hungary, its source is less clear but may have to do with continuing opposition to pension privatization.

[9] An immediate amendment was required to delay the launching of the private tier for three months in order to make minimal preparations.

[10] In 1999, a shift of collection responsibility from the PIF to the tax authority was mandated. However, under the new collection procedures, the tax authority's periodic revenue transfers to the PIF were made without sufficient information on the source and legal title of these funds to allow them to be assigned to individual workers.

no ready means to assess the compliance of particular firms with the statutory requirements. Given these difficulties, Parliament repealed the requirement for monthly employer reports identifying the individuals on whose behalf contributions are made. The PIF is still required to establish individual accounts, but without these reports it has so far been unable to do so.

Under the Polish reform, by contrast, it is the public pension authority, ZUS, that must collect and transfer workers' contributions to the private pension funds that they choose to manage their savings. Hence ZUS's establishment of individual pension accounts was an essential prerequisite to privatization.[11] The need for timely transfers was all the more vital in view of the fact that delays by ZUS in making the transfers entail heavy interest payments (30%) by ZUS to the funds. With no lead time for preparation, ZUS entered the implementation phase with its plans for the required information systems still on the drawing board. Most employers, therefore, used a newly devised surrogate paper form to report the contributions they were submitting on behalf of individual workers. Ambiguities on this form and general confusion among employers led to a very high rate of initial reporting errors, in the range of 50 percent. This effectively paralyzed the new system; ZUS initially failed to make 95 percent of the required transfers to private funds. As of the time of this writing, nearly three years later, ZUS is still working to process a large backlog of unrealized transfers and is still unable to complete 20-30 percent of the required monthly transfers (see Chłoń, sec. 3.3.a, this volume).

Disability vs. retirement

Another shared problem resulted from lack of coordination between the reformed old-age pension schemes and the unreformed disability schemes. In both countries this omission, unless addressed, will lead to rising disability expenditures and growing inequities between disability and old-age pensions. The roots of this problem in the two countries are different.

In Hungary, the 1998 reform gives workers who become disabled the option to transfer their private pension savings back to the public scheme and thereby

---

[11] This was also essential to the successful implementation of the new NDC scheme, to be launched in 2009.

receive disability benefits as if they had never entered the mixed system. While this option is attractive and useful from the perspective of individual workers, it distributes risk asymmetrically between the public and private pension tiers. It allows 'bad risks' (those for whom disability benefits will be likely to exceed the private savings transferred to the public scheme) to rejoin the public system, while the 'good risks' would rationally decide to forego this option. As the new private scheme matures, it could cause a substantial drain on public disability revenues (see Augusztinovics *et al*, sec. 3.3.a, this volume).

In Poland, the problem is broader. The new NDC system will substantially reduce retirement pensions but leave disability pensions unchanged.[12] However, upon reaching retirement, disabled pensioners may continue to receive their disability pension if it is greater than their retirement pension. This will advantage those workers who become disabled in comparison with workers with similar earnings and career histories but no disability, leading older workers to seek disability benefits. As the pension reform is phased in, the benefit differential will place a growing burden on disability financing (see Chłoń, sec. 3.3.b, this volume).

Deferred private benefit issues

There is a rough accuracy in the claim that pension reform in both countries replaced an earlier structure in which the relation between contributions and benefits was unclear with a reformed structure where the level of contributions is more transparent but the level of expected benefits is much less so. The decreased transparency of the benefit promise results on the one hand from the fact that both reforms establish defined contribution (DC) systems in which there is no benefit specified. Under these new systems, workers will receive the monthly benefit that their accumulated savings will purchase at retirement, given the yields on the securities in which they were invested.[13] Thus, the actual value of a worker's account will be subject to substantial variation during his or her working

---

[12] Projections indicate that this differential will grow over the next half century to approximately 25 percent.

[13] The loss from administrative charges of fund managers and the average remaining life expectancy of the worker's age cohort are also taken into account.

years according to the performance of the markets. While this increased uncertainty is inherent in the change from DB to DC benefits, the unknowns have been increased in both countries by the deferral of key issues concerning private benefit payments.

The uncertainties are more extensive in Poland, as legislation governing the calculation and payment of private benefits has not yet been enacted. In it absence, there are no rules governing the conversion of an individual's savings to an annuity at his or her retirement, i.e. whether this will be possible only through a single annuity company, through one of multiple competing companies, or through the insurance industry. Further, there is no guidance as to what factors will be taken into account in the life expectancy tables that are central to this conversion, i.e. whether men and women will have identical periodic benefits or whether women will have smaller benefits as a result of their greater longevity (that is, unisex versus gender specific life expectancy tables). The manner of cost of living adjustments in also an unresolved question (see Chłoń, framework 1 and surrounding text, this volume).

In Hungary, uncertainty arises due to a gap between the requirements of law and existing industry practice. The law provides two options for converting a worker's accumulated savings to an annuity at retirement: a private pension fund may do this directly or may purchase an annuity from an insurance company. Whichever method is used, annuities must be calculated using gender-neutral life tables; and they must be indexed in the same manner as public pensions, that is, the Swiss method, which requires adjustments reflecting wages and prices in equal proportions. Uncertainties arise with these requirements due to: (1) the posture of existing private funds, which have so far stated that they will not offer annuities themselves but will instead rely on the insurance industry; (2) the reluctance of insurance companies to use gender-neutral life tables, coupled with the lack of any legal guidelines as to how they are supposed to structure such tables; and (3) the absence of annuities on the market in Hungary (or anywhere) that would satisfy the indexation requirement, as well as of any government bonds indexed in a way that would enable private pension funds to cover their risks of future wage and price increases. Given the novelty and risk associated with the legal requirements from industry's perspective, whatever arrangements are devised are likely to be costly for workers (see Augusztinovics et al, sec. 2.2.c, this volume).

In sum, those workers who were given a one-time choice as to whether to join the private system as well as those who were required by law to do so were severely restricted, though for different reasons in each country, in their ability to forecast what level of retirement pension support they could contemplate.

Participation, market structure, and performance of the new pension funds

Given these uncertainties, the observer might expect those free to exercise a choice in the matter to be reluctant to join the reformed private schemes. Such was not the case, however, in either country. In fact, workers subscribed in numbers that significantly exceeded official projections.

In both countries, the option to join a private pension fund was extended to certain subgroups of the workforce. In Hungary, all current workers were given the choice. In Poland, the choice was given to all workers between the ages of 30 and 50. Younger workers were required to subscribe while older ones were excluded. Both choice cohorts opted for the mixed system in significantly greater numbers than expected. In Hungary the government estimated that 1.5 million workers would join a private fund, whereas two million, or 40 percent of the economically active population, actually did so. In Poland, the government estimated that 50 percent of the work force would join, but the actual total, 9.7 million workers, exceeded 60 percent (see secs. 3.2.a in both Augusztinovics *et al* and Chłoń, this volume).

The unexpected strength of worker preferences for private pensions appears to have two sources in common. First, it is attributable to so-called active errors, that is, switching by workers who lost more accrued rights under the public system than they stand to gain from private pension savings. Such over-switching seems to have been motivated by public disenchantment with the existing public schemes in both countries, resulting in part from *ad hoc* restrictions placed on benefits earlier in the 1990s, as well as by positive public expectations that investments in private pension funds would increase security and prosperity in retirement (see sections 3.2.b in both Augusztinovics *et al* and Chłoń, this volume). Second, decision making was skewed toward private pensions by that sector itself, which engaged in an advertising blitz and employed large teams of sales agents to recruit new members. In Hungary, funds backed by financial institutions with large sales forces captured more than 90 percent of the market. In Poland, the private pension industry outspent the government publicity campaign twenty fold and employed a sales force of 400,000.[14] The Polish study points to a strong, if unsurprising positive correlation between the success of firms in recruiting members and the number of agents they deployed.

It is clear then that those funds with large parent companies which provided initial injections of capital had a considerable advantage in consolidating their position in the industry, since these injections allowed high levels of spending on advertising and agent networks. In Hungary, of the 60 funds that initially applied for a license, only a third, or 21 funds, survived as separate entities for three years. The largest of these are backed by financial institutions, i.e. banks and insurance companies. Eighty percent of all subscribers belong to just five funds. In Poland, the government licensed a total of 21 firms in 1999, considerably fewer than the Hungarian government, especially given the disparity in populations. However, most of these were also established and backed by financial institutions. As in Hungary, a few firms dominate. The three largest Polish funds have nearly 60 percent of members and 65 percent of assets. As of June 2001, one Polish fund had been sold and four were in merger or acquisition proceedings (see secs. 3.4.a in both Augusztinovics *et al* and Chłoń, this volume).

In this situation, market consolidation seems likely to continue. While this trend offers the potential for greater economies of scale in pension adminis- tration, it also raises two troublesome prospects. First, as will be shown, it is smaller funds that have so far demonstrated the greatest efficiencies and the highest net yields in the Hungarian market. Second, in an environment with high market concentration, workers will be less able to rely on competitive forces to assure private firms' performance; and governments will face greater regulatory challenges in the face of possible anticompetitive practices.

A final common pattern relates to the early performance of the private funds. The brief period under examination does not allow confident extrapolations about the funds' future financial performance. Still, the early results have not been promising. Using a common methodology that takes account of administrative fees and inflation, the Hungarian and Polish studies both show

---

[14] The ratio of agents to members is thus 40 per thousand. This is high compared to countries in Latin America which undertook similar reforms and where the ratio of agents to fund members was five to 1,000.

that the private funds in both countries on average registered losses throughout their operation.[15] Significantly, workers' pension assets not only failed to grow but declined in real value in both countries. In Hungary, in 1998-2000, for the industry as a whole, the rate of return so computed averaged –4.1 percent (7.1 percent growth against average inflation of 11.2 percent). In Poland, net-of-inflation returns for all firms across the industry ranged from a high of –3 percent to a low of –14 percent[16] (see Augusztinovics *et al*, sec. 3.4.d, and Chłoń, Table 16, this volume).

What factors explain these early losses? Unlike private pension funds in the US and some Western European countries, these funds are not heavily invested in equities, so poor performance by equities markets does not appear to provide an explanation. In Poland, 60 percent of worker savings is invested in government bonds and 27.4 percent in equities. In Hungary, the private funds have invested 77 percent of worker savings in government bonds, 16 percent in domestic equities, and a tiny fraction in foreign equities. In both countries, rates on government bonds have been high in recent years. On this basis, the Hungarian study concludes that the reasons for the poor performance are not fully understood.

The studies do, however, point to two explanatory factors on the cost side of the ledger: high fund management fees and high marketing expenditures. In the Hungarian study, investment fees are shown to vary sharply between the two types of funds. In 2000, in those funds in which the fund manager is chosen competitively (the smaller funds), fees absorbed 8.5 percent of gross returns. On the other hand, in those funds that used an investment manager from another firm also owned by the same parent company, investments fees were 23.8 percent of gross returns, or nearly three times greater. This second group includes the largest funds in the Hungarian market with the largest market share. Since gross rates of return for the two groups were statistically indistinguishable, the superior performance of the smaller firms resulted from their lower fee structure. Despite the erosion of the returns of the larger firms by much higher fees, they have thus far experienced no attrition in membership. On the contrary, their market share is increasing relative to their smaller competitors.

---

[15] These are not calculations of gross returns on investments, as typically performed by private industry, but rather measures of the yield earned on a worker's *total* contributions, including administrative fees and charges.

[16] These rates were computed for the period September 1999 to June 2001.

The Polish study identifies marketing expenditures as the main factor contributing to funds' financial losses in 1999 and 2000. In December 1999, after the end of the open season where workers were free to select a fund, the private funds continued to spend heavily on advertising and sales agents. In 2000, marketing expenditures dwarfed other administrative costs, exceeding the industry's next largest expenditure category nearly fourfold.[17] Marketing costs alone exceeded total industry revenues by ten percent. Most of these operating deficits were covered by capital injections by parent or holding companies (see Chłoń, Table 17, this volume).

Distribution of the burden of transition costs

The shift from a pay-as-you-go pension scheme to a mixed pension system inevitably creates financial strains within a country, since it must build up reserves with which eventually to pay prefunded pensions while at the same time continuing to meet current pension obligations on a pay-as-you-go basis. Both Hungary and Poland are incurring these transitional financing costs, which magnify the fiscal difficulties already confronting both schemes. In Hungary, six percent of the 28 percent contribution (that is, just over one fifth) is being diverted to the private tier for each new member, creating a shortfall in the budget of the public scheme that is immediate and sustained. In Poland, the amount transferred is 7.3 percent out of the 36.59 percent (also just over one fifth).[18]

In both countries, heavy reliance is being placed on so-called internal financing to cover this deficit, meaning benefit cuts in the public scheme. These cuts do not imply a transfer of benefits from the public to the private tier, since no significant amount of benefits will be paid from the private scheme for at least one to two decades. Rather, the cuts amount to imposed belt-tightening on a generation of workers, who will receive lower benefits from the public pension system in order to offset, on a macroeconomic basis, the loss of public scheme revenues due

---

[17] Total marketing costs were 811,375 PLN, while total industry revenues were 726,614 PLN.

[18] The figures quoted are total contribution rates for old age, disability, and survivors, the two latter of which are still financed from the public pension scheme. In this sense, privatization of old age benefits is greater than a fifth.

to privatization. This pattern is most transparent in Poland, where long-term projections show that over the next half century, two-thirds of the transitional financing costs will be met by cuts in public pension benefits, one-fourth by increased government borrowing, and the remainder (roughly, one-twelfth) from privatization revenues. The Polish projections show that, without the extra burden of transitional financing, public scheme benefits would have been nearly twice their projected level in 2050 (see Chłoń, figure 21 and appendix B, this volume).

In Hungary, the transitional financing burden is harder to analyze due to the absence of long-term financial projections. What can be said is that the revenue loss to the public scheme is being offset by the combination of less generous indexation of pensions and the government subsidy to the pension fund. In this sense, pensioners and taxpayers are bearing the burden of the transition.[19]

These transitional costs make pension privatization very costly for a generation of workers: without them, pensioners in the lengthy transition period could have enjoyed significantly higher benefits; privatization revenues could have been used for other social purposes; and less debt would have been placed on the shoulders of the current and future workforce that will have to generate wealth to cover the interest payments (see Chłoń, sec. 3.3.c, this volume).

***

For readers seeking to learn from the experience of Hungary and Poland, what general conclusions can be drawn from these early experiences? Which of the observed patterns are inherent results of privatization? Which patterns are shaped by social or economic factors in the countries themselves? Which result from specific decisions by policy makers within the framework of the privatization effort? While these questions are both important and tempting, the answers to many lie beyond the scope of the studies. They must wait for further research which focuses on more cases and captures more variation.

---

[19] The picture is complicated, however, by additional changes made at the time of the reform: a two point reduction in the employer contribution and a modest benefit liberalization for widows. In this fuzzy situation, what can be said is that the reduction in the employer rate has increased the burden to be borne by pensioners and workers.

What can be concluded from this comparison is that the similarities between the two reforms efforts relate mostly to difficulties: they call attention to more pitfalls, glitches, and early problems than achievements or early successes, suggesting that privatization is proving to be a more complex undertaking than was expected. These patterns cannot of course be taken to mean that the reforms are unsuccessful. It is too early to judge this, and as the implementers gain experience, outcomes may move closer to those predicted at the time of adoption of the reforms. Moreover, it is the long-term performance of the new private funds that will determine their success rather than investment yields earned in early years.

Despite their focus on a short time period, we see these studies as providing a highly useful addition to the literature on radical pension restructuring. By highlighting risks, problems, and challenges in undertaking privatization, they enhance the potential for improved policy making and implementation by those in other countries who are aware of the details of these early experiences. Such insights are especially useful in the new democracies of CEE, since citizens in democracies are well known to resist changes in their social security with consistency and passion that few other legislative endeavors evoke. Given these schemes' natural resistance to change, it is important to get things right early – to plan, legislate, and implement reforms in a manner which minimizes the need for future revision and maximizes the probability of early success. It is in this spirit that the ILO joins the authors in offering these case studies to governments, workers, employers and all other interested parties in countries planning or considering similar reforms.

Chapter 1
The Hungarian Pension System Before and After the 1998 Reform

Mária Augusztinovics (coordinator), Róbert I. Gál,
Ágnes Matits, Levente Máté, András Simonovits, and János Stahl[1]

Terminology

Efforts are made in this report to avoid any possible confusion from the different taxonomies applied by various international institutions and from the somewhat ambiguous language in the Hungarian legislation on the pension system. However, some concessions have been made in translating current Hungarian usage, which sometimes employs more than one expression for the same concept. Furthermore, a few concepts crucial to understanding the Hungarian *public* pension scheme have to be referred to, even if the corresponding English terms may sound unusual to non-Hungarian readers.

The following specific usages should be noted:

The terms pension *scheme, pillar* and *tier* are treated as synonyms.

The terms *public* and *social security* are taken as synonymous in the pension context. Although the term social security covers a broader field, the study is not concerned here with anything other than the pension aspects of it.

The terms *first pillar* and *second pillar* are avoided, as these have different connotations in different taxonomies.

The term *mandatory* has been systematically inserted when referring to the private funded pillar established by the 1998 pension reform, to distinguish it clearly from the *voluntary* private pension funds in existence since earlier, but not discussed here.

Valorization refers to the reappraisal of a retiring individual's *past earnings*, (according to the average wage increase between two periods), for the purpose of assessing such earnings on retirement.

---

[1] Mária Augusztinovics, Levente Máté and András Simonovits are with the Hungarian Academy of Sciences. Róbert I. Gál is with TARKI Social Research Centre. János Stahl is with the State Financial Supervisory Authority. Ágnes Matits is an independent actuary.

Degression and *degressive* indicate that when valorized past earnings are used to compute amounts of benefit, higher brackets of income add decreasing (less than proportional) amounts to the notional sum of 'pensionable' past income on which the entry pension is based.

Indexation refers to linkage of periodic (annual) increases in pension benefits, usually to the trend in wage and/or price increases or to any predetermined percentage. Sometimes, however, the increase is defined as a specific sum of money and/or lower and upper limits to the increase apply. Whatever the case, 'indexation' is interpreted as a set of rules for determining the pension increase in a specific calendar year.

Entry pension means the initial pension assessed at retirement and paid during the calendar year of retirement. An entry pension is not subject to indexation.

Pension formula denotes the set of rules for calculating entry pensions.

Continued pensions are all pensions in a calendar year assessed prior to that year, to which the indexation rules apply.

Own pension or a pension in the beneficiary's *own right* is based on that person's working career (sufficient length of service and the notional pensionable income accrued).

Survivors' pension benefits include widows', widowers' and orphans' benefits. (In a negligible number of cases, parents and/or siblings without pensions of their own may be eligible for survivors' benefits if the deceased is the person responsible for their support.)

Disability benefits and *disabled persons* are distinguished according to whether they have also reached the statutory retirement age. The rules for the two groups, which have varied over time, are discussed in the relevant sections.

Acronyms

SSPS	Social Security Pension Scheme (Excluding those types of disability benefits that are handled by HIF.)
PIF	Pension Insurance Fund (A financial entity handling revenues and expenditures of SSPS. Formally separate from the central government budget. Notwithstanding the name 'Fund', the mode of finance is PAYG.)
HIF	Health Insurance Fund (public, PAYG)
PAYG	Pay-as-you-go
MPPF	Mandatory Private Pension Fund (actually, mutual savings association)
MS	Mixed System (the combination of SSPS and MPPFs)
SFSA	State Financial Supervisory Authority (supervising MPPFs among other financial institutions)
STCA	State Tax Collecting Agency
CSO	Central Statistical Office
TARKI	Social Research Centre (a private research institution)

1. The pre-reform scene

1.1. Demographic and economic background

1.1.a. Demography

Life expectancy at birth increased in Hungary from 37.3 years to 69.1 years between 1900 and 1970. Since then, however, male mortality rates have been deteriorating somewhat, particularly among the middled-aged, while female mortality has improved only slightly. Thus the average life expectancy has stalled at somewhat less than 70 years over the last three decades and the difference between male and female life expectancy has widened. Natality in the first half of the 20th century adapted gradually to the decreasing mortality, but remained relatively high. The gap between the mortality and natality trends resulted in a population increase, from 6.8 million in 1900 (in the current territory of Hungary) to 10.7 million in 1980. Since then, there has been a natural decrease, so that the population was slightly over 10 million in 2000.

Table 1 Age-structure and demographic dependency				
	Population shares		Dependency ratios	
	0–19	65–	Old age	Total
1970	28.3	13.1	22.4	70.6
1980	26.3	15.6	26.9	72.1
1990	26.2	15.8	27.2	72.4
2000	23.6	14.6	23.6	61.8
2010	21.1	15.6	24.6	58.0
2020	20.2	18.5	30.2	63.1
2030	20.2	20.1	33.7	67.5
2040	19.2	22.5	38.6	71.5
2050	18.9	26.2	47.7	82.1

Source: CSO Yearbooks and Hablicsek (1999).

The ageing of the population was relatively slow in the final decades of the 20th century. As Table 1 demonstrates, the present demographic dependency ratios are clearly favourable (lower than they were 10-20 years ago). This is due to the baby-boom generation born after World War Two and to their 'echo', the large cohorts born in the late 1970s and now in their earning span. Their retirement, in about 2020 and 2050 respectively, compounded by the present below-replacement rate of fertility will increase the old-age (and to a much lesser extent, the total) demographic dependency ratio, but both ratios are projected to remain relatively moderate until 2050, if viewed in a broader European context.

1.1.b. The economy

Hungary is roughly comparable in its level of economic development with such Central European countries as the Czech Republic, Slovakia and Poland and such Southern European countries as Greece and Portugal. The economy underwent a transition crisis due to the collapse of the Council of Mutual Economic Assistance (COMECON) in 1990 and the ensuing need for structural adjustment. Output, employment and net labour income contracted and the inflation rate reached double figures, peaking at 34 percent in 1991 and not subsiding below 20 percent again until 1997.

	GDP	Consumers' prices 1989 = 100	Real net earnings	Employment rate
	Table 2 Major macroeconomic indicators			
1990	96.2	129	96.6	75.9
1991	84.9	174	89.8	71.0
1992	82.3	214	89.1	64.5
1993	81.7	262	85.0	60.8
1994	84.2	311	91.2	59.8
1995	85.4	399	80.3	58.7
1996	86.8	493	76.2	58.3
1997	90.9	583	80.3	58.4
1998	95.3	667	83.0	59.5
1999	99.4	734	84.7	61.3
2000	103.6	806	86.4	61.9

Source: CSO Yearbooks

About 30 percent of previous jobs were lost in the early 1990s and the employment rate fell by 18 percentage points. GDP resumed growth in 1993, but it did not surpass its 1989 level until 2000 and net job creation has remained very low. Employment and real wages are still far below their 1989 levels.

Income differentials have widened drastically during the transition to a market economy. On the one hand, revenues from capital have become significant and employees in good jobs in the newly formed private sector earn relatively high pay. On the other hand, people who have lost their jobs and remain persistently or permanently outside the labour market have to live on very low sums of unemployment benefit and social aid. The Gini coefficient of net earnings jumped from 0.21 to 0.32 between 1989 and 1997 (Fazekas, 2000), while that of individual distribution of equivalent household income increased only from 22.5 to 25.4 percent (Flemming and Micklewright, 1999, cited by Fazekas, 2000). The difference is due to falling employment and a consequently increasing share of pensions, child allowances and various social-assistance benefits in household income, which has cushioned the wage differentials to some extent.

1.2. The pension system before the 1998 reform
1.2.a. A brief history

All Hungarian funded pension schemes collapsed during or after the Second World War, due to the damage sustained by real estate that the funds owned and to hyperinflation. A unified, unfunded PAYG system was introduced around 1950 for wage and salary earners. Initially, this covered about half the population, but the coverage and range of benefits were gradually extended. By the mid-1970s, the system was approaching maturation, with almost 100 percent coverage and a comprehensive range of old-age, survivors' and disability benefits. The Social Security Act of 1975 consolidated changes made over the previous quarter of a century.

Expansion of the system, rising wages and retirement by successive cohorts with entitlements from increasing numbers of years of employment raised the proportion of aggregate pension expenditure (including all disability benefits) to GDP from 3.5 percent in 1970 to 6.9 percent in 1980 and 8.8 percent in 1990. By the late 1970s, the system was under increasing strain from problems of rising wages and prices. Pension increases were inadequate and sporadic, so that only the lowest pensions kept pace with wages and inflation, while medium-sized and higher pensions were steadily eroded, at first only relative to wages, but later in real terms, relative to prices (Antal *et al.*, 1995).

1.2.b. Gradualist reform process in the early 1990s

Some significant changes were made in the pension system in the early 1990s. Parameter changes had become necessary to cope with the effects of the transition crisis and restore the system to long-term financial viability. Certain institutional and accounting alterations were made concurrently to improve system design, particularly its macroeconomic transparency. These successive changes can be seen as a gradualist process of reform within the public PAYG framework.

The fall in employment was decreasing the number of contributors while the number of pensioners was increasing sharply, as many employees close to the statutory retirement age were sent into early retirement or volunteered for it. Thus the *system dependency ratio* – the ratio of the number of pensioners to the number of contributors – jumped from 51.4 percent in 1989 to 83.9 percent in 1996. As a result, *aggregate pension expenditure* increased to 10 percent of the GDP by 1994.

The upward trend was reversed mainly by tightening the so-called 'pension formula', *i.e.* the set of rules determining the *entry pensions* first received by beneficiaries on retirement. This was effected mainly by two changes in the pension formula in the early 1990s.

First, past earnings as a basis for pension determination had been calculated as the average of the 'best' (for the beneficiary) three of the last five years before retirement. After 1992, however, earnings for the period from 1988 until the moment of retirement were considered, irrespective of what was 'good' or 'bad' for the beneficiary. Thus the period for assessing the past earnings of a retiree was increasing by one year each year, so that 'past earnings' would become lifetime earnings by the year 2050 (assuming retirement at a statutory age of 62).

Second, the valorization of past earnings for wage increases was truncated, by omitting to valorize the earnings of the last three to four years before retirement, which were accepted instead at their nominal value. Those who retired in the early and mid-1990s, during a period of extremely high inflation, lost heavily by receiving very low entry pensions.

Furthermore, *continued pensions* from 1991 onwards were indexed according to the rise in nominal, net wages, in other words, at a rate lower than the inflation rate, since real wages were falling sharply. Moreover, pensions were increased from 1996 according to the nominal wage index of the *previous year*. The lag of one year behind wages occurred amidst high inflation, which was around 20 percent in those years. This created great difficulties for pensioners, while achieving a significant 'saving' in aggregate pension expenditure.

Previously, entry pensions had always been higher on average than the average of continued pensions (benefits assessed in earlier years), which had a push effect on aggregate pension expenditure. In 1992, the relative figures became reversed, with low entry pensions exercising a pull (decreasing) effect and helping to contain the increase in aggregate expenditure on pensions.

As a result of these measures, and several others of less importance, the ratio of the total pension expenditure to GDP fell to 8.3 percent in 1997, which was below its 1990 level. Of that, aggregate old-age pensions and survivors' benefits amounted to 7.1 percent of GDP, while the remaining 1.2 percent covered disability benefits.

Most important for the future, the *statutory retirement age* was raised in 1996. It went up for men from 60 to 61 years (effective from 1998) and 62 years (effective from 2000), and for women, from 55 years by one year of age in every second calendar year until 2009, when it reaches 62. Benefit reductions for early retirement and some rewards for delayed retirement were introduced at the same time. These measures significantly contained the long-term upward trend in aggregate pension expenditure and injected into the system a modest element of actuarial fairness.

In 1992, an independent *Pension Insurance Fund* (PIF) was established and separated from the government budget, with its own administration, budget and elected Self-governing Body responsible to Parliament. A similar *Health Insurance Fund* (HIF) was created at the same time, to finance health-care institutions and distribute sick pay, among other duties. Responsibility for the disabled persons and their survivors was divided between the two funds. The HIF took responsibility for paying disability benefits for persons *below* the statutory retirement age, and in the case of their death, for their survivors. The same benefits were paid by the PIF for disabled people *above* the statutory age and their survivors. (As a disability pensioner reached statutory retirement age, the transfer of responsibility from the HIF to the PIF took place automatically.) Employers' and employees' social-security contributions were accordingly divided between the two new funds.

From 1992, the financial burden of *non-pension-type benefits* (inherited from the previous, comprehensive social security system, such as child allowances and some social-support schemes) was gradually transferred from the PIF to the central government budget. Simultaneously, the government budget started to pay old-age pension contributions to the PIF for some previously non-contributory activities to which pension claims accrued, for example years spent on maternity leave after childbirth and later also for men drafted into the armed forces. In subsequent years, the PIF was allotted a modest quantity of assets out of the revenues from privatization of state property. The intention was to begin building a reserve fund for the demographically critical period expected around 2020.

These measures lent much greater transparency to the macroeconomic situation with revenues and expenditures related to old-age pensions, survivors' and disability benefits. They also contributed significantly to a healthier PIF budget, in a period of high inflation. The contribution revenues of the PIF in 1997 happened to finance exactly 100 percent of the aggregate pension expenditure. Temporary forces were helping to produce this financially favourable situation, but deficits were again to be expected in the late 1990s, when diminishing inflation and slow real-wage growth were expected. For the more distant future, the promise of balance and financial sustainability for the public pension system came from the increases in the statutory retirement age.

In 1993, it became possible for *voluntary private pension funds* to be established. These were supported by quite significant tax exemptions and immediately became popular among wealthier groups able to utilize the tax breaks, but, as a rule, do not affect the old-age income of the majority of employees. For that reason, they will not be discussed further in this study.

1.3. Reasons for and expected results of the 1998 reform
1.3.a. Inadequacies of the system

While the measures described in the previous section restored the immediate financial viability of the PIF, they did not improve the microeconomic transparency or the fairness of the pension system. If anything, they went against equity among retiring cohorts, by making individual pensions strongly dependent on inflation-rate fluctuations in the years preceding retirement, and weakened confidence in the ability of old-age pensions to provide income security. Furthermore, anxieties persisted about the projected increase in the old-age demographic dependency ratio from 2020 onwards.

The prime inadequacy of the existing system was its design. It embodied an almost impenetrable mix of social assistance (solidarity through redistribution) and social insurance (partial but fair replacement of previous income, based on contributions). Pensioners had little idea why their pensions were exactly what they were or how they related to their previous contributions. It will be shown in Parts Two and Three that most of those weaknesses persist today.

The way *entry pensions* were calculated was extremely complex and far from actuarially fair. Past earnings (and therefore past contributions) were degressively approximated by the product of the pension scale (a decreasing function as years of service increased) and of estimated average valorized past earnings (hereafter 'estimated earnings'). According to the pension scale, ten years' service yielded an entry pension of 33 percent of estimated earning, while 40 years yielded 80 percent. In other words, four times the length of service gave 2.4 times the entitlement in terms of estimated earnings. Furthermore, estimated earnings were also included degressively: higher earnings did not make for proportionally higher bases for the entry pension.

In addition, 'pensionable income' was capped. This ceiling, above which further earnings did not produce any increment in the entry-pension entitlement, remained nominally constant from 1992 to 1996. The rapid inflation of the period reduced its ratio to average gross earnings from 3.36 to 1.63, which was a major factor in the decline in the real value of entry pensions over those years. Although employees' contributions were similarly capped – no contribution was paid on the neglected portion of earnings – the same did not apply to employers' contributions. The same proportion was levied even on the highest wages and salaries, without increasing entry-pension entitlements in the least. In this respect, employers' contributions were rightly seen as a payroll tax, rather than a pension insurance premium.

After many years of *ad hoc* increases, wage indexation of *continued pensions* was introduced in 1991, as already mentioned. However, the principle of indexation was frequently violated by imposing tight upper and lower limits on the increase awarded. Lower pensions were increased by proportionally larger amounts, while middle-range and higher pensions received proportionally smaller increases than the ones that strict average wage indexation would award. Such measures were effective in supporting the poorest pensioners, but were obviously inconsistent with the insurance principle.

One of the worst results of these practices was arbitrary discrimination. Different cohorts of retirees received entirely different treatment. Moreover, the actual date of retirement became a dominant determinant of the pension received. Two persons with an identical work history (in terms of length of service, estimated 'pensionable' income, *etc.*) could receive quite different pensions in the same month, depending on when they happened to have retired. Table 3 shows that those who retired in 1994 received in 1996 pensions that were an average of 23 percentage points lower than the ones received by 1990 retirees, although there is no evidence to indicate or reason to assume that their work histories had been significantly different.

Table 3 Pensions in 1996, by year of retirement		
Year of retirement	Distribution of pensioners (%)	Pension as percent of average
–1970	2.3	95.7
1971–75	4.8	99.6
1976–80	11.4	98.6
1981–85	17.7	101.8
1986–89	18.1	105.8
1990	7.9	113.2
1991	8.3	98.1
1992	6.8	94.0
1993	6.7	93.3
1994	6.2	90.4
1995	6.8	93.9
1996	2.9	97.0

Source: PIF Administration

To summarize, the pension system as a whole did not collapse during the transitional economic crisis. It continued to give albeit meagre support to pensioners and on average to sustain equity between the working and retired generation: at least until 1996, the real values of the average pension and the average wage sank in parallel. The system favoured the poorest pensioners at the expense of those with higher previous incomes and longer service. Even within this framework, the moment of retirement gained an unjustifiable importance. The system had become gradually too complex, illogical and unattractive over the decades since the 1975 codification. Citizens had decreasing incentives to contribute properly to its financing, at a time of increasing opportunities to evade contributions through the so-called black and grey economies.

1.3.b. Conflicting reform blueprints

By 1995, it was generally agreed among experts and politicians that a comprehensive reform was necessary. There should be a new pension system that created strong personal incentives for earners to pay contributions. Two essential requirements for this were fair calculation and individual record keeping. The ideas about how to achieve these goals, however, differed fundamentally. By and large, two reform blueprints emerged, one advocated by the PIF's Self-governing Body, trade unions and individual pension experts, and the other by the Ministry of Finance. The difference boiled down to what structure the mandatory system should have, there was no argument about the persistence of the existing voluntary pension funds or about support for them.

According to the reform concept advanced by the *PIF's Self-governing Body*, the public, mandatory pension system would consist of two tiers, to give a clear distinction between social assistance and social insurance. The first tier would consist of a basic, flat-rate pension scheme available to citizens (residents) as a right. It would be clearly redistributive and financed from general taxation, after requisite restructuring of the income-tax and pension-contribution rates. The second tier would be a financially viable, earnings-related, actuarially fair insurance scheme for employees and the self-employed. It would have been based on a simple points system, with individual record keeping and annual reporting to the insured person on the number of points accrued. There was to be no *ex post* tampering with the points or therefore with the proportionate pensions of individual beneficiaries. The nominal value of the pension benefit yielded by one point would be set annually by Parliament, in line with the net-wage trend in the economy. The system would be combined with a flexible retirement age, incorporating fair rewards and penalties for postponed and early retirement, respectively.

The system was to be calibrated to ensure that the average pension (deriving from the two tiers) would be equivalent to about 60 percent of the average net wage. There was to be a gradually increasing statutory age of retirement. At pre-reform contribution rates, the system would also have accumulated a trust fund over the two ensuing, demographically benign decades from the mid-1990s to the mid-2010s, to help mitigate problems arising with the retirement of the baby-boom generation, around 2020. The transition from the old system to the new was to be fast, but smooth. Overall, it was envisaged that nobody would receive a lower monthly pension than before, although people would have lower lifetime pension entitlements because of the rising retirement age. The main result expected from the blueprint was the creation of a viable, accountable and flexible public system of PAYG pensions, with effective incentives to contribute. The viability of the system reformed in this way was demonstrated by model calculations made by individual experts (*e.g.* Augusztinovics and Martos, 1996).

By contrast, the blueprint advanced by the *Ministry of Finance* and later supported by the *Ministry of Labour*, concentrated on introducing a mandatory, private, funded scheme, while largely neglecting the internal systemic problems of the public scheme. The concept relied mainly on the three-pillar scheme of the World Bank (as outlined in World Bank, 1994), although it contained some important deviations from it. The contribution-related, public PAYG system would have to be sustained rather than replaced by a modest flat system, so that the privatization would be only partial. Furthermore, the indexation of the public scheme, rather than returning to pure price indexation, was to follow the so-called 'Swiss-method', whereby continued pensions would rise annually faster than prices but more slowly than nominal wages. The expectations of the plan's proponents were along the lines of the World Bank's argument. It was to foster economic growth, deepen capital markets, and for pensioners, to produce returns on invested capital that would be higher than the internal rate of return in the PAYG system. Additionally, there was emphasis on the advantage of putting one's eggs in two baskets (splitting risks between two pension schemes).

A working document by the Ministry of Finance, arguing for the introduction of the mandatory, private funded pillar, warned that the reformed PAYG scheme would have to remain healthy enough to bear the costs of the transition to a multi-pillar system. The document estimated that the annual deficit of the unchanged public scheme would be equivalent to 4 percent of GDP by 2050, but claimed that this could be eased to 1.4 percent by raising the statutory retirement age and introducing 'Swiss' indexation. The requisite calculations used quite realistic parameters and considered various scenarios. Thus the projections themselves belied the much-publicized claims that the public scheme was 'financially unsustainable' without privatization.

By contrast, experts from the World Bank (Palacios and Rocha 1998) published much more dramatic figures suggesting that without a reform, the deficit of the public pension scheme would reach an alarming 6 percent of GDP by 2050. They added that the combined effect of indexing continued pensions (with tax-base expansion) and increasing the pensionable age could delay the emergence of pension deficits until about 2014 and contain the deficit-GDP ratio at about 4 percent in 2050. This article is still widely cited in international literature because it was the only published paper by the proponents of the Hungarian pension privatization.

It is hard to judge the soundness of the various projections, mainly because the underlying calculations have hardly been made public. It is even harder to reflect the ideas of the radical reformers with respect to expected benefit levels in the reformed system, because there were very few official publications. The Ministry of Finance and Ministry of Labour (1997) considered a wide menu of assumptions about growth, inflation and interest rates that is hardly penetrable to the lay people expected to reach their individual decisions. However, the assumptions that most experts regarded as reasonable gave results suggesting it was inadvisable to opt for the new mixed system if a period longer than about 17 years had been spent in the pre-reform public system. In that case, the losses in benefits from the public scheme would exceed the gains to be expected from the private pillar.

The paradigmatic controversy between the two concepts, briefly described here, lasted for several years and led to a few compromises. For example, the Ministry of Finance gradually decreased the proposed size of the private pillar to 25 percent of the contributions. When the government made the final political decision in favour of the radical, partial-privatization concept, only a few months were allowed for working out the legal and financial details of the legislation to be presented to Parliament. Several *ad hoc* changes in the submitted text were made during the parliamentary debate itself, when there was no time left for experts to check the consistency of the amendments proposed by members and subsequently adopted by Parliament.

2. Substantial elements of the 1998 reform

The Hungarian Parliament enacted in the summer of 1997 a reform package effective from January 1998 that split the hitherto unified mandatory pension system into two schemes. One scheme remained public and PAYG, while the other was private and funded. The package did not affect the voluntary pension funds established earlier in the decade.

The legislative package consisted of four laws. Act LXXX deals with contributions, Act LXXXI regulates the Social Security Pension Scheme (SSPS), Act LXXXII establishes the legal framework for the Mandatory Private Pension Funds (MPPF) to be created,[2] and Act LXXXIII relates to the health-care system.

The reform offered a choice to those already employed. They could either remain full members of the SSPS or join an MPPF of their choice, while retaining membership of the SSPS with diminished contributions and pension rights. (Exclusive membership of an MPPF was not an option.) Those who opted for the latter solution, known as members of the Mixed System (MS), surrendered 25 percent of the pension rights that had accrued to them hitherto in the SSPS. Those switching to the MS were legally allowed to return without loss to full SSPS membership up to the end of 1999. No alternative was offered to new entrants to the labour market, for whom the MS became compulsory, implying that in the very long run, the mixed system would become universal. Entrants who fail to make a voluntary choice are allocated to a fund.

The Contributions Act required employers' contribution to the SSPS to decrease from the pre-reform 24 percent of gross wages to 23 percent by 1999 and 22 percent by 2000. On the other hand, the employees' contributions (up to the ceiling on 'pensionable income' discussed in Part One) were to increase from the pre-reform 6 percent to 7 percent by 1998, 8 percent by 1999 and 9 percent by 2000. Of this, MS members were to pay 1 percent to the SSPS and the rest to their MPPF. Thus the mandatory private pillar rests entirely on the employees' contributions, while employers contribute only to the public scheme. However,

---

[2] The Acts avoid using the term 'mandatory' and simply call the new funds 'private'. For sake of clarity, however, the attribute mandatory will be systematically applied here, to avoid confusion with the *voluntary* private pension funds in existence since 1993. It is not mandatory for all to join a 'mandatory' fund, but those who do so will remain within the mandatory pension system.

employers have to deduct from wages and transfer the employees' contributions of MS members directly to the requisite MPPFs.

2.1. Changes in the public pillar

The reform has left the systemic deficiencies of the public old-age pension scheme practically unchanged or postponed corrections in it until around 2010.

Rules of eligibility and measures concerning *old-age entry pensions,* received in the beneficiary's own right, have been sustained with a few minor exceptions. The pension scale (according to years of service) will not change until 2013, when it will become linear, with each year yielding 1.65 percent of the estimated income for full SSPS members and 1.22 percent for MS members. Degression in the estimated pension-base income will be eliminated gradually, ceasing only around 2009. The ceiling on 'pensionable income' (and the employees' contribution base) will always equal twice the expected annual average gross wage. On the other hand, elimination of the incomplete valorization of earnings is not planned for any time in the future. A rather ambiguous provision in the act concerned stipulates that pensions in 2013 should be switched from the 'net' to the 'gross' principle, meaning that pension benefits will become taxable, but the necessary adjustments in the tax and contribution rates are not outlined in the act.

The reform did change the *indexation rules* for continued pensions. A gradual change from the previous net-wage index to the 'Swiss' index is prescribed. The SSPS act stipulated that the wage indexation should be sustained partially for 1998 (reduced by 2.5 percentage points, to cover the costs of increased survivors' benefits, to be discussed later) and fully for 1999. For 2000, there was to be a 30–70 mix, and for 2001, the final 50–50 mix of the annually projected price index and the net wage index.

While the system for old-age pensions was left largely unchanged, quite important changes were made in survivors' and disability benefits.

With *survivors' benefits,* the 'one-pension-for-one-person' rule had applied before the 1998 reform, with those persons eligible for more than one pension being allowed to choose the greater benefit of the two. The reform changed this rule, allowing a maximum of two benefits to accrue to each person. Thus a widow or widower could receive benefit in that capacity in addition to his or her own pension. However, the level of widow's (widower's) benefit was decreased from 50 to 20 percent of the deceased spouse's pension. (Later a 50 percent level was restored under a Constitutional Court ruling for those not eligible for a pension in their own right.)

The rules on the calculation and eligibility of individual *disability benefits* were not changed. However, an important alteration for the finances of the public scheme was made. Responsibility for providing the benefits of the disabled persons below statutory retirement age who had completely lost their ability to work was transferred back from the HIF to the PIF, but without a corresponding alteration in the allocation of social-security contributions between the two.

The act on *contributions* called for the establishment of a personal contribution register for the SSPS, requiring employers to register each employee's contributions individually, along with each contribution payment. However, this requirement was postponed after a few months until 1999 and later revoked.

The act on the SSPS gives a full *government guarantee* for the public scheme, including compensation from the government budget for losses resulting from the employees' contributions of MS members being paid to MPPFs rather than the SSPS. This budget obligation, on the other hand, implies increased leverage in pension issues for the Ministry of Finance.

2.2. Enactment of the mandatory private pillar

2.2.a. Governance structure

To some extent, the mandatory private pension funds of the mixed system are modelled on the voluntary mutual pension funds, regulated by Act XCVI/1993. Their legal structure was finally reached under a compromise acceptable to all the parties that had some chance of asserting their interests while the reform was prepared.

An MPPF is a non-profit organization for collecting contributions from its members in personal accounts and investing them to assure their members income after their retirement. Conspicuously, however, the provision of annuities (pension-type benefits) is not listed specifically among the obligatory tasks of an MPPF. Rather, funds may *decide* whether they want to provide annuities themselves or buy annuities for their retiring members from an insurance company. This implies that the personal accounts represent personal savings over the accumulation period and that members belong to an investment association not significantly different from a mutual fund. Only on retirement does a member (or the capital endowment accumulated in his or her personal account) become part of a real insurance pool that shares the mortality risk.

MPPFs may be founded by employers, chambers of commerce and trade unions, singly or jointly, and by voluntary pension funds. The *owners* of a fund are its members, who exercise their rights through the general assembly. The general assembly elects a board of directors and a board of supervisors, to direct and control the operation respectively, and it approves the basic statutes of the fund. Obviously, the general assembly is a formal rather than an operational body in a large fund with hundreds of thousands of members, so that the founders have wide scope to assert their own interests.

The *operation* of the fund is carried out by several appointed persons (appointment of a managing director, an auditor, an actuary, an investment manager, a legal officer and an internal auditor is mandatory) and outside institutions. (A bank and an external custodian are mandatory, while outsourcing asset management, administration and record keeping is optional.) A fund has to meet statutory investment, disclosure, reporting and accounting obligations, and to publish a simplified version of its audited annual report, containing its balance sheet, profit and loss statement and financial report. Each fund member has to receive a statement of his or her personal account at least once a year. The accounting rule applied is accrual accounting. Both market and book values for the assets have to be recorded, with the market values being updated every quarter.

The funds and the financial firms to which asset management of the fund, for example, is outsourced, are supervised by the *State Financial Supervisory Authority* (SFSA), whose president is elected by Parliament for a six-year term. The president reports to the government and has an advisory board, stipulated by law. The SFSA features in the government budget but also has its own revenues from the supervisory fees paid by the MPPFs. These were originally 0.2 percent of members' contributions and will become 0.4 percent in 2002. The fee is included in the operational costs.

The SFSA plays a role in the *licensing procedures* for the funds (licensing of foundations and separate licences for operation). It issues and enforces regulations, partly defined by law. A fund wishing to provide the annuities for its retired members requires a further licence from the SFSA.

MPPFs must file quarterly and annual *reports* to the SFSA. The annual report has to include an *actuarial report*. The legislation prescribes some aspects of the form and content of these reports. The SFSA is currently drawing up a rule requiring funds to conduct and report daily asset evaluations. This is due to enter into force in 2002.

2.2.b. Contributions and capital accumulation

A member's contributions to an MPPF are divided into three parts. One part (4–5 percent in most funds) covers the fund's *operational costs*. About 1 percent goes into various contingency *reserves*. The remaining 94–5 percent is credited to the member's *personal account*.

A fund has to design and implement an *investment policy* that specifies a benchmark or benchmarks corresponding to its goals. The benchmark value or values have to be published annually. (Benchmarks are discussed in more detail in Section 3.4.)

The *investments* of the funds are regulated on two legislative levels. Sections of the act contain some general statements, for example on controlling risks and maintaining solvency. The government decree implementing the act contains several prescriptions of a quota type concerning the securities in which the assets may be held. For example, a fund may not hold too high a proportion of its assets from the same origin or own too high a stake in the registered capital or equity of a business association.

Costs of investment (*e.g.* costs of asset management) are deducted from the fund's gross returns. The net returns that remain are credited quarterly to the personal accounts of the fund members.

The act prescribes the creation of several reserves. One is the *liquidity reserve*, whose purpose is self-evident. Some of the more important additional reserves are described briefly in the following paragraphs, and some consequences of these are noted in Section 2.2.f.

If a fund does not outsource its investment management or annuity-providing operations, it must establish out of its members' contributions a *self-activity reserve* (about fifty thousand USD) to protect against incidental losses on such activities.

If the fund provides its own annuities, it has to create a *service reserve* and a separate *demographic reserve*. When a member retires, a small portion of the balance in the personal account is transferred into the demographic reserve and the rest into the service reserve.

All MPPFs must create a *return-adjustment reserve*. The object here is to stabilize or even out the rate of return over the years that the personal accounts and service reserve obtain. There is an expected band of return for each fund in each year, determined annually in advance by the board advising the president of the SFSA. The band depends on performance parameters of the economy and the

MPPF concerned. (In practice, it has been set as the rate of return attainable by holding a certain portfolio of government bonds.) At the end of the year or somewhat later, it becomes possible to calculate the fund's actual rate of return and compare it with the band that was prescribed.

Nothing happens if the fund's rate of return lies within the band. If it is higher, some of the surplus yield will be transferred into the return-adjustment reserve from the personal accounts to which higher rates were applied. If it is lower, some money will be transferred from this reserve into the personal accounts to which lower rates were applied. (Normally, the rates of return applied to the various personal accounts differ only because the incoming contributions during the quarter are made at different times. However, the act leaves open the possibility of the MPPF varying the personal rates, but it does not specify the permissible reasons for doing so. This is a serious deficiency in the regulations, which could allow various accounting manipulations to occur.)

2.2.c. The pension promise

An MPPF provides its members with benefits in case of death or disability before retirement, and ultimately, on retirement.

If a member *dies* during the accumulation period (*i.e.* before retiring), a previously designated beneficiary of the insured may withdraw the endowment from the personal account as a lump sum. This is designed to be an equivalent of the survivors' benefit awarded under the public scheme. However, the act defines for the public scheme who the recipients of the survivors' benefit may be and takes care of them all, while a member of an MPPF is free to appoint anyone as the beneficiary and the bequest is not a function of the number of beneficiaries, *e.g.* orphans.

A member who becomes *disabled* during the accumulation period may choose between an annuity from the MPPF, based on the capital endowment in the personal account (along with another from the public pillar, which will make a specified percentage of the disability benefit of a full SSPS member), or returning the accumulated capital to the SSPS, which provides full disability benefit.

On *retirement*, the basis for calculating the annuity to be received is the amount accumulated in the member's personal account. Members may choose among various types of annuity, which the act describes:

a) A single-life annuity to be paid until the annuitant's death.

b) Annuities on two or more lives, paid while at least one beneficiary survives.

c) A guaranteed life annuity paid at least until a date previously agreed. If the annuitant survives after that date, the annuity becomes a life annuity. If the annuitant dies earlier, the annuity is paid instead to the appointed beneficiary until that date.

In cases other than a single-life annuity, the distribution among the beneficiaries applicable for various periods is regulated by the fund. If the MPPF provides its own annuities, the range it offers must include the single-life annuity and at least one other annuity type.

The *indexation rule* for the annuities is the same as for the public pillar, *i.e.* the indexing has to reflect wage and price increases in equal proportions. Many experts are sceptical about this provision, which introduces into the system the further risk of unforeseeable wage increases. Moreover, it is not clear how insurance companies will relate to this rule, as there are no products currently on the annuity market that satisfy these requirements.

Even when the MPPF provides its own annuities, a member retains the right to purchase the benefit due from another MPPF or instruct his or her own fund to buy the benefit from an insurance company. In that case, a transaction fee set by the fund has to be paid. Some sections in the act imply that the provider can be changed even after retirement, *i.e.* in the service period. This possibility could certainly have an adverse selection effect, well described in the pension literature. Similar effects may also derive from the possibility of choosing among various types of annuities, and of inheritance by another of the capital endowment in the personal account of the insured.

2.2.d. Guarantees

The act introduces the concept of 'guaranteed capital'. If the capital endowment in a member's personal account on retirement is less than the capital required to provide a prescribed annuity on two lives, the member's capital endowment should be brought up to such a level by the *Guarantee Fund*. This applies only after a minimum contribution period to mandatory private funds of 180 months. Although no age limit is imposed for voluntary switching to the mixed system, the legislators were concerned to limit the chances of 'irrational' switching. Members with less than 180 months' membership may take the accumulated capital at retirement as a lump sum. The act's definition of the annuity to be assured by the guaranteed capital is rather ambiguous.

However, there are also provisions at the opposite end. If the capital endowment in the personal account exceeds twice the defined guaranteed capital, the member may withdraw the excess as a lump sum. (From a technical point of view, it may be seen as advantageous that the lower and upper limits on the capital restrain the variance in the annuities, since probability calculations are easier and safer if the variance is smaller.)

The object of establishing the Guarantee Fund was to safeguard the rights of MPPF members and to assist pension funds in providing annuities. The Guarantee Fund accordingly performs additional functions in the system. It pays out the capital endowment in the personal account when a member switches from one fund to another, if the MPPF is unable to pay (which would occur in practice in a case of fraud or negligence). It will also lend capital to funds whose reserves do not cover their liabilities.

The fee payable to the Guarantee Fund by the funds, which is included in the operating costs of the latter, will vary from time to time between 0.3 and 0.5 percent of members' contributions, as decided by the board of the Guarantee Fund and endorsed by the SFSA. The portfolio of the Guarantee Fund consists exclusively of government bonds. If its resources should be depleted, the government guarantees its borrowing.

2.2.e. Equity between genders

The act states that the benefit provided by an MPPF may not be influenced by the sex of the member. However, the legal grounds for 'unisex' treatment of annuities are actuarially unclear and controversial. The main legislative rules are the following.

The actuary of an MPPF is obliged to apply the 'unisex' life table of the fund in taking account of the mortality of male and female members. Starting from the endowment in the personal account, the annuity is to be calculated by applying the standard principle of actuarial equivalence. However, the actuary has to take into account the member's sex when calculating reserves. All these rules, along with the leeway allowed to providers, frustrate the calculation of actuarially prudent 'unisex' annuities whose redistribution is transparent.

It is even less clear what happens to the annuities provided by an outside insurance company. There is a provision in the act stating that the insurance company has to sell products specifically devised for MPPF members. Presumably the intention behind this was to extend the requirement of 'unisex' annuities to the insurance companies. However, an earlier act regulating insurance-company activity makes no mention of such special products and such companies do not generally apply 'unisex' life tables.

2.2.f. Redistribution

It is customary in pension literature to assume that privately funded pension schemes, unlike public PAYG schemes, are not redistributive, for which they are often specifically praised. It is usually emphasized that the capital in the personal account is personally owned, which implies that each MPPF saves exclusively for his or her own retirement. This section will show that this assumption cannot be sustained under the Hungarian legislation.

A mandatory private pension scheme necessarily involves an *underlying redistribution* of members' retirement savings due to their varying life spans. However, sharing of the mortality risk in Hungarian MPPFs takes place only after retirement, as the personal capital endowment of the fund member is inheritable in case of death during the pre-retirement accumulation period.

Since longevity is not unrelated to sex, social status, income and education, even sharing of the 'purest' *mortality risk* produces a redistribution among social groups when pension funds are precluded from discriminating according to such criteria, for example, by the imposition of 'unisex' life tables and annuities. Such requirements are natural, on the other hand, if pension funds are regarded as parts of a mandatory system of social insurance. Depending on the demographic composition of an MPPF, 'unisex' annuities may generate either a surplus (if there is male predominance among the annuitants) or a deficit (if there is female predominance). How this kind of imbalance is to be tackled remains unclear and is compounded by other unanswered questions, such as who will ultimately provide the annuities and what role and approach insurance companies will take.

Various guarantees are built into the system, such as the reserves to be created by MPPFs in addition to the obviously required service reserve, and the various functions of the Guarantee Fund. These are intended to make the system safer, but they do not necessarily do so. For instance, future demographic developments may belie the assumptions on which the creation of the *demographic reserve* was based. At the same time, these rules decrease the portion of the contributions credited to the personal account and produce an unwanted redistribution inconsistent with the philosophy of a privately funded scheme.

The *return-adjustment reserve* exemplifies unnecessary, opaque redistribution well. The smooth and even rates of return over many years that it is designed to promote constitute a questionable objective, since the defined-contribution, funded system rests on the principle of higher returns for higher risks. The proper objective of the system, according to its theoretical foundations, is to collect as much capital in the personal accounts as possible at any time (assuming that none of the personal accounts can be discriminated against).

The return-adjustment reserve is inconsistent with this goal. This is obviously the case if the investment-return rate of the reserve is greater or less than that of the personal accounts, when the mere existence of the reserve will affect the overall returns credited to members. However, redistribution among fund members may still ensue if the rate of return of the reserve is the same as that of the personal accounts, due to variations in the times of contributions and/or retirement. For example, someone who retires after many years of high rates of return loses the portion of the returns on the capital endowment that has been transferred to the reserve. Conversely, someone retiring after an extended period of low returns gains because the balance in his or her personal account has been supplemented from the reserve, which has been replenished previously from returns taken from other members.

In effect, the return-adjustment mechanism and the concept of 'guaranteed capital' blur the *defined-contribution* feature of the system, by breaking the strict correlation between individual contributions paid and annuities received, thereby inducing redistribution within and among the funds.

In MPPFs that pay their own annuities, the personal accounts and the investments of the accumulating fund are strictly separated from the *service reserve*, which contains the combined capital endowments of retired members. The only link between the contributing members and the retired members is their membership of the same legal entity. It follows that the rate of return on the personal accounts that are still accumulating may differ significantly from the return on the service reserve. The only exception is the return-adjustment reserve, where the rates of return of both the benefit reserve and the personal accounts must be taken into account by law and the necessary transfers made. Such transfers can present difficulties, since the technical interest rate already provides a guaranteed rate of return for the service reserve.

As for the *self-activity reserve*, the flat-sum provision will have to be replaced sooner or later by a more sophisticated solvency capital, dependent on the level of the services provided by the fund. This would be more reasonable and closer to the practice of insurance companies.

If the reserves of a fund do not cover its liabilities, the bailout provided by the *Guarantee Fund* must be paid back. This is another strange feature of the system, as it is hard to conceive who will make the return payment and when. If it later becomes possible for the fund to pay, the result will again be an opaque redistribution among successive generations of members. Instead, the Guarantee Fund should be established in such a way that it can cover certain risks clearly specified by legislation. This would offer a more transparent redistribution among the funds and fund members.

Some problems to do with the reserves are currently under consideration by professional and legal committees, so that modifications can be expected. Deficiencies in the legal framework will have to be addressed sooner or later, but they will not be easy to remedy.

3. Early post-reform experience

3.1. Subsequent legislative changes in 1998–2000

Parliamentary elections in 1998 resulted in a new coalition government consisting of political parties that had previously been in opposition. There is no reason to assume that the pension reform had any effect on this outcome. Nevertheless, subsequent legislation has significantly altered the institutional arrangements and several parameters of the pension system enacted in 1997. The changes that required legislation were approved by Parliament, while others fell within the competence of the government.

The *relative independence* of the public pension scheme was abolished. The Self-governing Body of the Pension Insurance Fund was disbanded (along with its counterpart for the Health Insurance Fund) and the PIF placed under direct government supervision, mainly by the Ministry of Finance, which also presents the PIF's annual budget to Parliament.

The *collection* of social-security contributions was transferred from the PIF and the HIF to the State Tax Collection Agency (STCA). This may seem a purely technical measure, but it reinforced the view (mainly held by employers) that social security contributions are simply a form of tax. The clause in the Act on Contributions requiring employers to record each employee's contribution individually within each contribution payment was deleted, as the STCA was neither able nor willing to develop or maintain the huge register that this would require.

The *deadline* before which MPPF members may still return to the pure SSPS without loss has been extended year after year. The option is still open until the end of 2002.

The rules of *indexation* for continued pensions were already changed in 1999. Rather than retaining the gradual transformation prescribed in the act – sustained wage-indexation with a one-year lag in 1999, a 30–70 mix of the price and wage indices in 2000, and the so-called Swiss method (a 50–50 mix) in 2001 – the government declared that the indexation rules of the act were not 'affordable' in 1999. The reason was that the gradual rules implied a 18.4 percent increase in all continued benefits in that year. Instead, the rather inadequate practice of defining flat sums and upper and lower limits was reapplied. Benefits generally were increased by HUF 3500 per month, but low benefits were not to be increased by more than 25.5 percent and all benefits had to be increased by at least 11 percent. These complicated limits yielded an increase of less than HUF 3500 for about 3 percent of pensioners and more than HUF 3500 for about 23 percent. The average increase, however, came to only 14.2 percent, i.e. by more than 4 percentage points less than prescribed in the 1997 act for 1999. Naturally, the loss to pensioners spilled over into the following years, as the 1999 base for later increases was significantly lower than it should have been. The overall result of this is discussed further in Section 3.3.

Probably the most drastic changes affected *contribution rates*, as Table 4 shows.

Table 4 Pension insurance contribution rates (gross wage = 100)					
	Employers	Employees	TOTAL	MS members to MPPF	to SSPS
1998	24 (24)	7 (7)	31 (31)	6 (6)	1 (1)
1999	22 (23)	8 (8)	30 (31)	6 (7)	2 (1)
2000	22 (22)	8 (9)	30 (31)	6 (8)	2 (1)
2001	20 (22)	8 (9)	28 (31)	6 (8)	2 (1)
2002	18 (22)	8 (9)	26 (31)	6 (8)	2 (1)

Rates legislated in 1997 are shown in brackets.

As mentioned already, the Contributions Act of 1997 sought to keep the total rate constant at 31 percent of the gross wage, while gradually reallocating two percentage points from the employers' to employees' contributions, to widen the field for the mandatory private pillar which depends exclusively on employees' contributions. Instead, the total rate will be down by 5 percentage points in 2002, to 26 percent. This makes the long-term sustainability of the entire system questionable in the light of the expected demographic changes. The major beneficiaries of these provisions are the employers, whose 'burden' is to be decreased by 6 percent of the wage bill, from 24 to 18 percent. Employees enjoy one percentage point of the cut. They continue to pay 8 percent (instead of the pre-reform 6 percent), rather than the envisaged 9 percent. Within that, however, the rate to be paid to the mandatory private pillar has been frozen at 6 percent, while 2 percent rather than 1 percent goes to the public pillar. The results in terms of gains and losses are summarized in Table 5.

Table 5		
Contribution gains (+) and losses (–) in 2002 as proportions of the annual wage bill		
	As compared to	
	1997 actual	legislated in 1997 for 2002
Employers	+ 6	+ 4
Employees	– 1	+ 1
Together	**+ 5**	**+ 5**
SSPS	– 5	– 3
MPPFs		– 2
Together	**– 5**	**– 5**

While the MPPFs are not happy with this outcome, the changes have placed the SSPS at an even graver disadvantage. The rationale advanced is to improve the profitability and competitiveness of the economy. Most importantly for future pensioners, accrual rates in the public pillar have not been adjusted to the somewhat increased contribution and the obviously diminished prospects of capital accumulation in the private pillar.

In November 2001, important changes were made to do with membership of the mixed system and guarantees for mandatory pension fund members. In provisions attached to the act concerning approval of the previous year's budgetary activities, Parliament made it *voluntary* to join the mixed system, even for entrants to the labour market, and ended the obligation of the Guarantee Fund to top up the personal capital endowment to the guaranteed-capital level.

3.2. Transition of people to the mixed system
3.2.a. The process
Employees had 20 months (from January 1, 1998 to August 31, 1999) to choose whether to remain full members of the SSPS or join the mixed system. Eventually, the number of those who joined exceeded expectations. The official projection suggested there would be 1.5 million MPPF members, while the true figure was about 2 million – 48 percent of the economically active population (including the unemployed), of whom almost one hundred and fifty thousand were mandatory members (entrants into the labour market). The difference between the two figures may reflect the effects of two counteracting factors:

1. *'Active' errors:* Some people switched to the mixed system even though the value of their eventual capital endowment is likely to fall short of the value of the accrual rights they lost at the SSPS.

2. *'Passive' errors:* Some people failed to switch to the mixed system even though they would have done better to do so.

The process of switching reflected various kinds of behaviour. TARKI polled public opinion on the new funds on several occasions in 1998 and made predictions of the number of switchers, which varied between 1.7 and 1.9 million (TARKI, 1999) and clearly outlined the group of potential members. People who were sure about joining registered early, especially employees in early middle age, who are less likely to ignore their future than those in their twenties. After the early months had elapsed, the age composition of the funds became remarkably different, with enrolment of new members proceeding for over a year at an almost constant speed of some fifty thousand recruits a month. This reflects the impact of the network of agents put into the field by the large funds. Finally, there was a rush by several hundred thousand, mainly younger employees, to sign up in August 1999.

A follow-up survey in 2000, more than a year later, showed that there would have been even more switchers if the funds had been reopened to those who missed the deadline. Less numerous were the actual and potential flows in the opposite direction. By the end of the first quarter of 2001, only 38 thousand members of MPPFs (1.7 percent) returned their savings to the SSPS. According to the 2000 survey, only 3–3.5 percent were considering such a course. If an individual returns, the capital in the personal account is transferred back to the SSPS and all accrual rights there are restored as if nothing had happened.

3.2.b. The choice situation

The choice between staying in the pure pay-as-you-go scheme or moving to the mixed system is usually assumed in the literature to depend on the number of service years that a worker has already attained, the number of future service years, the slope of the age-earnings profile, the rate of return on the capital, the internal rate of return on contributions to the PAYG scheme, and differences in risk-structure of the competing pillars.

Age is probably the single most important explanatory variable for switching. It affects the previous contribution period (*i.e.* the pension rights hitherto earned in the public scheme, which have to be given up) and the expected length of future service (*i.e.* the predictable future capital endowment). However, the age limit above which it is no longer profitable to switch becomes blurred by the slope of the *age-earnings profile*. People who can expect steeper profiles (who usually have a higher education) are likely to suffer relatively less by losing their past contributions, because their future earnings will be higher. So people with a high level of educational attainment are likely to switch until a relatively higher age.

As for the *returns on funds*, many economists agree that dynamic efficiency holds in practice: yields on the stock exchange are higher than the internal rate of return from PAYG schemes. On the other hand, the operating costs of organizing the collection of contributions and the payment of pensions in a decentralized way exceed those of a social security system. In passing the legislation on the Hungarian pension reform, Parliament accepted the assumption made by the majority of experts that the investment returns of the MPPFs would exceed the implicit rate of return in social security by enough to outweigh their higher operating costs.

The effects of differences in *relative risks* are more difficult to pinpoint, even theoretically. Funded schemes face investment risk and annuitization risk. Pension funds can be mismanaged and inflation may hit the yields on capital. The member's portfolio of assets may offer high gains most of the time, but he or she is unprotected against sharp fluctuations on the stock exchange around retirement time (Alier and Vittas, 1999). Annuities may become too expensive, as insurance companies and pension funds try to protect themselves from risks resulting from superior information available to others about the member's health status and hence life expectancy (Mitchell *et alia* 1999). Moreover, private funds may be better shielded from political risks in the accumulation period, but at the time of converting the endowment into an annuity, they are less protected against the government's propensity to levy tax. On the other hand, a PAYG scheme is even more exposed to political risks (Diamond, 1997) and tends to be heavily redistributive within and between generations (Geanakoplos, Mitchell and Zeldes, 1999). It is also seen as more vulnerable to demographic risks, especially ageing, since it is easier to export assets through capital markets to countries with a younger population than it is to import labour from them.

The net effects of returns and relative risks are fervently debated by experts, let alone lay people trying to make up their minds about switching. The TARKI polls already mentioned suggest that respondents were expecting higher pensions from private funds, and as the number of fund members increased, they even tended to consider them safer.

Apart from such general considerations, the switching decision was subject to several *individual characteristics*. First, the effects of current decisions about pensions follow only much later and people tend to devalue future effects. So the choice is likely to have been influenced by discounting the future and myopia. The former displays increasing strength with the length of the individual prospects ahead, so that it would cause younger people to tend to switch less than expected. The combination of the two opposing impacts of age – the higher future gains (discussed already) as opposed to the stronger tendency to discount the future – gives a mixed impact. The rules that favour those switching at a younger age will tend to leave young cohorts over-represented among the MPPF members, but stronger discounting the future will make for passive errors: failure to switch when it would have been advantageous to do.

To look at another dimension of human character, *myopia* causes people to care less about their prospects. Fortunately, there was a question that captured myopia in the TARKI poll and a variable in the model to be introduced later, so that this relation can be tested.

Another important feature of the choice situation was *uncertainty about the consequences*. As mentioned earlier, there is no general consensus among experts about the investment, annuitization and political risks entailed. Moreover, individuals were facing a double choice: whether or not to switch, and if so, which MPPF to join. The choice was difficult in terms of collecting the requisite detailed information on the legislation (largely impenetrable to lay people anyway), assessing the prospects of the entire private sector and particular pension funds, and acquiring or hiring the expertise necessary to make this analysis. This gave selling agents and employers importance in guiding potential switchers.

3.2.c. Switching behaviour

This sub-section examines the roles of five explanatory factors behind switching behaviour, based on the successive TARKI polls: age, education, time horizon (myopia or foresight), size of employer (where applicable) and income.

The *age* of fund members, as expected, is significantly lower than the age of non-members. While non-members averaged 40 years of age in the sample taken in 2000, members averaged only 34. The relative youth of later entrants increased the age difference between the two groups in the TARKI samples from 4.8 years in 1999 to 6.2 years in 2000.

The frequency of active and passive errors could be captured by relating the number of MPPF members to the number of economically active by age group. This is shown in Table 6.

Table 6			
MPPF members among the economically active population by age group			
Age	**Percent**	**Age**	**Percent**
15–19	89	41–45	36
20–24	81	46–50	15
25–30	84	51–55	3
31–34	76	56–60	1
35–40	60	61–	0

Source: SFSA 1999 Quarterly Reports, economically active population including the unemployed

Although the highest rate of switching to the mixed system can be found among the youngest age group and the rate declines by age in all but one age group, 11 percent of the 15–19 age group are very likely to have made a passive error. The same applies to most of the non-switching 19 percent of the 20–24 cohorts. (Only 89 and 81 percent of these groups switched.) Passive errors were probably lower among the 35–40 and 41–45 cohorts, but active errors are likely to have occurred above the age of 45.

It had been expected that fund members would be *more educated* than non-members, for two reasons. (1) As mentioned earlier, people with a higher educational attainment usually have a steeper age-earnings profile, so that the age borderline separating the cohorts for whom it is better to switch from those for whom it is better not to switch shifts upwards. (2) On average, the level of education attainment is higher in younger age groups, due to the expansion of higher education in recent decades. The expected age effect automatically pushes up the level of education among members. Other reasons why a growing difference in educational attainment can be expected are because younger cohorts tended to register later and because only labour-market entrants were permitted to sign up after the deadline of August 31, 1999.

As the annual TARKI Household Monitor showed in 1999 and 2000, fund members were indeed better educated and the difference grew with time, again in line with the hypothesis. While the difference between the means for the switching and non-switching groups was 0.73 years of educational attainment in the TARKI Household Monitor in 1999, it was almost a full year in 2000.

The *time horizon* of respondents was captured by a question about the ways in which they were preparing for old age. Respondents were offered nine potential preparation strategies, which can be grouped under the following titles: prolongation of labour-market activity, traditional types of saving, saving through financial market products, and reliance on the family network. Three out of the nine strategies could be chosen. This aspect divided the sample into two groups: (1) those who named at least one strategy, and (2) those who were myopic and gave the 'don't prepare' or 'don't know' responses. Fund members were expected to have clearer views about coping with their fall in income in old age.

The TARKI data show that MPPF members indeed have a different time horizon. Almost 80 percent had some idea of how to prepare for old age, while the corresponding figure among non-members was only 50 percent.

With *employment*, the prediction is for greater economic activity among switchers, for three reasons. (1) The unemployed have higher chances of disrupted labour-market careers and lower future earnings paths, making them more likely to fall into the group for which it is better not to switch. (2) The transaction costs of joining a fund are higher for the unemployed, who cannot call on administrative help from the employer in arranging membership. (3) Finally, the unemployed have fewer chances of meeting a pension-fund recruiting agent, simply because people can be more easily reached on workplaces and the employed make more attractive recruits to the fund. For the last of these reasons, a positive relation is also predicted between the size of employing organization and the probability of joining a fund.

Both expectations are supported by the figures. Non-switchers are three times as likely to have no job as switchers are. To a lesser extent, they are also more likely to work for small firms (including self-employment).

Finally, for reasons not dissociated from the earlier ones (notably education and employment), members have significantly *higher incomes*: 30 percent higher in the case of the TARKI sample.

3.2.d. A regression analysis

Since some of these variables produce overlapping effects, an attempt was made to separate them by a logistic regression analysis. The purpose was to see how well this group of variables explains switching behaviour, how strong the separate effects of the individual variables are, and what order of relative importance pertains among them. The results appear in Table 7. This displays four values for every variable: the logistic regression coefficient (B, the marginal effect of the independent variable on the logit of the dependent variable), the so-called Wald statistic created by transformation from the coefficient, which in large samples has a χ^2 distribution, its level of significance (P), and the partial correlation coefficient (R) measuring the relative importance of an individual variable.

Table 7
The logistic regression model for choice of switching

	B (regression coefficient)	Wald-statistics	P (level of significance of the Wald-statistics)	R (partial correlation coefficient)
Education	0.08	10.0	0.002	0.05
Age	−0.10	267.6	<0.005	−0.31
Time horizon	1.42	134.1	<0.005	0.22
Employer(*)	–	129.2	<0.005	0.20
Income	<0.05	2.1	0.148	0.01

(*) Degree of freedom is 5 for this variable and 1 for all the other

Table 7 shows that all the variables except income have a significant effect on switching, even if cleaned of interaction with other variables. The significant income difference between members and non-members seems to derive from a background effect, probably the fact that switchers are more educated and more likely to have a job. A person with a higher income but the same type of employment and education as another person is not noticeably more likely to switch.

In line with the expectations, the strongest individual effect is produced by age. The other two variables exerting strong influence are the time horizon and the type of employer. Those who have at least some idea of how they will deal with the problem of falling income in old age are much likelier to join an MPPF. The difference between members and non-members is significant at all levels if the time-horizon variable is coded to differentiate between more than two levels, based on how many preparation strategies respondents name (the lowest being 0 and the highest 3). Furthermore, if the preparation strategy of saving through financial market products, of which fund membership is just one of many possibilities, is eliminated, the significant difference between members and non-members still prevails.

Possession of a job and the size of the employing company both influence switching. The unemployed are significantly less likely to be MPPF members than those working for small firms. On the other hand, those employed by larger firms are even more likely to switch.

The results of the model are demonstrated here through the examples of two, extremely different persons representing largely different social groups:

> This is a 50-year-old whose educational attainment is the eight grades of elementary school. He or she is unemployed, has no idea of how to prepare for old age, with an income only half the national average. The probability of such a person switching to the mixed system is 1.7 percent.
>
> This is a 25-year-old with a university degree working for a company with over 500 employees, with a long time horizon as defined earlier, and earning an average wage. In this case the probability of switching is 92.8 percent.

In conclusion, it is safe to say that the incentives built into the switching rules affected the decisions of individuals, whose behaviour can be described in terms of a rational choice. The age distribution follows a clear age pattern in line with international experience (Disney, Palacios and Whitehouse, 1999) and the inten-tions of those devising the switching rules. Nevertheless, targeting was not perfect. The larger-than-expected number of switchers to the mixed system, particularly those above 40–45 years of age, suggests that active errors (joining when remaining in the pure SSPS would have been more advantageous) were strongly at work. On the other hand, the fall of the switching rate among the youngest active cohorts to 90 percent shows that passive error (not switching when it would have been advantageous) was not rare either.

3.3. Results and problems in the public pillar

The underlying, paradigmatic feature of the 1998 reform was its creation of a privatized, mandatory funded pillar. The essential problems of the public system either remained unsolved or were shelved by the act until some ambiguous solution scheduled for around 2010. Nevertheless, the SSPS has been affected by a number of less important, though significant changes in the public pillar, such as the alteration of the survivors' benefit system and the reallocation of certain types of disability benefit from the HIF to the PIF (see Section 2.1.). Further modifications came with the successive legislative changes in 1998–2000 (see Section 3.1.).

It is virtually impossible to disentangle the effects of the earlier, unreformed problems from those of the 1998 reform and subsequent legislation.

3.3.a. Survivors' and disability benefits

The changes brought by the 1998 reform had an immediate impact here. In 1997, there were 724 thousand survivors' benefits being paid. This jumped to 860,000 when the possibility of receiving two concurrent benefits came in 1998. The ratio of widows' (widowers') benefit paid to all benefits jumped from 23.1 to 26.2 percent. This was not through an increase in the number of recipients. On the contrary, the number of beneficiaries living solely from widows' (widowers') benefits decreased from 8.8 percent to 8.3 percent of all pensioners. It was a case not of new pensioners appearing, but of existing pensioners becoming eligible for a second benefit.

The reform has left survivors' and disability risks to the public pillar, even where the beneficiaries have joined the mixed system. At the same time, the actuarially necessary funding for them is not covered by the SSPS contribution rate, as explained below. In the early years of the maturation period of MPPFs, the burden on the SSPS has not yet proved financially significant, but if the situation remains unresolved, it may cause grave difficulties in the long run.

The beneficiaries of MPPF members are appointed by the members themselves. If an active (non-retired) member dies, the benefiting survivor or survivors may decide to return to the SSPS with the endowment inherited from the personal account of the deceased, with full survivors' right in the SSPS. However, such beneficiaries are not necessarily the same as legal survivors. Some of the beneficiaries may not be survivors in the legal sense and some of the survivors may not be beneficiaries. (Non-beneficiary survivors will receive 75 percent of the normal SSPS survivor's benefit, as compared with the 75 percent expected SSPS pension benefit of the member.) At present, there are no forecasts of the consequent long-term financial burden on the SSPS.

The rules are more or less similar with disability. If an MPPF member becomes disabled, he or she may switch back to SSPS, transferring the capital endowment that has built up in the personal account and having full rights to SSPS disability benefits restored. Currently, almost all newly disabled choose to return because their accumulation period in the MPPF has been short. This situation will probably change very slowly if at all.

Obviously, in case of a member's death or disability, the beneficiaries will choose for themselves the best benefit bargain. All those who have less on their personal accounts than the discounted lifetime value of the expected SSPS benefit will return to the SSPS. In insurance parlance, the SSPS has to readmit the 'bad risks' of the MPPFs. Since survivors' benefits currently amount to about 14 percent of aggregate pension expenditure and the disability-benefits account for more than 16 percent (including disabled persons above statutory retirement age), the consequences for SSPS may well become serious.

These problems have been addressed in quite a number of expert calculations and publications in recent years (*e.g.* Bod, 2000; Réti, 2000), but nothing has been done to remedy the problem of asymmetric risk handling between the two pillars.

3.3.b. Inadequate information system

Efforts to create an up-to-date information system for social security reach back as far as the late 1980s. A sizeable World Bank loan was granted to a project with this aim in the early 1990s, but implementation was halted and finally frustrated by rivalries between different government agencies.

Nevertheless, considerable progress has been made in digitalizing the previously paper-based tasks of assessing entry pensions at the time of retirement, recalculating continued pensions sometimes twice or three times a year as haphazard indexation rules require, and meticulously paying out monthly pensions. Such efforts were previously concentrated on providing proper service to individual beneficiaries, as this was always considered a politically sensitive issue. In more recent years, even aggregate statistics have become available on various groups of pensioners, distinguished by age, sex, and certain previous parameters descriptive of previous work record, year of retirement, *etc.* Unfortunately, important social characteristics such as educational attainment are still missing, because they play no role in the pension formula.

To sum up, it might be said that the amount of information on the *benefit* side is more or less satisfactory, although the administration is still working with pre-21st century types of hardware and software. The system is still not capable of running standard regression and/or sensitivity analyses. So it is not possible, without considerable intellectual outlay by experts and researchers, to separate the effects of various factors and measures, for instance to contrast the impact of the changing composition of pensioners with that of a changing indexation rule.

On the *contribution* side, the situation can be described as deplorable. Since 1988, employers have been required to report at the end of each year the contributions paid on behalf of each employee, as the pension formula now calculates pensionable income from 1988 until the moment of retirement. This mass of paper-based information continued to build up in damp cellars at regional offices of the PIF Administration, without being completely digitalized. Meanwhile there is a shortfall in the monies actually transferred by employers because of deficient payments and/or an excess because of *ex post* payments, fees, penalties for late transfers, *etc.* Thus the PIF's actual cash flow of contribution receipts would be neither compatible nor comparable with the individual employee records, even if the latter had been completely processed.

The 1998 reform required employers to transfer their contributions to the SSPS, plus 1 percent (later 2 percent) of the gross wages of MPPF members and 7 percent (later 8 percent) for non-members, along with a 6 percent employees' contribution from members directly to the MPPFs. Subsequent legislation (see Section 3.1.) authorized the STCA, the tax-collecting agency, to collect the contributions intended for the SSPS as well. These two measures made the situation much worse, as demonstrated by the Chart 1, which does not even indicate tax and other transfers from employers to the STCA (*e.g.* health contributions).

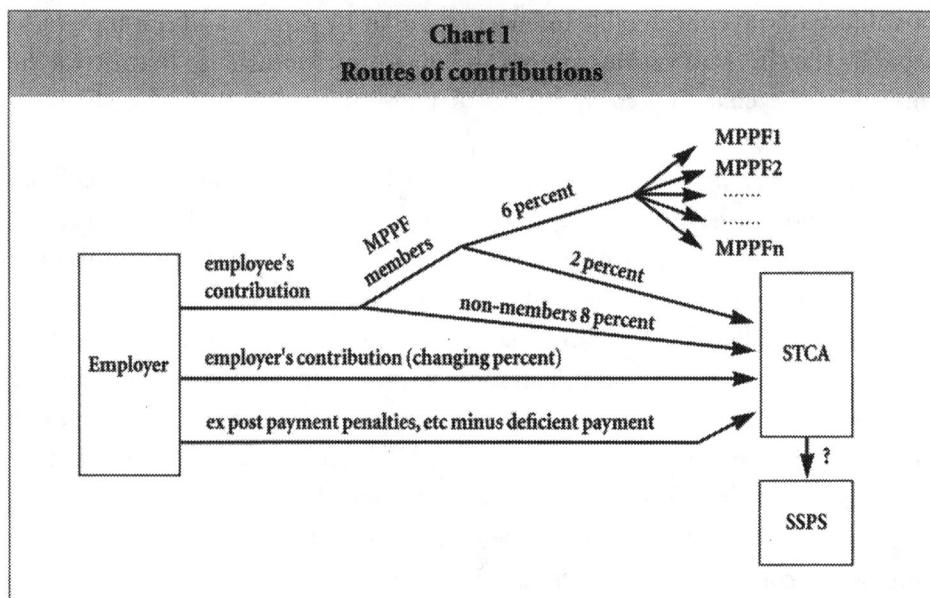

Chart 1
Routes of contributions

The STCA collects the money, but it is not obliged to process and maintain personal records until 2003. Nor has it any knowledge of the employees' contributions paid directly to mandatory private funds. It periodically transfers money to the PIF through the Treasury, but without supplying adequate information about the source of and legal title to its contribution revenues. Obviously, such revenues are even less comparable than before with the employers' reports on individual contributions. This prevents the SSPS from keeping continuous personal contribution records for its members. By the end of 2001, the insured were being notified by the PIF Administration about their pension-base income in 2000, but the information was based on the employers' annual reports to the SSPS, not on the actual, current contribution payments to the STCA.

In the circumstances, it is impossible to keep track of the actual contributions. Separation of the contributions of MPPF members from those of non-members, for example, is based on various estimates. Thus the compensation from the government for 'lost' SSPS employees' contribution revenue is also haphazard, relying on preliminary estimates built into the annual budget as approved by Parliament, rather than on the actual losses. Table 8 shows how various numbers for employees' contributions appear.

Table 8
Divergence in the data on employees' contributions
(Billion Hungarian Forints)

		1998	1999	2000
1	MPPF contribution revenue[1]	29.8	54.7	81.4
2	16.7 and 33.3 percent of above[2]	5.1	18.2	27.1
3	SSPS revenue from MPPF members[3]	n.a.	16.8	26.0
4	Government budget compensation[3]	20.0	57.2	63.2
5	Discrepancy (4-1)	−9.8	+2.5	−18.2

[1] Source: MPPF reports to Supervisory Authority

[2] The MPPFs are entitled to 6 percent of wage. SSPS share was 1 percent (16.7 percent of 6) in 1998 and 2 percent (33.3 percent of 6) in 1999–2000.

[3] Source: PIF Administration annual Yearbooks

Row 1 in the table indicates the actual flow into the MPPFs. Calculated on this basis, the SSPS revenue from fund members should have been the figure shown in Row 2, while Row 3 shows the *actual* revenues reported by the SSPS. The missing HUF 1.4–1.1 billion is not a large sum in terms of the PIF budget, but it raises questions about the efficiency of contribution collection. On the other hand, the discrepancy between the budgetary compensation and the contributions flowing into the MPPFs (Row 5) reached an appreciable magnitude already in 2000.

The 1997 Act on the SSPS calls for annual projections of the financial balance of the PIF over a ten-year period and demographic projections over a fifty-year period. However, it is not clear whose responsibility it is to provide such projections. In the light of what has been said so far, it is not surprising that no reliable projections have yet been published. The PIF Administration is currently at the stage of preparing a fairly large-scale simulation model, which may become capable of the task in some years' time.

The quality of the information system will probably improve in the medium term, but at present it makes it difficult even to summarize the current, early post-reform effects on the financial position of the SSPS. The following have to rely heavily on expert conjectures.

3.3.c. The financial balance

The cash-flow report of the PIF is a complex document, complete with minor items on both the revenue and expenditure sides and not free of accounting manipulations irrelevant to this study. The comparison here is between pure contribution revenues and aggregate pension expenditures.

First, in Table 9, a contrived, *ex post* situation is presented as if there had been no reform. It reconstructs a scenario in which the pre-reform parameters have remained applicable. There are no MPPFs. Employers' contributions are 24 percent of gross wages and employees' contributions 6 percent. Pensions are indexed to the net wage index for the previous year. There is no second survivor's benefit for widows (widowers) and no expenditure on disability benefits. These pre-reform parameters, however, are applied to otherwise real data for the 1998–2000 period (*e.g.* for the number of pensioners). The analysis is confined to this period for want of precise financial projections for the future. The 'no-reform' scenario serves as a background for assessing the effects of the changing parameters.

Table 9 The 'no-reform scenario' for contributions and pensions (Billions of Hungarian Forints)				
	1997	1998	1999	2000
Employers' contributions	499.4	593.7	686.2	790.1
Employees' contributions	95.6	125.9	142.0	171.7
Other contributions[1]	13.2	21.0	25.9	46.9
TOTAL CONTRIBUTIONS	608.2	740.6	854.1	1008.7
Old-age pensions[2]	527.3	662.2	786.3	888.7
Survivors' benefits	81.2	91.0	105.3	112.7
TOTAL PENSIONS	608.5	753.2	891.6	1001.4
BALANCE	–0.3	–12.6	–37.5	+7.3
For comparison: GDP	8540	10087	11393	12877
Pensions as percent of GDP	7.1	7.5	7.9	7.8

[1] Mostly from the government budget for non-contributory years. The jump in 2000 was due to an increased government contribution to the pensions of military personnel.

[2] Including disabled beneficiaries above the statutory retirement age

As discussed in Section 1.2, high inflation and falling real wages contributed to an extremely favourable financial situation for the PIF in 1997, while worsening the situation of pensioners. As inflation eased and real wages increased in subsequent years, pensioners would have been partly compensated for their previous losses by the pre-reform indexation rule. Aggregate pension expenditure would have increased from HUF 753 billion in 1998 to HUF 892 billion in 1999 (see Table 9), *i.e.* by 18.4 percent – faster than wage-related contribution revenues. This explains a notional deficit of HUF 37.5 billion, which would have been a mere 4.4 percent of total contributions, but 'unaffordable' for the government budget, which provides full guarantee cover for the PIF deficit. The expected increase in the aggregate pension expenditure prompted the government to withdraw the indexation rules legislated in 1997 and award *ad hoc* pension increases in 1999 (see Section 3.1). The combined effect of the indexation change appears in Chart 2.

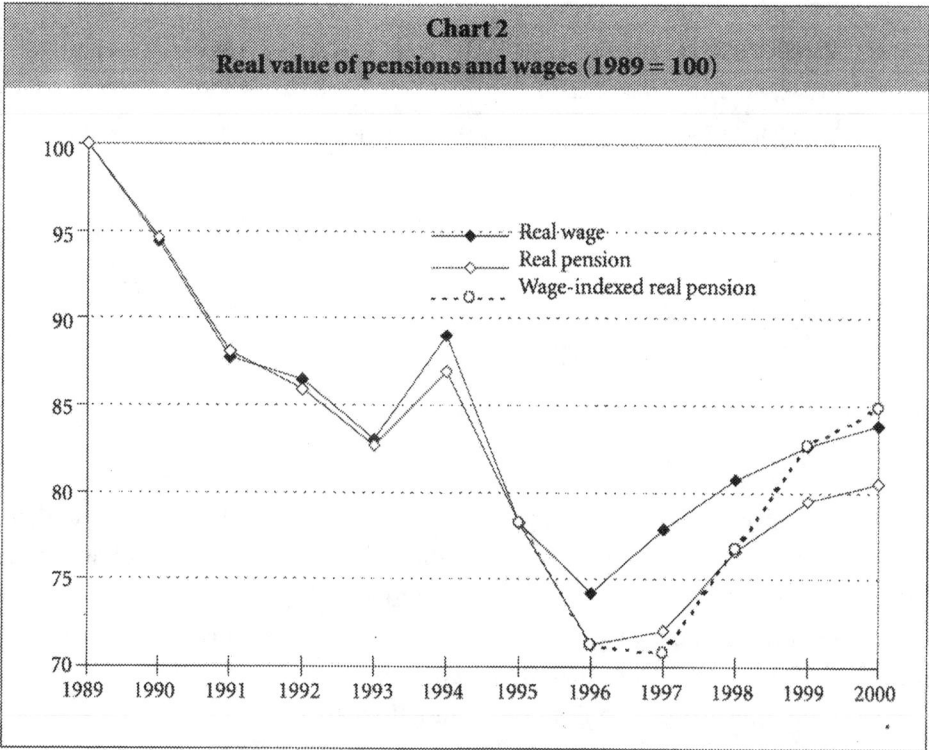

Chart 2
Real value of pensions and wages (1989 = 100)

Real wage
Real pension
Wage-indexed real pension

While real wages and pensions decreased in parallel almost until 1995, a gap originated in 1996 at the expense of pensioners and has been sustained rather than addressed since then, through the elimination of wage indexation of pensions.

Other parametric changes since 1997 have been described in Section 3.1. Here it is sufficient to summarize the effects of the various measures on the financial balance of PIF.

Table 10
Effects of reform and post-reform measures on the financial balance of the public pillar
(Billion Hungarian Forints)

	1998	1999	2000
1. Indexation	+15.3	+48.6	+64.4
2. Second widows'(widowers') pensions	−16.7	−19.7	−23.2
3. PENSIONERS (1+2)	−1.4	+28.9	+41.2
4. Increased employees' contribution	+21.0	+47.4	+57.2
5. PENSIONERS AND EMPLOYEES (3+4)	+19.6	+76.3	+98.4
6. Disability benefits returned to PIF	−23.7	−27.5	−30.9
7. From employees to MPPFs	−29.8	−54.7	−81.4
8. Decreased employers' contribution	−57.9	−65.8	
9. GAINS OF OTHER SECTORS (6+7+8)	−53.5	−140.1	−178.1
10. Compensation from government budget	+20.0	+57.2	+63.2
11. ALTOGETHER (5+9+10)	−13.9	−6.6	−16.5

There are several ways of looking at the figures in Table 10. On the one hand, it might be said that the end result (Row 11) did not deal a catastrophic blow to the PIF, simply increasing the 'no-reform' deficit to a negligible extent (see Table 9). On the other hand, the changing indexation of old-age pensions (even with some reallocation in favour of survivors) and the increase in the employee's contribution rate from 6 to 7 percent and then to 8 percent created a huge reservoir for various other purposes. The price paid by these two groups (Row 5) has even overcompensated for the fact that a high proportion of the employees' contributions has been directed to the MPPFs (Row 7). However, since the latter sum is larger than the total excess in employees' contribution (Row 4), it can be said that the price is actually being paid by the pensioners and by the employees who did not join the mixed system. In this sense, the 1998 reform has been 'self-financing', at least in the first three years.

There have been further complications not intrinsically tied to the underlying goal of the 1998 reform. Reallocation of some of the disability benefits from the HIF to the PIF had nothing to do with the creation of the mandatory private pillar and did not affect the recipients of disability benefits. It was simply intended as a minor relief for the hard-pressed HIF. A much more significant contribution to the increased PIF deficit has come from the decrease in the employers' contribution rate. Although it might be a random, temporary coincidence, it is interesting to see that the compensation from the government budget (Row 10) is much closer to the 'missing' employers' contribution (Row 8) than to the amount of employees' contribution diverted to the mandatory private funds (Row 7).

It should be underlined that for lack of detailed data, the analysis just given relies on several crude estimates, and for want of reliable medium-term financial projections, it has no direct implications for the years after 2000.

3.4. The initial performance of the mandatory private pillar[3]
3.4.a. The MPPF market

As mentioned in Section 3.2, about 1.5 million people were originally expected to join the new mandatory private funds. From this point of view, the 60 MPPFs applying for an operating licence was quite a high number. In this environment, the concentration that took place in the private pension market could be taken to be a natural consequence of market competition. As a result, 21 licenced funds (35 percent of the total) managed to survive the first three years and the number is sure to decrease further. There were several reasons why licensed funds disappeared.

---

[3] All the data in this section are based on official, annual reports of MPPFs. The data are supplied by courtesy of the SFSA.

Table 11 Changes in the numbers of MPPFs							
	1997	1998	1999	2000	2001*	TOTAL	
New founding licences	41	16	2	0	0	60	100%
Cancelled founding processes	0	17	3	0	0	20	33%
Closures of operations	0	4	9	2	4	19	32%
NUMBER OF FUNDS IN OPERATION	0	36	27	25	21	21	35%

* Projections

One third of the funds that applied for licences failed to start real operations, the commonest reason being an inability to attract the minimum membership required by law.

Another third of the funds that applied for licenses started operations, but ceased to be independent after a few months. The commonest form in which they became subsumed was acquisition by one of the largest funds. Only a few true mergers were detected during the concentration process. Typically, only small funds were involved in the early acquisitions and mergers. The average size of the funds acquired or merged was under ten thousand members. Probably the only exception was a transnational insurance firm that was late in entering the Hungarian market compared with its competitors and in practice bought itself a fund of some size with about fifty thousand members. At present, some medium-sized funds with about fortyfive to fifty thousand members are also considering mergers for reasons connected with pure market forces.

The founders of the funds can be classed in three different groups: financial institutions such as banks and insurance companies, large employers or groups representing employees' interests, and other bodies such as accountancy firms or private associations. Each of the three groups prove to have markedly different chances of survival.

	Number of funds		Chance
Table 12			
Numbers and survival changes of MPPFs by groups of founders			
	established	operating in 2001	of survival (percent)
Banks, insurance companies	17	13	76
Employers	24	9	38
Others	19	3	16

The chance that operations would cease was very high for funds with founders from a non-financial background. This might be ascribed to the financial nature of pension-fund management. However, since MPPFs are allowed to outsource their financial operations, funds with no financial founders behind them could also have been expected to be viable, but this has not been the case in practice.

Table 13 summarizes the main features of the MPPFs as a whole and in the three groups distinguished by the type of founder.

Table 13
The main characteristics of MPPFs in 2000, by groups of founders

	Banks, insurance companies	Emp-loyers	Other	TOTAL
1 Market share by members (percent)	89	10	1	100
2 Average number of members (1000)	153.7	9.1	5.9	90.0
3 Growth of membership (percent)	7	1	1	6
4 Mobility of membership (percent)	11	6	3	10
5 Average indiv. account (1000 HUF)	90.4	165.9	120.4	81.6
6 Average monthly contribution (HUF)	3121	6123	2154	3241

1 Number of members in group as a proportion of total membership (%)
2 Number of members in group divided by number of funds in group
3 Increase in total membership as a proportion of initial membership
4 Turnover of members (entries and exits) as a proportion of average membership
5 Year-end value of pension assets in personal accounts divided by year-end membership
6 Total annual contribution divided by average annual number of members, divided by 12

The summary in the table reveals the following aspects:

1. There is considerable concentration towards funds backed by financial institutions. Almost 90 percent of the total membership belongs to this group.

2. Almost all the funds showing a growth capability in 2000 belong to the first group. This may simply be the result of the network of agents working for the financial institutions.

3. Funds organized by employers attract twice as big an average contribution as the largest funds backed by financial institutions. This implies that the viable employer funds may be the ones where the average pensionable income is considerably higher than the national average.

4. The third group of funds has poor membership quality, with an average contribution far lower than 6 percent of the average wage. They probably have many members on the minimum wage and/or not paying contributions.

By the end of 2000, only 7 funds had attained an economically rational size with a membership exceeding a hundred thousand. Most funds are very small in size.

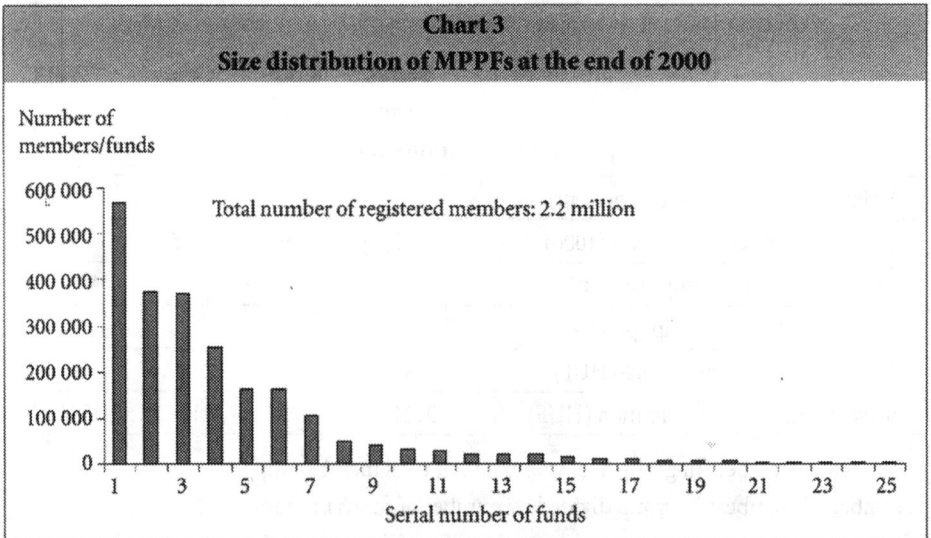

Chart 3

Size distribution of MPPFs at the end of 2000

Number of members/funds

Total number of registered members: 2.2 million

Serial number of funds

The age distribution of the funds is rather similar. Chart 4 illustrates the typical age distribution.

Chart 4
Two examples of the age distribution of the MPPF membership in 2000

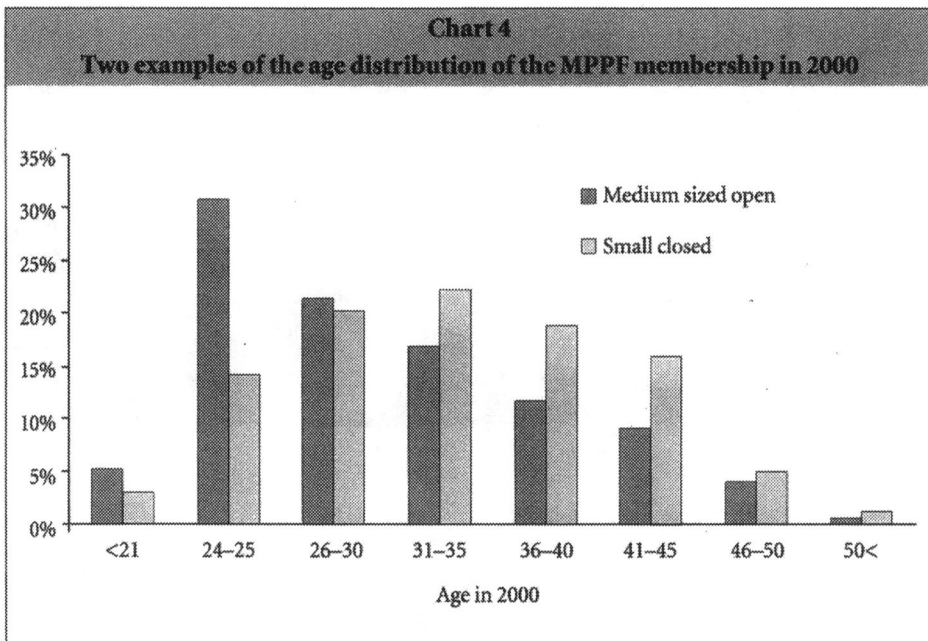

There are three points worth noting about the age distribution:

1. Those joining the MPPFs have not been confined to the younger generations.

2. About 20 percent of the total membership had no rational financial reasons for joining. Their length of service means they will probably lose more in the public pillar than they gain in the mandatory private pillar. Their explanations for their action (if any) are distrust of the social security system and/or an expected greater reliability of future performance from the private pillar.

3. The open funds have been able to enrol more of the young people starting out on their career, for whom it was compulsory to join the private system. As a consequence, the age distribution of these funds is generally more advantageous for their future operations.

The asset size of the funds is going to be considerable. By the end of 2000, the two largest funds already had total assets exceeding Euros 150 million, so that they would rank among the top 500 European pension funds, while the five largest would rank among the top 750 in Europe. (See *IPE Europe's Top 1000*, September 2001.)

Chart 5
The total asset values of MPPFs, 1997–2000

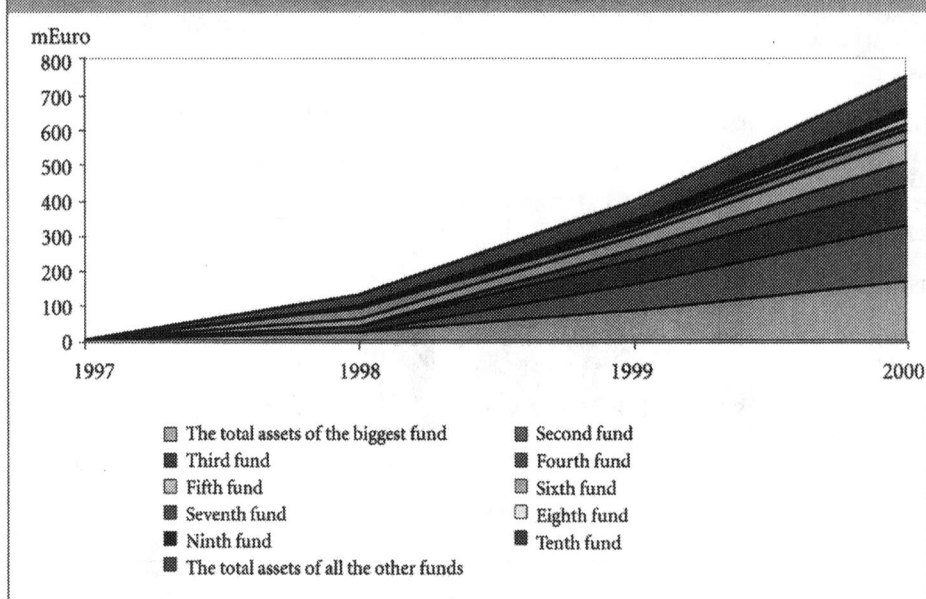

Legend:
- The total assets of the biggest fund
- Second fund
- Third fund
- Fourth fund
- Fifth fund
- Sixth fund
- Seventh fund
- Eighth fund
- Ninth fund
- Tenth fund
- The total assets of all the other funds

The value of assets is growing faster than it was projected in spite of the fact that the mandatory contribution rate to MPPFs has remained 6 percent of the pensionable income instead of the originally legislated 8 percent. This results from the larger membership and the faster growth of wages and thus pensionable incomes.

The market share of the large funds – each of the first ten has a financial institution in the background – was shaped at the very beginning of the operation. Chart 6 shows that the largest fund reached the market share of 20 percent in the first year and managed to maintain its position. Only the smaller funds lost their positions in the second year, and their positions are continuing to decline.

The first division of the market had been completed by 1999. As a result, the Hungarian market for MPPFs became dominated by the funds established by financial institutions. The concentration process had not ceased by the end of 2000. It is noteworthy that the large funds are growing faster than the smaller ones and the obligatory payment of contributions provides a guarantee for their future growth as well, if they are able to retain their members.

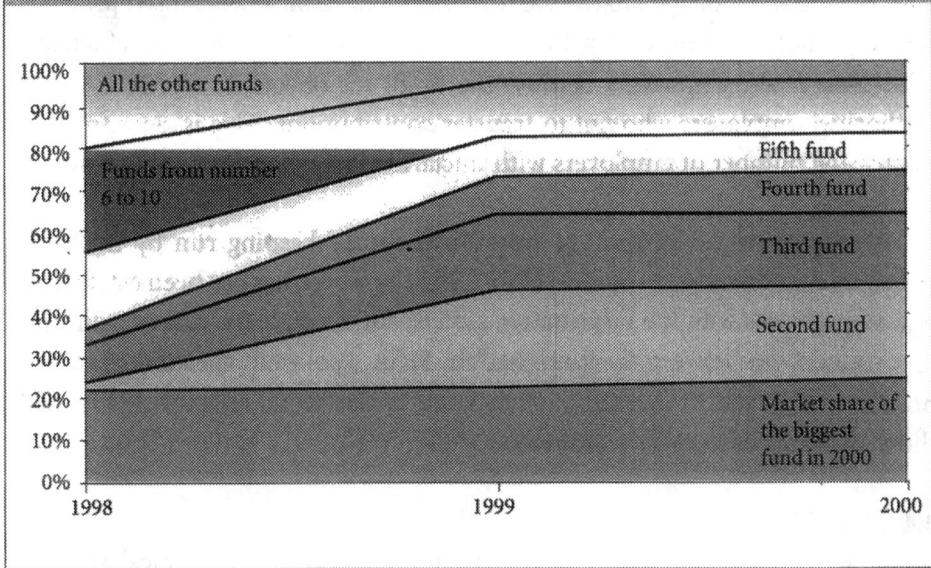

Chart 6
The concentration of assets in the MPPF Market

3.4.b. Contribution compliance

One important goal of the 1998 pension reform was to raise contribution compliance by means of private incentives. This goal has been attained only in part. In fact, it was not too rational to expect better payment discipline from employees, since the lack of it is dependent on other, mainly economic factors. The significance of the black and grey economies remains high, so that many people are reported as being paid only at the minimum level of taxable income. This has meant a low level of average contribution also for MPPFs.

On the other hand, a significant number of those who joined MPPFs do not pay contributions at all. A few of these are phantom members who joined simply to earn commission for a recruiting agent, but there are more who had to join because the definition of a person's 'first job' (entry into the labour market) was ambiguous or who were hustled into doing so by the restricted time available for those choosing to join voluntarily.

The main technical problems, for the funds and for the members, are unidentifiable payments: even today, these make up almost 6 percent of all payments paid into the MPPFs. Reliable identification of participants requires the cooperation of many employers, persons and institutions. It takes time to arrive at smooth reporting and collection of contributions in a huge, decentralized system. The decentralized nature of the system and the direct contacts between the funds and the employers obliged to transfer contributions to them has caused problems for all parties involved, but in the end, it has started to work quite efficiently. Discipline is also improving because the funds are obliged to report to the tax authorities employers who fail to transfer contributions. This is clear from the decreasing number of employers with unclarified payments and a shortening of the delays.

Initially, there were plans for centralized record-keeping run by the SFSA, based on monthly reports by the MPPFs. This, however, has not been established, due to problems with the information system, for example the sub-standard on-line connections between the funds and the SFSA. As a result, the authorities have no efficient means of linking contributions to the social security system with those to the mandatory private system.

3.4.c. Portfolios

There are big differences among European countries in their typical styles of portfolio management. The traditional players in the pension market tend to prefer to invest more in the stock market. (The investment share of equity is often higher than 50 percent in the Netherlands, the United Kingdom, Ireland and Norway.) Funds in other countries (Austria, Finland, Portugal or Germany) follow a more cautious approach, with portfolios dominated by less risky assets such as government bonds or even cash deposits. However, the share of equities in pension-fund investment is growing in the latter group of countries as well. In Hungary, it is not yet possible to identify a typical pension-portfolio policy among MPPFs, whose investment portfolios are extremely varied.

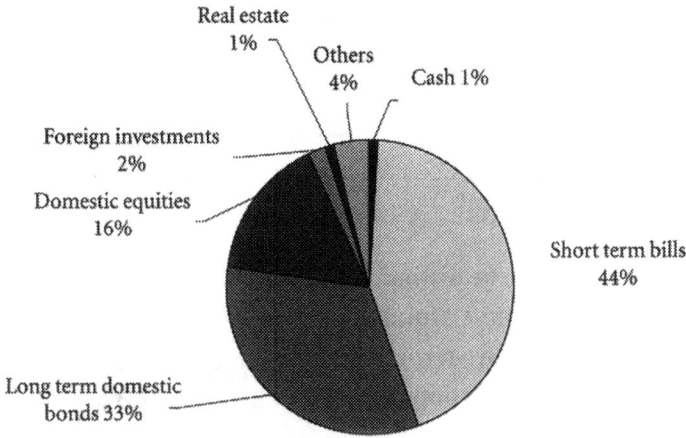

Chart 7
The portfolio of total assets of MPPFs at the end of 2000

The low proportion of foreign investment in these portfolios is not due to legislative limits, as the law permits 30 percent of all MPPF assets to be invested abroad. The explanation is more that the funds are at the beginning of their accumulation period. At the same time, asset managers are still not familiar with foreign markets and they had anticipated that the Hungarian market would perform better. Somewhat later in this section, it is shown that their confidence was misplaced.

Low-risk investments dominated throughout the period investigated, as Table 14 shows. In the table, 'low risk' indicates short-term bills, 'limited risk' includes long-term bonds or other assets backed by government guarantees, and 'higher risk' everything else.

		1998	1999	2000
Table 14				
The changing portfolios of MPPFs				
Percent of total:				
Cash and deposits		27	5	1
Investments	low risk	47	48	44
	limited risk	24	42	50
	higher risk	2	5	6

Four common types can be distinguished among the portfolios:
1. Those holding no equity (2 funds).
2. Those holding only short-term bonds and domestic equities (7 funds).
3. Those with a high proportion of equity in their assets, exceeding 20 percent (8 funds).
4. Mixed portfolios (7 funds).

Even within these four groups, the portfolios of different funds vary widely. There are funds at the extremes and others between the extremes. There are funds whose portfolios are practically free of risk, and on the other extreme, those with portfolios consisting entirely of stocks and long-term investments.

3.4.d. Investment performance and rates of return

It would be easy to explain the significant differences in performance by the fact that different classes of assets performed in very different ways in the three years examined. For example, the composite nominal rate of return on short-term bills and long-term bonds was 18 percent in 1999 and 12 percent in 2000 (with an inflation rate of about 10 percent in both years). Meanwhile the BUX, the official index of the Budapest Stock Exchange, soared by 40 percent in 1999 and plunged to minus 11 percent in 2000.

In fact, the portfolio differences do not fully account for the differences in performance. To demonstrate this, a simplified benchmark for each fund in 2000 was set. We considered each item in the fund's own, specific portfolio separately and applied to it the rate of return characteristic of that type of asset in 2000 generally, on average in the Hungarian economy. These returns that could have been obtained were then divided by the total asset value of the fund to arrive at its 'benchmark' rate of gross return, *i.e.* the rate that could have been expected and would have reflected the effect of the portfolio on the fund's overall gross rate of return.

As Chart 8 shows, almost half the funds *underperformed* their own, fund-specific benchmark in 2000. (Funds are obliged to calculate their own benchmark, but the method of defining it is not regulated and therefore not uniform. Asset managers generally prefer a calculation that shows they have outperformed their benchmark.)

Moreover, gross return was lagging not just behind the fund-specific benchmark in half of the funds. All but two funds achieved yields that fell short of the inflation rate, implying negative real rates of return, *i.e.* a loss in the real value of the assets invested.

Chart 8
The performance of MPPFs in 2000

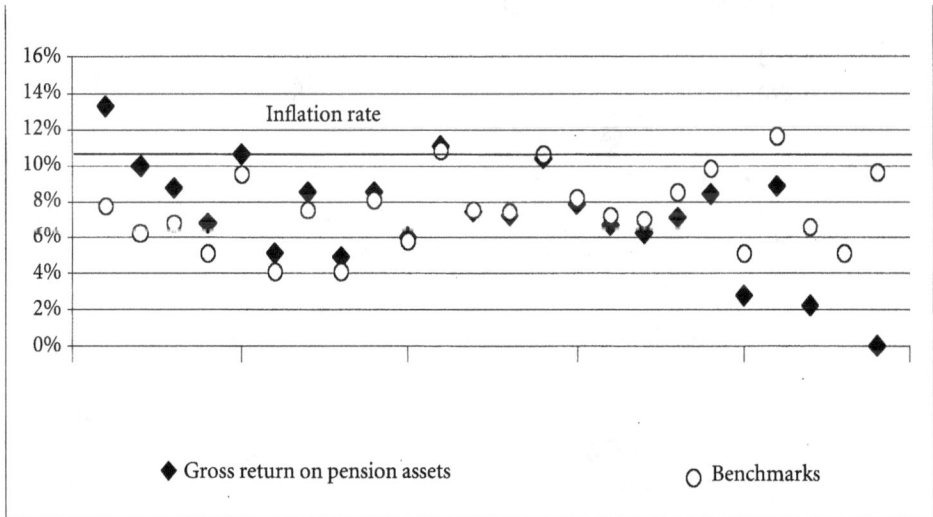

◆ Gross return on pension assets   ○ Benchmarks

The low level of average performance disguises a wide dispersion among the scores of the funds. A significant difference can be detected between two groups of funds: (1) where the asset manager has been chosen from the competitive market, and (2) where the asset manager is an insider from the interest group of the founding bank or insurance company. It is notable that all funds backed by financial institutions use an asset-management company (most often the only one) that belongs to the same group as their sponsor, so that these funds belong to Group (2).

Table 15
Investment management performances in 2000

| | Fund management | | TOTAL |
	Competitive (Group 1)	Insider (Group 2)	
Number of funds	11	13	24
Share in assets (percent)	9	91	100
Investment return (percent)			
gross	7.7	7.4	7.5
net	7.1	5.9	6.0
Cost of fund management as percent of			
total value of assets	0.6	1.5	1.5
total amount of gross return	8.5	23.8	22.3

Averages calculated with weights of asset values.

A few comments can be made on the findings in Table 15:

1. No effects of economies of scale can be detected.
2. There are no significant differences between the gross market returns of the funds managed on the basis of market competition and the funds managed by the financial institutions in the background but the difference in net returns is considerable.
3. The competition-based market prices of asset management in the first group are far lower than the management fees charged by insider asset manager companies in the background of the funds in the second group.
4. Almost 25 percent of the gross investment returns in Group (2) went from the funds to the asset-management institutions.

These facts imply a possible conclusion: members' interests would have required that market competition among asset managers be guaranteed by the regulations.

Naturally one year's performance is less significant than long-term performance, but there is no long track record in Hungary yet. The short-term performance is important only if members are overly sensitive to performance, but this has not been the case in Hungary. The mobility figures show that the number of members leaving a fund (transferring to another or switching back to the public pillar) was practically unrelated to the fund's rate of return. The number of people leaving funds is generally low, but the highest proportion of leavers were found in the group of funds founded by employers, where the average return was above the market average. On the other hand, the fund with the highest membership growth achieved a relatively low performance in the last two years.

The *method* of measurement is an essential issue when comparing performance. Some definitions for calculating net returns are laid down by law. The main problem with these is that the calculation of the average value of assets invested cannot be checked from outside. There is no regulatory obligation to publish only those rates of return that are audited by the actuary of the fund.

To calculate the *fund-specific, annual* net rates of return here, the net return on all personal accounts (the difference between the year-end and the opening market value, less the credited contributions) is arrived at from a rather crude approximation of the annual average capital stock (the sum of the opening stock of the personal accounts plus half the yearly contribution and the payments made from the personal accounts). Chart 9 shows the results for each of the 25 funds in existence at the end of 2000, each being represented by a line.

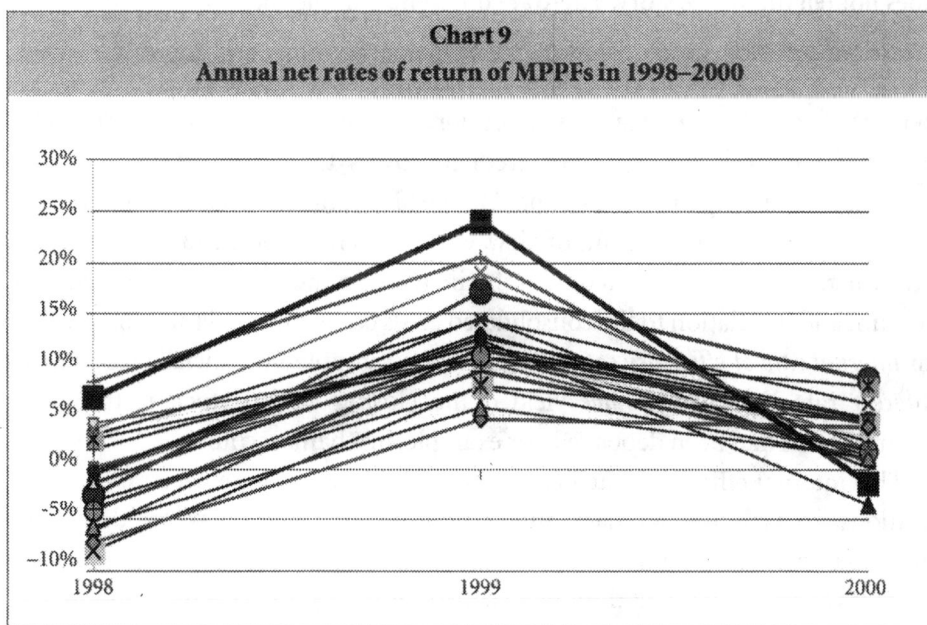

Chart 9
Annual net rates of return of MPPFs in 1998–2000

The overlapping and crossing of the lines in Chart 9 justify the following remarks:

1. There are notable differences in annual rates of return for various funds in each year. The *relative range* (the difference between the highest and lowest fund-specific rate as a percentage of the latter) was 16 percent in 1998, 19 percent in 1999 and 12 percent in 2000.
2. There is considerable *fluctuation over time* in the annual rates. (The fluctuation for a fund is measured as the difference between the maximum and minimum rate over the three years, as a percentage of the minimum.) The average fluctuation was about 14 percent.
3. Even *negative nominal rates* can be detected for 1998 and 2000.
4. No funds have always been good or always been bad. For example, the best fund in 1999 became one of the worst in 2000. Thus the factors affecting the dispersion of the annual rates of return are not yet fully understood.

3.4.e. The internal rate of efficiency

The other problem with comparisons is that the rate of return on investments does not tell the whole story. There are differences in the share of members' gross contributions that funds credit to the personal accounts and thereafter invest. These vary from 50 percent of the first contribution (upon joining) to 92–97 percent of consecutive, regular contributions. As for the latter, 94 percent can be said to be typical. The part not credited covers the administrative costs of operation, including the fees to be paid to the SFSA and the Guarantee Fund.

So from the members' point of view, what matters is not the rate of return on investment but the final outcome – the increase in the balance in the personal account and its relation to the consolidated gross contribution. From this relation an *internal rate of efficiency* can be derived as an imputed (artificially calculated) interest rate that *would have* yielded the closing capital stock if the gross contributions had been deposited, for example, in a bank account.

This internal efficiency rate has been calculated, with some necessary simplifications, for each fund annually, and then for the entire sector, averaged over the first three years of operation.

It was assumed that half the annual contribution was made at the beginning of the year and the other half in mid-year. This makes the number of half-year accrual periods for each payment an integer. (This simplification slightly underestimates the internal rate, as the contributions are spread in reality over the half-year period and so do not earn a return throughout the half-year.) If the internal rate to be computed is denoted x, a payment is made of C and the number of half-year accrual periods for the payment is n, the value of that payment at the end of the last period will be $C(1 + x)^n$. Crucially, it is known for a fact that the aggregate market value of the stocks in the personal accounts of all MPPFs was HUF 181.4 billion on December 31, 2000. The value of x – the internal rate of efficiency – can be calculated from this and from the available data on aggregate annual contributions.

Table 16
Calculation for the six-months internal rate of efficiency

	Aggregate gross contribution (billion HUF)	Accrual factor until End Date	Value at End Date if $x = .0355$ (billion HUF)
1998 January	14.9	$(1+x)^6$	18.3
1998 July	14.9	$(1+x)^5$	17.7
1999 January	26.9	$(1+x)^4$	31.0
1999 July	26.9	$(1+x)^3$	29.9
2000 January	40.1	$(1+x)^2$	43.0
2000 July	40.1	$(1+x)$	41.5
TOTAL			181.4

End Date: December 31, 2000.

The result, as indicated at the head of the last column of Table 16, is a 3.55 percent half-yearly internal rate. Again with a slight simplification, this can be taken as an **average 7.1 percent annual rate of internal efficiency** for the 1998–2000 period. As the average annual rate of inflation in the same period was 11.2%, the conclusion is that the MPPF sector in the first three years of operation earned a **negative real return** on contributions.

The usual argument against private pension systems is that the risks of investment are borne by the members, which could give rise to an inefficient pension. To avoid this, the problem of risk management needs to be considered in a more detailed and better regulated way, so that members are protected against the possibly detrimental effects of the new mixed pension system.

4. Conclusions

4.1. The costs of transition

There are two intrinsic difficulties in summing up the costs of the transition from a purely public, PAYG system to a mixed system. One is a *conceptual* problem: 'transition cost' is an ill-defined notion. The other is *specific to Hungary:* the process of creating the private funded pillar was obscured by a number of parametric changes, which need not have been coupled to the paradigmatic transition.

It is customary in the literature to refer to the costs of transition as a 'double burden' on the working generation. They are supposedly having to pay for the pensions of those already retired while shouldering the new burden of saving for their own, future pension. No working generation, however, would be able or willing to carry a real double burden. Yet transitions have proved possible in many countries. Eliminating the 'double-burden' theory, however, means that there is no clear definition left.

First, there are some who gain and some who lose by the process of transition. Is the transition cost to be defined as the sum of the losses or as the aggregate, macroeconomic balance of the gains and the losses? (The latter is probably zero, as money, like matter, does not disappear, but simply gets transferred.) In other words, whose costs need to be totalled?

Secondly, a decentralized, private funded system is known to be more expensive because of its higher administrative costs. In a switch from an economical to a more expensive system (conceivable in many sectors of the economy for several, sometimes justified reasons), should the *difference* between the two rates of cost be considered the cost of transition, or simply the cost of achieving the assumed goal or goals of the switch?

Thirdly, the new mixed pension system will not mature fully until the youngest present-day people to remain in the old system have died off, which will be in about 60–70 years. Transition costs will continue until full maturity is reached. Over what time-horizon should the costs of transition be considered?

There are no clear-cut answers to these or many similar questions.

The time-horizon at least is not an issue in present-day Hungary because the absence of reliable projections leaves nothing but the factual data for the first three years after the reform to analyse. This chapter presents the relevant data, but leaves several conceptual questions for readers to ponder.

4.1.a. 'Pure' transition

'Transition' is defined for this sub-section as the partial privatization of the mandatory pension system. As the pension benefits from the privatized segment are not yet due, the privatization consists at present of diverting some of the mandatory contributions from the public pillar to the mandatory private pillar. The attribute 'pure' implies that some accompanying but not intrinsically necessary parametric changes will be disregarded temporarily.

There are three cornerstones on which to build the virtual case of 'pure transition': (1) The sum of employees' contributions diverted from the SSPS to the MPPFs. (2) The government compensation to the SSPS for these lost contribution revenues. (3) The aggregate stock of capital in the personal accounts of MPPF members by the end of 2000.

The first two items, however, represent money flows that occurred at various times in the 1998–2000 period. Their compounded value at the end of 2000 must be calculated before they can be compared. (In the work that underlies this analysis, the cash flows for each calendar year are calculated at 'constant' 2000 values and then totalled, but for brevity's sake, the annual details are omitted here.) The method is basically the same as the one applied in Section 3.4 for calculating the internal rate of efficiency of the MPPFs: half the annual cash flow is assumed to occur at the beginning of the year and the other half at mid-year. As this simplification is applied to both revenues and expenditures, gains and losses, the resulting distortion cannot be significant. However, the procedure differs from the one with the internal rate of efficiency, where the rate is the *result* of the calculation. Here a quasi-interest rate must be selected *ex ante*, and there are several possible ways to do so. Table 17 shows the effects of this selection through the various compounded values of the contributions diverted to the MPPFs that result from various rates.

Table 17	
The compounded value of 1998–2000 contributions to MPPFs at the end of 2000 (Billion Hungarian Forints)	
Actual	181.4
Using the consumers' price index	191.8
Using the net nominal wage index	197.5
Using the BB (Bill-Bond) rate[1]	201.7

[1] Combined rate of return on short-term bills and long-term bonds, weighted by their shares in MPPF portfolios.

All imputed variants would have yielded significantly higher values than the actual HUF 181.4 billion in the personal accounts. Compounding with the consumers' price index represents preserving the real value of the contributions, so that there has been an *absolute* loss of HUF 10.4 billion (5.4 percent) for fund members over the three years. However, when pensions are assessed on retirement in the public pillar, previous earnings are valorized according to wage increases, so that this can also be regarded as a relevant measure, in the light of the SSPS pension rights forfeited by MPPF members. By this measure, their *relative* loss is HUF 16.1 billion (8.2 percent). Alternatively, it can be argued that if fund members had bought government securities for themselves rather than contributing to an MPPF, the market value of their year-end assets in 2000 would have been HUF 201.7 billion. (Naturally there would have been an unknown deduction for transaction costs and taxes in this case, so that the net result would be less than the market value of the securities.) No matter which of these arguments is embraced, the fact remains that the actual stock in the personal accounts of MPPF members was HUF 181.4 billion at the end of 2000.

On the other hand, it has to be considered that the government budget was in deficit in 1998–2000 and the deficit was financed by issuing government securities. Hence it is justifiable to assume that additional bills and bonds had to be issued to offset the compensation due to the SSPS, as additional government expenditure, and that the government is paying interest on this additional debt at the BB rate. The same applies to the remaining losses of the SSPS, since it forms part of the general government. So all items in what follows are calculated by applying the BB rate to the annual cash flows given in Table 16. This is compatible with the assumption that any individual or institution could have bought government securities on the open market.

Table 18
A summary of 'pure' transition compounded values at the end of 2000
(Billion Hungarian Forints)

1. Contributions diverted to the MPPFs	201.7
2. Additional government debt[1]	170.4
3. SSPS loss (1–2)	31.3
4. MPPF members' capital in personal accounts	181.4
5. 'LEAKAGE' (1–4)	20.3

[1] Resulting from compensation to SSPS

The government debt accumulated over the first three years is not too significant in itself, amounting to 1.1 percent of GDP in 2000. Nor, however, is it negligible, in light of the 60 percent Maastricht requirement and the further compensation from the budget to the SSPS that will be required after 2000.

Naturally, the HUF 20.3 billion 'leakage' does not imply that the MPPFs became that much 'richer' – they are non-profit organizations. As Section 3.4 explained, part of this would-be revenue has not been realized at all, because of poor investment performance. Another part financed the administrative costs, and some has been absorbed by exorbitant fees charged by insider asset managers associated with founding financial corporations.

Whether the HUF 201.7 billion of contribution revenue lost to the public pillar, or the HUF 170.4 billion in additional government debt, or the HUF 31.3 billion net SSPS loss, or only the HUF 20.3 billion 'leakage' is regarded as the 'pure transition' cost is an undecided conceptual issue. It has to be left to personal judgement.

4.1.b. Obfuscated transition

This sub-section turns to the parametric changes that accompanied the paradigmatic transition to a mixed pension system. These were not intrinsically tied to the transition, but they helped to obscure the effects, including the costs.

The employees' contributions diverted to the mandatory public pillar did not constitute the only major loss to the SSPS. There was a further loss, comparable in magnitude, through the effect of the two-percentage-point decrease in the *employers' contribution rate* from 1999.

At the same time, the *employees' contribution rate* increased by one percentage point in 1998 and two percentage points from 1999. It might be argued that minus two and plus two made zero, so that nothing had changed in this respect. However, this is not true. First, gross wages have not been adjusted, hence the additional two percentage points of employee contribution mean a decrease in net wages, while the two percentage points less paid by employers means a decrease in labour costs that improves profitability and hopefully enhances employment. Secondly, *total* contribution revenue decreased, since there is a ceiling on employees' contributions, while there is no such ceiling on employers' contributions.

A major improvement in the SSPS's financial situation (at the expense of pensioners) came with the change in the *pension indexation rules* (from indexing according to the previous year's wage increase to indexing by the current year's 'Swiss' index, *i.e.* 50 percent prices and 50 percent wages.) Moreover, this change was made practically immediate by subsequent legislation, while the original reform package envisaged phasing it in over three years. A relatively small part of this saving for the SSPS has been devoted to improving widows' (widowers') pensions. Somewhat more has been spent on disability benefits, for the disabled under statutory retirement age, responsibility for whom was reallocated to the SSPS from the HIF (to slow a looming catastrophe at the latter).

Table 19	
A summary of 'obfuscated' transition compounded values at the end of 2000 (Billion HUF)	
LOST GENERAL GOVERNMENT REVENUES	
1 Employees' contribution diverted to MPPFs	– 201.7
2 Reduction of employers' contribution (*)	– 144.1
3 Together (1+2)	–345.8
COMPENSATORS	
4 Pensioners (indexation)	+153.9
5 Pensioners (widows'(widowers') increase)	– 74.9
6 Employees	+153.1
7 Together (4+5+6)	+232.1
8 NET LOSS OF GENERAL GOVERNMENT (3+7)	–113.8
REALLOCATION WITHIN THE GENERAL GOVERNMENT	
9 Disability benefits reallocated to SSPS	–103.5
10 Government compensation to SSPS	+170.4
11 NET LOSS TO SSPS (8+9+10)	–46.9

* This item is not fully comparable with the rest as it relates to only two years.

This rather confusing picture raises at least one question. What exactly is the government (*i.e.* the general taxpayer) paying for? Is it really the employees' contribution diverted to the MPPFs but only partially offset by the government budget? Is it a surreptitious subsidy to employers, including the government itself, which is the largest single employer in the country? Or is it assistance to widows (widowers) and support for the health insurance system, by relieving it of some of its disability payments? In reality, these various sums of money are interchangeable, so that any of these answers can be justified.

However, one thing is certain. If the employers' contribution rate had not been decreased, there would have been at least two options. (1) No additional government debt would have emerged, if pensioners and employees had been made to pay amply for the transition. (2) If the government had still compensated the SSPS for the contribution revenues directed to the mandatory private pillar, it would not have been necessary to deprive pensioners and/or employees of a significant slice of their income.

4.2. Other major issues

The 1998 reform had been preceded by a long period in which there were competing reform blueprints and political controversies. The decision to implement it was followed by only a few months, which was insufficient for prudent preparation of the legislation to be submitted to Parliament.

Although the reform sustained the *public* pension scheme as the dominant pillar in the new mixed system, it postponed or left unresolved many of its *systemic problems*. Subsequent legislation worsened rather than improved the situation. A few of the measures taken were intended to boost actuarial fairness, for example by equalizing the impact of years of service, effective only from 2013, and eliminating the degressive element in pensionable income, which is to be introduced gradually, but not completed until around 2010. Other counter-productive features of the system were left unaddressed, for example the incomplete valorization of previous income in the pension formula, or the lack of a ceiling for employer's contributions. By and large, the public pillar is still an impenetrable web of justified, redistributive social assistance and contribution-based, income-replacing social insurance, just as it was before the reform.

The major systemic change in the public pillar was the change in the indexation basis for pensions, from wage increases to the 'Swiss' formula of half wages and half prices. This made the transition financially feasible. The resulting decrease in aggregate pension expenditure,[4] along with the previously legislated increase in the statutory retirement age, may have secured the public scheme financially at least until about 2050, according to pre-reform calculations. Notwithstanding the often advanced argument that the system would be 'unsustainable without privatization', the sustainability of the public scheme was not a goal of the transition to the mixed system, but a prerequisite for it.

The *paradigmatic goal* of the 1998 reform was to create the mandatory private pillar. This was the cornerstone of the preceding controversies, the political compromise and the hasty legislation, and at the focus of the public's attention.

---

[4] It should be noted, however, that 'Swiss' indexation can be a double-edged weapon. As long as the economy grows and real wages increase, it impairs the relative situation of pensioners and makes savings for the budget, but if a lasting recession arrives and real wages decline, it may favour pensioners and result in pension expenditures far above contribution revenues.

A switch in contribution rates, reallocating two percent of gross wages to decrease employers' contributions and increase employees' contributions without adjusting the gross wage level, was a much less publicized, but nonetheless significant accompanying *parametric* change.

According to the enacted structure of governance, the new *mandatory, private pension funds* (MPPFs) are non-profit organizations owned by their members, bearing all the risks of the fund's saving and investment performance. However, the largest funds that dominate the market, have been founded by banks and insurance companies and find several opportunities to assert the interests of their founders, not their members. For example, members' interests are unprotected by any regulation establishing obligatory, prudent market competition in the asset-management field. The assets of such funds are usually handled by asset managers from the founding financial corporation.

The legislation regulating the operation of MPPFs is ambiguous in many ways and not fully consistent with the assumed *'defined-contribution'* character of the private pillar. It prescribes the creation of several reserves, leaves open the possibility of applying various rates of return to various accounts, demands transfers among reserves and members' personal accounts in case of non-compliance with the fund's 'expected rate of return' (a rather obscure concept in itself), and builds up a less than transparent system of guarantees. These requirements were intended to make the system safer, but it is not clear whether they can achieve this. On the other hand, they make operation difficult and result in excess *redistribution* within and among funds, beyond the type of interpersonal redistribution inherent in a risk-sharing pool.

The major deficiencies in the legislation concern the *pension-type benefit* to be expected by fund members. The law describes several types of annuities from which retiring members may choose, but it does not oblige the funds to provide such annuities. They may, if they wish, *buy* annuities for their retiring members from insurance companies, out of the capital accumulated in the retirees' personal accounts. Obviously, in a rather underdeveloped annuity market, this may turn out to be a very expensive transaction. Furthermore, the law demands that annuities should be 'unisex' (no discrimination against women based on their longer expectancy of life) and that the indexation rule of the annuities should be the same as in the public pillar. On the other hand, insurance companies are not obliged by the law regulating their operation to offer such products.

None of the leading MPPFs is currently planning to provide annuities, while the insurance companies remain unprepared and possibly unwilling to sell the types of annuities required of the MPPFs by the law. In light of the uncertainty surrounding the pension promise, it may be wondered whether the Hungarian MPPFs, in their present legal and financial structure, are really pension funds at all, or simply mandatory savings devices designed for the accumulation period.

The *public* was less than well informed about the fine details of the legislation. The emerging MPPFs, and the government, emphasized the advantages to be expected from a mixed system and were rather vague about the risks to members, some of them natural and some of them resulting from the inadequacies of the legislation. The hope for better returns on one's 'own money' in the funds, the crumbling confidence in the social security system and an efficiently conducted recruiting campaign led almost two million people – about half the employed work force – to join the mixed system voluntarily. This number exceeded the official expectations considerably. It probably includes a few hundred thousand persons who lost more by forfeiting a quarter of their pension claims in the public pillar than they can hope to gain form the MPPFs, even assuming that the investment performance of the latter improves with time and experience, so that returns indeed become higher in the private than in the public pillar in the long term.

There are several signs that the 1998 reform and subsequent legislation failed to regard the public and the mandatory private schemes as *interdependent pillars* of one pension system.

One is the *asymmetry* between the public and the mandatory private pillar, with respect to risks other than longevity. While the public scheme provides lifetime survivors' and/or disability benefits, the MPPFs do not offer such provisions. In principle, disabled fund members or previously appointed beneficiaries of members who have died before retirement have a choice of retaining the capital endowment in the personal account in the MPPF or of taking it as a lump sum. In most practical cases, however, it will be more advantageous for them to return to the public scheme, which will be obliged to provide the benefits irrespective of the amount of the endowment transferred, which may be quite small for various reasons.

Another important sign is the haphazard meddling with *contribution rates* and seemingly complete neglect of the actuarial consequences affecting *replacement rates*. Subsequent legislation obliged members of the mixed system to keep paying less to the MPPFs and more to the public scheme than legislated for in the 1998 reform package, but their pension claims from the public scheme have not been increased correspondingly. Some experts believe that such an increase is not actuarially justified, but publicly the problem has not even been acknowledged. The employers' contributions to the public pillar – and with it the total contribution rate – are currently being decreased further by post-reform legislation, without considering the possible future effect on pension claims from the public pillar. Within the general government, the payment of some disability benefits has been reallocated from the health to the pension scheme, without a corresponding adjustment in their shares of total social security contributions.

A further example is the lack of efficient sharing and exchange of *information* between the two pension pillars. Each is struggling with its own problems of inadequate information about members and contributions, while cooperation is not properly organized.

Last but not least, government responsibility for pension issues is divided and unclear. Three ministries (Finance, Welfare and Health) and three agencies (the Pension Insurance Administration, State Financial Supervisory Authority and State Tax Collecting Agency) are involved, not to mention the powerful Prime Minister's Office. It is no wonder that none of them is accountable.

These are probably the main reasons for the disgraceful absence of any officially published long-term macroeconomic projections on the performance of the pension system as a whole. Neither are there official estimates available on some other crucial issues. These include the amount of the public pension claims forfeited by entrants into the mixed system, the remaining pension liabilities of the public pillar, actuarial calculations of future capital accumulation and expected replacement rates in the mandatory private pillar, the benefits to be expected by various types and groups of people from the two pillars, separately and combined. This names just some of the things that contribution payers and retired citizens are entitled to know. They are also indispensable for the design of a far-sighted pension policy.

The 1998 reform of the Hungarian mandatory pension system cannot be seen as completed. There will inevitably have to be some house-cleaning done both in the public and the private pillar sooner or later. What is needed before such action is taken is not another round of ideological debate or another package of hastily contrived legislation, but a significant improvement in the information system, careful actuarial foundations for several possible scenarios, and a wide, well-informed social consensus.

References

ALIER, M.-VITTAS, D. (1999): 'Personal Pension Plans and Stock-Market Volatility'. World Bank Conference, Washington, D.C.

ANTAL, K., RÉTI, J. and TOLDI, M. (1995) 'Loss of Value and Distortions in the Hungarian Pension System'. In Ehrlich and Révész (eds.) Human Resources and Social Stability during Transition in Hungary. San Francisco, International Center for Growth.

AUGUSZTINOVICS, M. and MARTOS, B. (1996): 'Pension Reform: Calculations and Conclusions'. Acta Oeconomica, Vol. 48 (1-2).

BOD, P. (2000): 'Reflections on the Perspectives of the Functioning of the Private Pension Funds' (in Hungarian). In Király, J., Simonovits, A., and Száz, J., eds. (2000): Rationality and Fairness. Budapest, Közgazdasági Szemle Alapítvány.

DIAMOND, P. (1997): 'Insulation of pensions from political risk'. In Valdes-Prieto, S. (ed.): The Economics of Pensions, Cambridge UK, University Press.

DISNEY, R., PALACIOS, R. and WHITEHOUSE, E. (1999): 'Individual choice of pension arrangement as a pension reform strategy'. London: The Institute for Fiscal Studies, Working Paper Series W99/18.

FAZEKAS, K. ed. (2000): 'Labor Market Mirror: 2000'. (in Hungarian) Budapest, Institute of Economics.

FLEMMING, J. and MICKELWRIGHT, J. (1999): 'Income Distribution, Economic Systems and Transition'. Innocenti Occasional Papers, Economic and Social Policy Series 70, Florence, UNICEF.

GEANAKOPLOS, J., MITCHELL, O. S. and ZELDES, S. P. (1998): 'Social Security Money's Worth'. NBER WP 6722, also In Mitchell, O.S., Meyers, R.J. and Young, H., eds. (1999): 'Prospects for Social Security Reform'. Pension Research Council, University of Pennsylvania Press, 1999.

HABLICSEK, L. (1999): 'Aging and Diminishing Population: Demographic Scenarios 1997-2050' (in Hungarian). Demográfia 42.

MINISTRY OF FINANCE and MINISTRY OF LABOUR (1997) 'Background Information for the Pension Reform'. (in Hungarian). Budapest, April.

MITCHELL, O.S., POTERBA, J.M., WARSHAWSKI, M.J. and BROWN, J.R. (1999): 'New Evidence on Money's Worth of Individual Annuities', American Economic Review 89.

PALACIOS, R. and ROCHA, R. (1998) 'The Hungarian Pension System in

Transition'. In Bokros and Dethier (eds.) Public Finance Reform during the Transition: The Experience of Hungary. Washington, World Bank.

RÉTI, J. (2000): 'The Pension Risks at the End of the Nineties: (On the History of the Pension Reform)' (in Hungarian). In Király, J., Simonovits, A., and Száz, J., eds. (2000): Rationality and Fairness. Budapest, Közgazdasági Szemle Alapítvány.

TÁRKI (1999) 'The Emergence of the Private Pension System in Hungary' (in Hungarian), Budapest, Mimeo.

WORLD BANK POLICY RESEARCH REPORT (1994): 'Averting the Old Age Crisis', Oxford, Oxford University Press.

Chapter 2
The Polish Pension Reform of 1999

Agnieszka Chłoń-Domińczak[1]

Acronyms

CBOS	Public Opinion Research Centre
FRD	Demographic Reserve Fund
FUS	Social Security Fund
NDC	Notional Defined Contribution System
NUSP	Social security number for contribution payer
OFE	Open pension fund
PIT	Personal income tax
PTE	Pension fund society – manager of a pension fund
SEKIF	System for Registry of Accounts and Funds
UNFE	Superintendency of Pension Funds
ZUS	Social Security Institution

1. The pre-reform scene

From the period preceding the political changes, Poland inherited a social security system similar to that of most of the former socialist countries. This system was financed from social security contributions, paid entirely by employers. During and after a period of martial law in the early 1980s, generous extensions of early retirement privileges had been made. As early retirement did not require termination of employment, there was a strong incentive to 'retire' as early as possible, and in 1990, a new law even allowed for early retirement by those laid-off from their companies. These policies led to a significant increase in the number of pension beneficiaries. As a result, the ratio of beneficiaries to insured

---

[1] Ms Chłoń is with the Gdansk Institute for Market Economics.

persons (the dependency rate) grew from less than 30 percent in the 1980s to almost 40 percent in 1990, and by 1995, exceeded 50 percent. Poland also suffered hyper-inflation in the late 1980s, which led to *ad hoc* benefit adjustments, thus increasing pension expenditures. This generous pension policy required additional financing. As a result, the social security contribution rate in the employee pension system, financing old-age, disability and survivor pensions as well as sickness, maternity and work-injury benefits, was raised from 15.5 percent of the net salary prior to 1981 to 38 percent in 1987-89, and finally to 45 percent in 1990. This was still not enough to finance expenditures, however, and the pension system constantly had to be subsidised from the state budget.

During the transition period, economic reforms commonly known as a shock therapy were introduced, and changes in social policy, including the area of pensions, were high on the agenda of the Polish government. The pension debate lasted throughout the 1990s, but it was difficult to reach a consensus despite many efforts. As decision-makers were reluctant to reform the pension system comprehensively, smaller changes were introduced. The changes were aimed at reducing pension expenditures and included, for example, an increase in the period of earnings used for pension calculation, lowering pension indexation, and reducing the wage base used for new benefit calculation. Incremental changes to the pension system were not sufficient to ensure long-term financial stability, however, and more radical reform was seen as necessary.

The remainder of this section sets the stage for analysing the major reform which eventually occurred. To this end, the demographic and economic situation in Poland of the 1990s is described, an overview of the pre-reform pension system and the changes made in the course of the 1990s is provided, and the reasons for and the expected results of the pension reform introduced in 1999 are explained.

1.1. Demographic and economic background
1.1.a. Demographic changes in Poland

Until the mid 1980s, Poland experienced rapid population growth (the average growth rate was around 0.9 percent annually). In the 1990s, this trend decreased significantly – in the second half of the decade growth was only around 0.02 percent per year. In 1999 and 2000, the size of the population actually decreased, as a result of very low natural growth combined with negative net migration. Net imigration is a long-term phenomenon in Poland: in the 1990s, it was at a level of approximately minus 12–14 thousand annually, and in 2000 it approached minus

20 thousand. Future projections show a small amount of natural population growth until 2018, related to the fact that the baby-boom generation born in the 1980s is at reproductive age. After 2018, a sharp decline in the population size is expected.

Chart 1
Births and deaths in Poland, 1990–2050

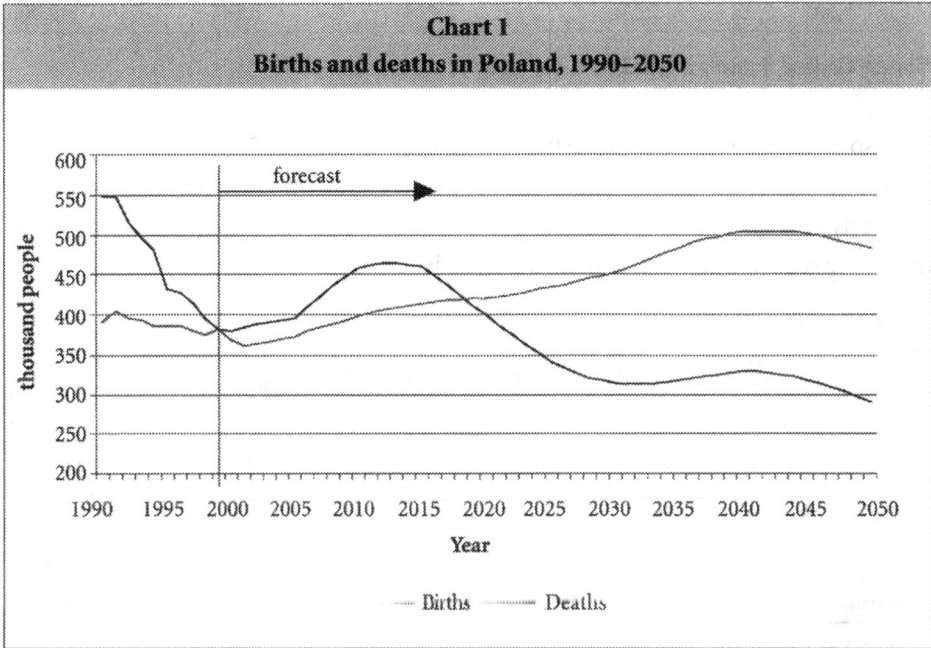

Source: Central Statistical Office, the Gdansk Institute for Market Economics (projection)

A decrease in births, resulting from a lower fertility rate, is the most significant reason for this decline. In 1998 there were fewer than 400 thousand children born. In the course of the 1990s, the fertility rate fell from 2.04 in 1990 to 1.37 in 1999 (Table 1). This means that the current fertility rate is much too low to guarantee net maintenance of the population. Changes in the fertility pattern have also been observed. In the 1990s, the average age of mothers increased, the predominant age for child bearing shifting from 20-24 years to 25-29 years. This reflects the choices of young people, who have decided to achieve a certain level of education and economic stability before starting a family.

Table 1				
Total fertility rate in Poland, 1970–1999				
Year				
1970	1980	1990	1995	1999
2.200	2.276	2.039	1.611	1.366

Source: Central Statistical Office

Also in the 1990s, the average life expectancy of Poles increased by two years to 68.5 years for men and 77 years for women. The number of deaths remained relatively constant at around 400 thousand. The above changes are due to a long-term increase in longevity, which was already observed in the 1970s (Table 2).

Table 2				
Longevity in Poland, 1970-1999				
	Year			
	1970	1980	1990	1995	1999
Average life expectancy at:					
Men:					
0 years	66.62	66.01	66.51	67.62	68.83
60 years	15.68	15.18	15.33	15.84	16.29
Women:					
0 years	73.33	74.44	75.49	76.38	77.49
60 years	19.23	19.38	19.96	20.52	21.13

Source: Central Statistical Office

A slight increase in life expectancy is forecast for the future, but this is still below the level needed to ensure population maintenance. In the long term, further increases in longevity are expected.

	2000	2005	2010	2015	2020	2025	2030	2035	2040	2045	2050
	Table 3 **Demographic assumptions**										
Fertility rate	1.34	1.31	1.50	1.59	1.59	1.59	1.59	1.58	1.58	1.58	1.58
Life expectancy (male)	69.86	70.88	71.95	73.07	74.24	74.92	75.57	76.25	76.96	77.71	78.50
Life expectancy (female)	78.19	78.78	79.40	80.05	80.7	181.31	81.91	82.56	83.24	83.96	84.73

Source: The Gdansk Institute for Market Economics

Over the next 50 years, a decrease in the proportion of persons of pre-working age is expected. At the same time, the percentage of people of post-working age will increase. According to population projections, the latter will exceed the former by 2015, and by the mid 21st century, this trend will have increased very dramatically. By 2050, the old-age dependency rate, measured as a ratio of people of post-working age to those of working age, will grow considerably from the present value of 25 percent to 64 percent (Chart 2).

Chart 2
Demographic projections

a. Demographic structure of the Polish population 1998-2050

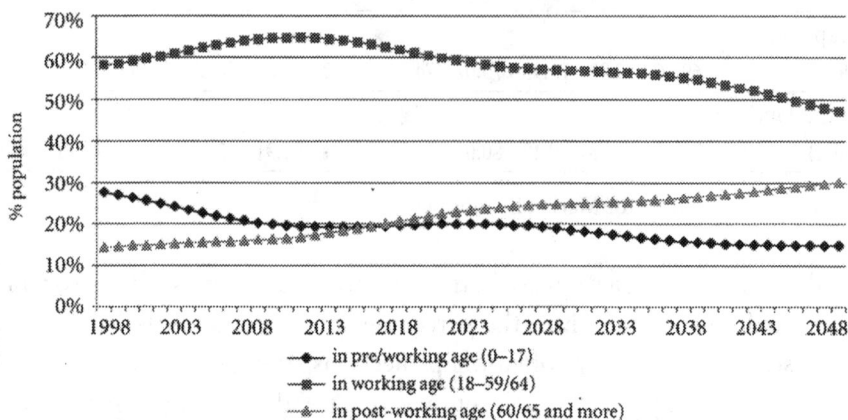

- in pre/working age (0–17)
- in working age (18–59/64)
- in post-working age (60/65 and more)

b. Old-age dependency rate (population of post working age as percent of population of working age)

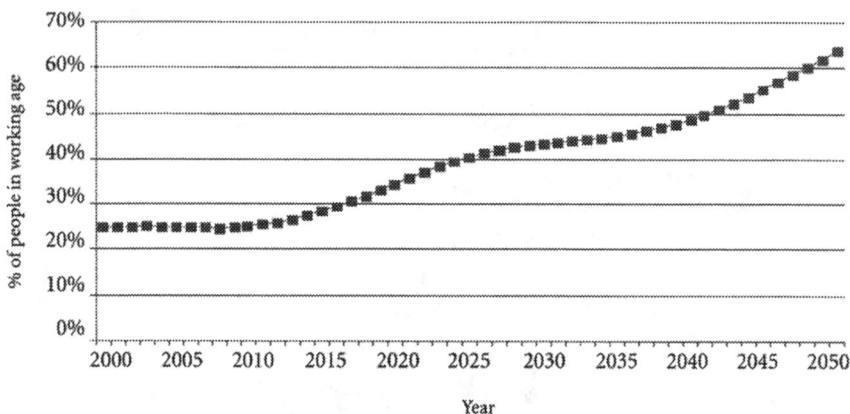

Year

Source: The Gdansk Institute for Market Economics

1.1.b. The economic situation in the 1990s

Like other transition economies, Poland suffered an economic recession at the beginning of the 1990s. By 1991, the Gross Domestic Product had lost about 18 percent of its 1989 value. The fall in the GDP was accompanied by a reduction in employment and real wages, though the former was initially less severe than the latter (see Chart 3).

While the GDP started to increase again beginning in 1992, the situation on the labour market did not improve. Employment continued to fall until 1993, and the increase after this time was not as rapid as the increase in the GDP. The unemployment rate peaked at just above 15 percent in 1995.

Wages also decreased after 1989. The fall in wages was highest in 1990, then the level stabilised until 1994. After 1995, the value of real wages started to increase, following the increase of the GDP.

It is noteworthy that in the period 1998-2000, wages and unemployment grew simultaneously. This phenomenon is due to two factors: firstly, the rigorous Labour Code and the relatively strong position of the trade unions make lowering wage levels difficult, and secondly, the labour market is fragmented – there is unemployment in some sectors (i.e. heavy industry) and a labour shortage in others (i.e. services).

Chart 3
GDP and employment in Poland (cumulative indices, 1989=100)

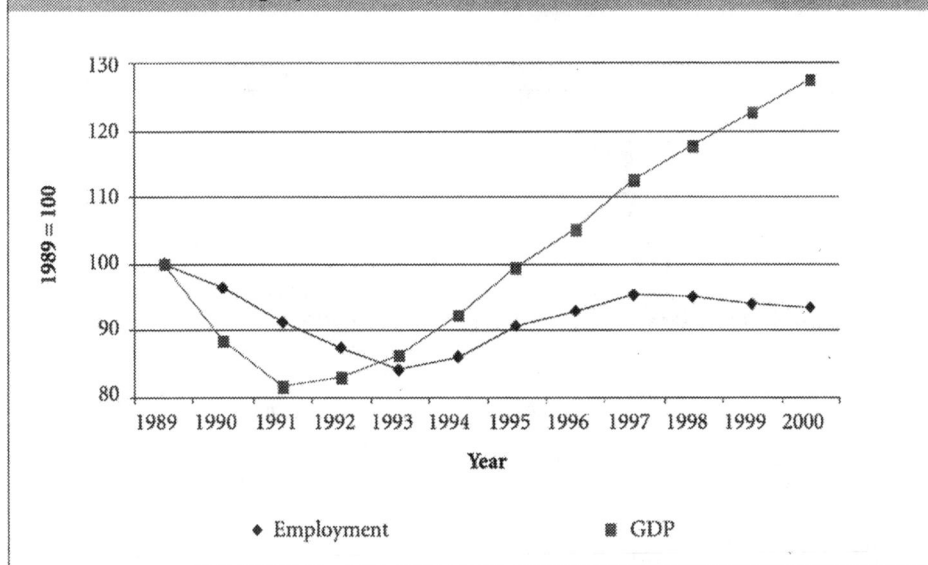

Chart 4
Unemployment rate in Poland, 1990–2000

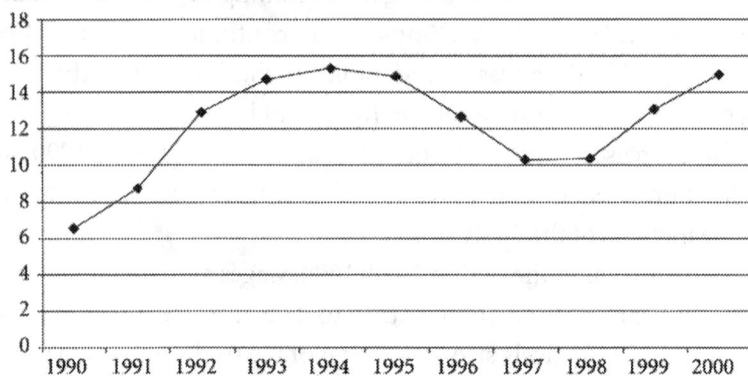

Chart 5
Wages and GDP per capita in Poland (cumulative indices, 1989=100)

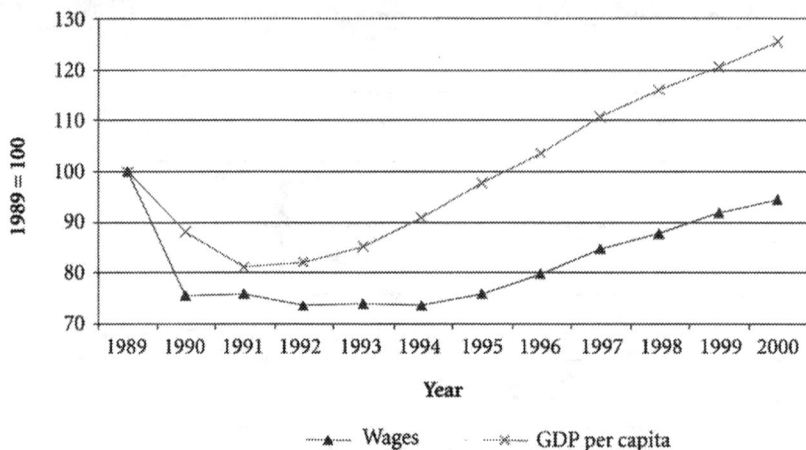

Source: Central Statistical Office, author's calculations

1.2. The pre-reform pension system

Until 1999, the Polish pension system was based on traditional defined benefit (DB) and pay-as-you-go principles. Pensions were financed from current contributions and, as noted earlier, fully paid by employers. The system covered a wide range of risks: old-age, disability, survivorship, sickness and maternity, work-injury and professional diseases. It provided protection for all employees in the public and private sectors as well as the self-employed.[2] All contributions were paid into the Social Insurance Fund (hereafter: FUS), from which benefits were drawn. The Fund was managed by the Social Security Institution (hereafter: ZUS).

1.2.a. Legislative changes in the 1990s

In the early 1990s, in marked contrast to other transition countries, Poland introduced legislation that increased the value of pensions relative to average wages. In the early and mid 1980s, the value of pensions had deteriorated, especially for older pensioners, as pensions were not indexed to wages. The indexing policy changed in the late 1980s, and wage indexing was provided for a period of several years. However, in order to eliminate the differences in sizes of pensions that persisted in the pension system from early 1980s, the so-called Revaluation Act of 17 October 1991 included a provision allowing for revaluation of all pension benefits. As a result, the amount of pension paid was no longer dependent on the time it was granted.

The Act also introduced changes aimed at strengthening the link between past wages and the size of the pension. At the same time, a minimum benefit guarantee for all pensioners was fixed at 35 percent of the average salary. There was still no reduction in benefits for early retirement, but restrictions were placed on the possibility of combining gainful employment with the receipt of old-age pensions and other benefits.

The Act introduced a new pension formula which was used to calculate old-age pensions for persons born before 1949 and disability pensions for all insured persons. This consisted of three parts:

– A flat component, equal to 24 percent of the base amount (economy-wide average wage);

– An earnings-related component, equal to 1.3 percent of the applicant's assessment base (countable average earnings) for each year of contributions paid;[3]

---

[2] Farmers and military services had their own separate pension schemes; expenditures on these are not included in the figures quoted.

[3] The assessment base is equal to an individual's average earnings over a period of ten consecutive years, chosen from the last 20 years, indexed for wage inflation. The averaging period was gradually increased from three years in 1993 to ten years from 1999 onwards. Additionally, there is a maximum cap on the assessment base equal to 250 percent of the average salary.

– A supplement of 0.7 percent of the applicant's assessment base for each year of non-contribution during his or her career. These other eligible years (e.g. spent bringing up children, university education) could not exceed one third of the contribution years.

Over the next three years, Parliament made two adjustments aimed at cost control. First, in December 1992, it amended the above law so that the base amount used to calculate newly granted pensions was reduced from 100 percent to 91 percent of the national average wage. However, this reduction proved to be unacceptable to society. As a result, this was increased to 93 percent in 1994, and then by one percentage point with every subsequent benefit indexation, until it reached 100 percent again in 1999. Second, at the end of 1994, the government decided to introduce price-based indexation of pensions, this change being implemented in 1996. Using prices, as opposed to wages, for indexation would reduce program costs significantly. The move was questioned by President Wałęsa, who asked the Constitutional Tribunal in October 1995 whether it was in line with the Constitution. The Tribunal agreed that changes in indexation were necessary in order to stabilise financing of the scheme in anticipation of reform. According to the Tribunal, '*Taking legislative action leading to radical restructuring of the pension system, and carrying out social consultation on the proposed changes sufficiently justifies introduction of the special indexation mechanism in 1996*'. The government was obliged by the Tribunal to implement a pension reform that would create a stable system for the future.

In 1996, however, the new indexation rules were changed. Parliament adopted legislation that allowed for some real growth of pensions, the growth factor being set each year in the budget law based on resources available in the state budget.

In 1996, the government also proposed a change in disability pensions that was adopted by Parliament. This change was aimed at reducing Poland's very high rate of disability pensioners by providing stricter rules for eligibility determination. The most important provisions of this legislation were as follows:
– eligibility for a disability pension was to be assessed based on the ability to work, not strictly on a medical condition, as had been the case before 1996;
– the former doctors' commission was replaced by social security doctors who would be trained in how to apply the new standard and would actually examine applicants for disability pensions; and
– the former three disability groups based on state of health were replaced by two groups – partial and total inability to work.

1.2.b. Operation of the pension system in the 1990s

The legislative changes described above exerted a strong influence on pension financing. The impact was felt in two phases: an increase in pension expenditures until the mid 1990s, followed by reduced expenditures from that time on. Other elements influencing the pension system in the 1990s, as previously noted, were an increase in the number of pensioners, and the general economic situation in the country.

In 1991 alone, outlays of the FUS (Social Insurance Fund) grew by 50 percent relative to the GDP (from 9.6 percent of the GDP in 1990 to 14.2 percent). This explosion in pension expenditures resulted from a combination of the following:

- the re-calculation of all paid pensions caused an increase in the average pension from 53 percent of the average wage in 1990 to 61 percent in 1991; and
- an influx of new pensioners: in 1991 the number reached almost one million, compared with approximately 600 thousand the previous year.

In 1992, personal income tax (PIT) was introduced. This law called for all pension benefits to be increased by the value of taxes paid, and after the introduction of income tax, pension expenditures grew from 14 percent of the GDP in 1991 to around 16 percent of the GDP during 1992-1994. This increase was not caused by wage indexation of pensions, as the real value of wages did not increase.

In addition, benefit levels rose during this period. Even with the reduced wage base, newly granted pensions were still quite high. In 1994, new pensioners received benefits on average equal to 72.8 percent of their final salary (which means that the new pension formula increased new pensions by 11 percentage points compared with those paid to new pensioners in 1990).[4]

Beginning in 1995, the expenditures of FUS in relation to the GDP started to fall (see Table 4). This was partially a result of economic growth, but also due to the fact that the government did not index pensions in line with wages in the fourth quarter of 1995, which was against the law. From 1996, pensions were modified in line with prices rather than wages. The influx of new pensioners was also lower, and the total number of pensioners was thus not increasing as rapidly

---

[4] In contrast to Poland, in other CEE countries (Czech Republic, Slovakia, Hungary and Slovenia), the replacement rates were reduced in the same period. For details see Golinowska (1996).

as at the beginning of the 1990s. In 2000, the total expenditures for FUS in relation to the GDP had fallen back below the 1992 level.

Table 4											
Expenditures of FUS as a percentage of the GDP in the 1990s											
	1990	1991	1992	1993	1994	1995	1996	1997	1998	1999	2000
Expenditures on cash transfers, including:	9.64%	14.23%	16.30%	15.84%	16.12%	13.67%	13.04%	13.71%	12.79%	12.34%	11.45%
Old-age	3.37%	5.51%	6.55%	6.67%	6.98%	6.58%	6.43%	6.48%	5.75%	5.67%	5.64%
Disability	2.47%	3.39%	3.85%	3.87%	4.06%	3.80%	3.65%	3.65%	3.15%	3.37%	3.25%
Survivors	1.12%	1.53%	1.89%	1.94%	2.08%	1.71%	1.96%	1.99%	1.70%	1.76%	1.75%

Source: ZUS

In the first half of the 1990s, the number of those insured in the social security system was falling, mostly due to the reduction of employment as described in the previous section, while the number of pensioners was increasing. This increase resulted in part from the early retirement policy adopted in order to reduce pressures on the labour market. In the second half of the 1990s, the number of insured stabilised and the increase in the number of pensioners was lower than previously. Between 1990 and 1999, the number of pensioners increased from 5.42 to 7.23 million. In 2000, the total number of pensioners decreased slightly to 7.21 million, mostly due to a decline in the number of disability beneficiaries, resulting from the 1996 reform. The net effect of all these changes is that the system dependency rate rose from 38 to 55 percent during the course of 1990s.

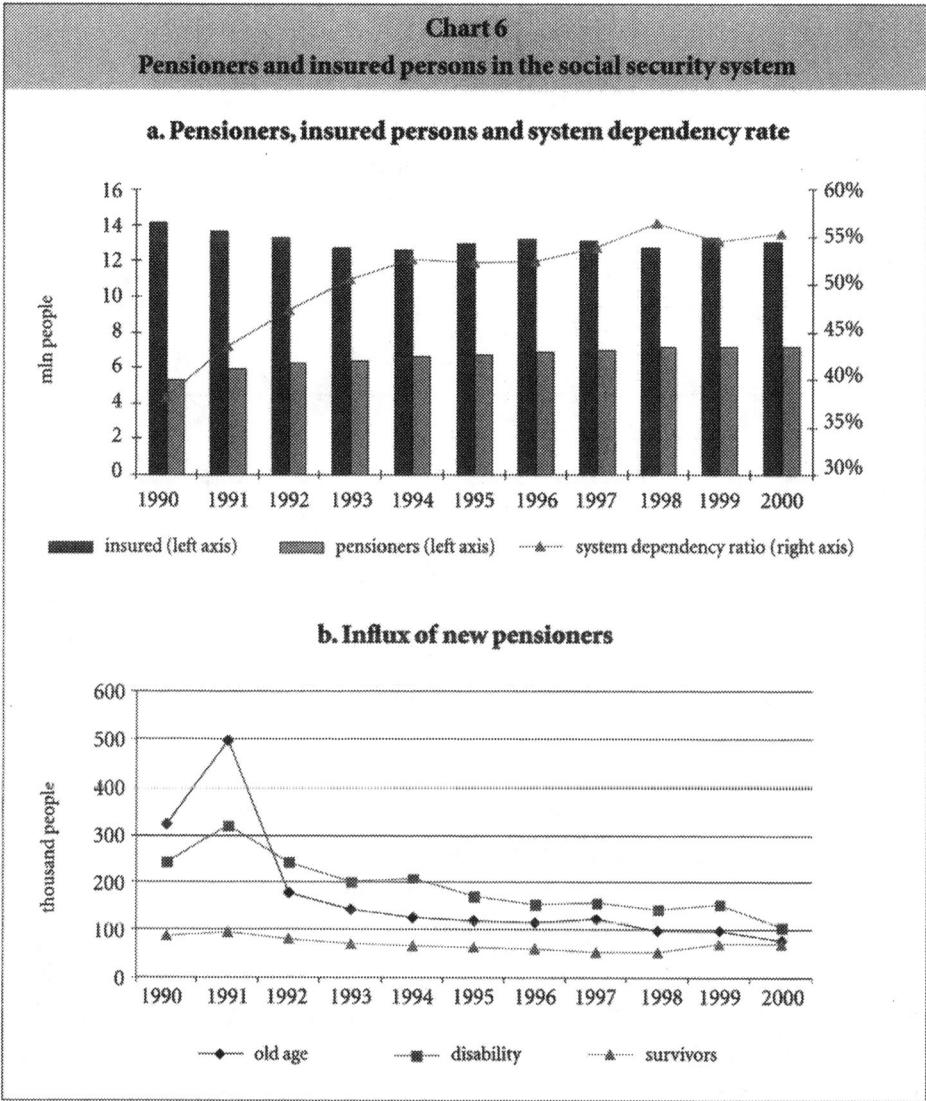

Chart 6
Pensioners and insured persons in the social security system

a. Pensioners, insured persons and system dependency rate

insured (left axis)   pensioners (left axis)   system dependency ratio (right axis)

b. Influx of new pensioners

old age   disability   survivors

Source: ZUS

The value of the average pension relative to the average wage also increased until the changes in the indexation method were introduced in 1995. After that, the ratio of the average pension to the average wage began to decline, and it is currently slightly higher than 50 percent (net of social security contributions).

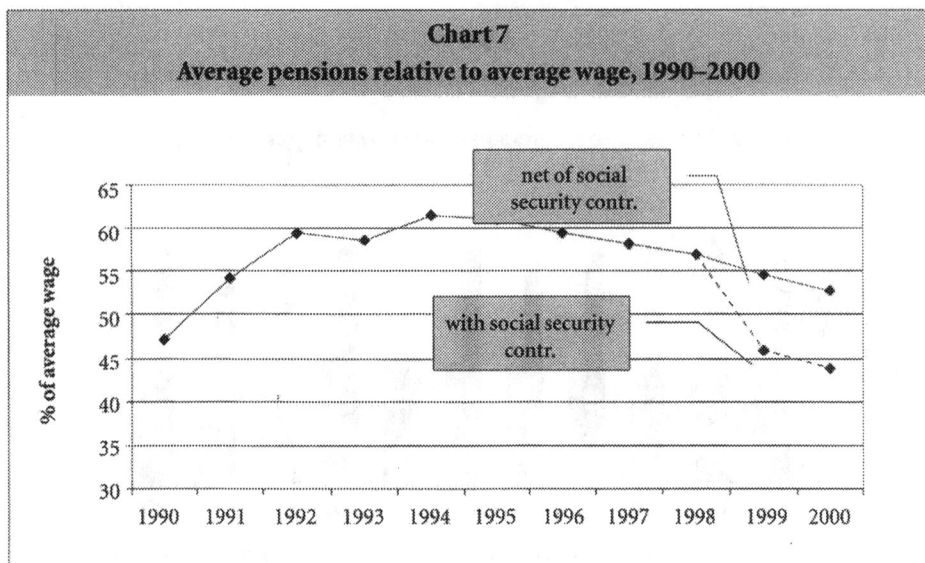

Chart 7

Average pensions relative to average wage, 1990–2000

Source: ZUS

The expenditures of the social security system were covered from contribution revenues and a state budget subsidy. As contribution revenues were falling in the 1990s, the government was forced to increase the state budget subsidy, the size of this subsidy reaching almost four percent of the GDP in the period 1992-1994. After 1995 this started to decrease, but throughout the entire period of 1990s the social security system was not self-financing, despite the high contribution rate.

1.3. Reasons for reform and expected results

There were several reasons for the major pension reform which occurred in 1999. First of all, the numerous changes to the pension system which had been made during the 1990s had undermined public confidence in the existing system. Many felt that the government and Parliament were manipulating the parameters of the pension system in an unfair manner, just to reduce expenditures. People could not understand the pension formula and indexation principles, which were complex and not transparent. In 1996, 73 percent of Poles were not aware of the basic rules by which the social security system functioned.[5] Secondly, the financial difficulties of the system created an urgent need for stabilising measures. As social security contributions were already at such a high level that they could not be increased further,

---

[5] According to a public opinion poll conducted by CBOS (Public Opinion Research Centre).

adjustments were necessary on the expenditure side. Finally, projections showed that an increasing demographic dependency rate would place an even higher burden on the pension system in the future. As was stated in the reform programme:

> The Polish social insurance system is universally criticised as costly, obscure and unjust. Most significantly, the system is threatened with breakdown over the next 10-15 years. Pension costs are high and the benefits provided unsatisfactory. Future benefits are not related to contributions made. Many people are of the opinion that their pension is based on imprecise criteria and arbitrary decisions, often made ad hoc by government authorities under the pressure of short-term economic needs. The proposal to reshape the Polish pension system based on fixed principles, long-term valuations and safety guarantees is therefore very important. Providing pensions based on such principles is the objective of the proposed reform plan. [6]

The main objectives of the reform outlined by the government were to create a transparent pension system that would resist demographic and macroeconomic pressures, while at the same time ensuring the highest possible level of benefits for future generations.[7] The authors of the reform concept believed that a multi-tier system would best fulfil these criteria. This would involve adding two new pre-funded tiers to the existing system, one being mandatory and the other voluntary. Both were to be privately managed and invested. At the same time, the public system would be made more transparent through establishing a stronger link between contributions and benefits.

1.3.a. Pension reform debate in the second half of the 1990s

Discussion on how to reform the pension system continued through most of the 1990s. The first proposal including the introduction of a prefunded tier was formulated in 1991 by Topinski (president of ZUS) and Wisniewski (an economist and actuary from Warsaw University), but this proposal did not attract the attention of the government, which was not yet ready to discuss (partial) privatisation of the pension system. The coalition pact (a blueprint for government action) of the SLD-PSL government, which took office in the autumn of 1993, included only a very general clause stating that the social insurance system should be reformed.

---

[6] See: *Security through Diversity*, a programme of the pension reform in Poland.
[7] See: *Security through ...*

Before 1995, alternative proposals for reform of the pension system were prepared by two ministries – the Ministry of Labour and the Ministry of Finance – that of the latter being part of the 'Strategy for Poland' programme presented by Minister Kolodko.

The Ministry of Labour proposal followed a more conservative and incremental path, along the lines of countries having traditional PAYG systems (e.g. France or Germany), and called for rationalisation of the PAYG system with the introduction of prefunded pensions on a voluntary basis. The Ministry of Finance proposal followed the Latin American example and included creation of a mandatory prefunded tier. It also limited the PAYG system to providing a flat-rate social benefit. The proposals were very different, and no agreement could be reached.

Besides proposals being prepared within the government, other institutions were also active. In the mid-1990s, both the Institute for Labour and Social Policy (IPiSS) and the trade union 'Solidarity' presented ideas for reforming the pension system. Their proposals included strengthening the link between wages (contributions) and benefits. The 'Solidarity' plan included creation of a mandatory prefunded savings tier, while IPiSS proposed the introduction of a system of voluntary prefunded pension savings, supported by preferential tax treatment. The basic elements of the four proposals are listed in Table 5.

The disagreements on how to reform the pension system were observed and analysed by journalists, one observer summing up the situation as follows:

> This reform is a political issue. So far nothing has been done, as politicians are afraid of the seven million voters who are pensioners, and these are afraid of any changes. ... The pension reform already has many godfathers, but pensioners are not interested in which minister introduces it.[8]

In December 1995, the government accepted a new proposal from the Ministry of Labour which could be described as a first attempt at a more radical change. The government called for draft laws to be produced in 1996. The most important elements in the proposal were:

– tightening the link between earnings history and pension benefit,
– increasing the retirement age for women (to 65 years),

---

[8] 'Liczymy emerytury', Gazeta Wyborcza, June 1995

- making the method of indexation more flexible – the annual increase in pensions would not be lower than planned inflation or higher than the planned increase in wages,
- tightening the eligibility rules for disability pensions, and
- withdrawal of some occupational privileges (e.g. higher benefits, lower retirement age).

This plan did not call for the establishment of a prefunded tier to supplement the pay-as-you-go pension scheme. The initial version of the proposal did not gain approval, as many politicians and trade union representatives were against an increase in the retirement age and the withdrawal of occupational privileges. In the end, only the changes to the indexation method and the disability pension eligibility rules were adopted.

There was still no comprehensive plan for pension reform that could gain the acceptance of Parliament and the government. In April 1996, by which time a new Prime Minister (Cimoszewicz) and a new Minister of Labour and Social Policy (Baczkowski) were in office, the government decided to appoint a Plenipotentiary for Pension Reform – a politician formally responsible for the preparation of a pension reform plan. The Minister of Labour (Baczkowski) was the first appointed Plenipotentiary. He was a strong supporter of fundamental pension reform, so he announced in Parliament that the government programme was still in need of 'final touches'. In particular, he announced his intention to develop prefunded pensions, which had previously been included in the plans of the opposition (i.e. the Solidarity union proposal). Baczkowski created the Office of Government Plenipotentiary for Social Security Reform (hereafter the Office for Pension Reform), consisting of a team of experts given the task of developing the reform proposal. Michal Rutkowski, a World Bank official on leave from the Bank, was appointed head of the Office. Together with Marek Góra, a professor from the Warsaw School of Economics, he co-ordinated the work of this team, which included both Polish and international experts. The work on pension reform was also supported by a World Bank grant.

In April 1997, the reform programme designated *Security through Diversity* was presented to the government and to the academic community by the Office and the new Plenipotentiary, Hausner, who had taken over the post on the sudden death of Baczkowski. The programme provided a framework for the creation of a multi-tier system in Poland, with a mandatory prefunded second tier.

Table 5
Basic elements of the preliminary proposals for pension reform in Poland

Main elements of the proposal	Reform proposals formulated between autumn 1995 and spring 1996			
	Ministry of Finance	'Solidarity' trade union	Institute of Labour and Social Policy	Ministry of Labour
Basic pension – first tier	Flat pension at the level of 20 percent of the average wage	Basic pension consisting of two elements – constant element financed from taxes and insurance element financed from contributions (individually determined)	Benefit dependent on the length of time contributions paid and size of contribution. Contribution is financed by employee and employer with cap on contributions and pensions (gradually attaining the level of 100 percent of average wage)	Benefit based on the length of working career and individual's salary, financed from contributions and state subsidies with a cap of 250 percent of average wage (falling to 200 percent of average wage)
Additional pension – second tier	Mandatory saving in pension funds	Mandatory saving in pension funds by transferring part of social security contribution plus privatisation bonds, given to all employees	Voluntary savings in pension funds for those earning more than average salary. Additional system integrated with basic one and combined with tax preferences	Voluntary savings in pension funds for those with highest incomes. Expected participation – marginal
Transition path	Mandatory participation for new entrants; a choice between systems for the employed; very high transition costs	Expected transition period for establishing pension funds (ca. 10 years), social security contribution divided between PAYG and funded tiers, significant subsidies from the state budget	Change in the first tier at the start of the process. Lower replacement rate in the pension system introduced when first pensioners take out pensions in the second tier. Transition costs covered by lower expenditures from the first tier	Beginning of the legislation process by the end of the 90s, implementation in the first decade of the 21st century

Source: Gospodarka i Przyszlosc, special edition on Social Security after Orenstein (2000).

1.3.b. Public opinion on the pension system

The attitude of society towards pension reform has been measured by CBOS (Public Opinion Research Centre) since 1995, when the public debate on the reform began. At that time, the opinion polls showed that support for the reform resulted from the negative assessment of the existing pension system rather than positive opinion about the proposed changes. Dissatisfaction with the level of benefits was accompanied by a lack of knowledge concerning the basic rules by which the system functioned. This source of dissatisfaction is rather striking, as the level of benefits in Poland is higher than in other transition economies. Thus, dissatisfaction must be seen as the subjective perspective of the persons surveyed (both of working age and pensioners), rather than a reflection of the actual income levels of pensioners. Panek, Podgórski and Szulc (1999) show that there is a significant discrepancy between actual levels of poverty among pensioners and their subjective perceptions.

In December 1997, 66 percent of respondents believed that pension reform was necessary and urgent. A quarter of respondents believed that reform was needed, but other issues were more important. Others either thought that no changes were required (2%) or they did not have an opinion on the subject (8%).

During 1997 and 1998, the Office of Plenipotentiary worked closely with journalists to disseminate information on the pension reform. Brochures were distributed widely among the general public (in return for coupons printed in newspapers) as well as among trade unions. The results of a survey from June 1998 captured public opinion before the introduction of pension reform.[9]

These results showed that more than half the population still did not know what kind of changes the pension reform would bring. A third knew about the changes, five percent had not heard about pension reform at all, and ten percent were not interested in the subject. Almost a third of Poles surveyed were hopeful about the pension reform, while the same number perceived it with uncertainty and 20 percent, with anxiety. The highest hopes related to the reform were expressed by the youngest people, those below the age of thirty who would participate in a fully reformed system, as well as by more highly educated and qualified people and those in a better financial situation. Those most fearful of the reform were unskilled workers (44%).

---

[9] CBOS survey, 'Current problems and events', 17–23 June 98, representative sample of adult Poles (N=1117).

One quarter of those surveyed (24%) believed that in the future the situation of pensioners would be better. A much lower number (around 8%) feared that the reform would worsen the situation of all pensioners. 29 percent believed that some pensioners would be better off and some worse off. One in three (36%) was convinced that in the future differences between the highest and lowest pensions would be larger than at present.

A large majority of those surveyed (73%) supported creating individual pension accounts. Almost two fifths (39%) believed that pensions should be financed from savings accumulated during an employee's working career. Almost the same proportion (37%) held that the best pension system was one with mixed funding – partially PAYG and partially prefunded. More than half of those surveyed (58%) considered a close link between contributions and benefits to be fair. Half of the respondents (51%) stated that individuals should decide for themselves when to retire once they reached retirement age. Similarly, 53 percent believed that pensions should be actuarially adjusted if someone continued working after reaching retirement age.

1.3.c. Economic projections

The impacts of the various reform proposals can be observed most readily when compared to a baseline scenario. The no-reform scenario presented below is based on the extended version of the Social Budget Model, prepared at the Gdansk Institute for Market Economics (in co-operation with the International Labour Office and the Ministry of Labour and Social Policy).[10] The model has been used to project the impact of an ageing population on social security expenditures, including old-age pensions and other benefits. The simulations presented were prepared in mid 2001 for the purpose of this study. Economic assumptions underlying the projections are presented in Table 6. These assumptions reflect the economic situation in Poland at the beginning of the 21st century, in order to allow for comparisons with the reform projections presented in Section 3.[11]

---

[10] For the methodology of the model, see Wóycicka (1999a) and for the results of projections as of 1999, see Wóycicka (1999b).

[11] For the pre-reform projections of the outcome of the pension reform see: Chłoń, Góra, Rutkowski (1999).

	1995 level	1995	2000	2005	2010	2015	2020	2025	2030	2035	2040	2045	2050
Table 6													
Labour market and GDP assumptions, 1995=100													
Participation rate	47.1	100	102.82	112.91	119.67	117.38	114.84	114.4	115.8	116.9	115.4	113.0	111.2
Unemployment rate	0.13	100	124.1	77.2	77.2	77.2	77.2	77.2	77.2	77.2	77.2	77.2	77.2
Labour force	17.07	100	101.9	110.9	117.4	116.0	112.3	108.1	104.7	102.0	98.0	92.7	86.6
Employment	14.79	100	98.2	114.8	121.5	120.0	116.2	111.9	108.4	105.6	101.5	95.9	89.6
Labour productivity	20.71	100	131.0	136.0	141.0	148.2	157.9	170.4	185.7	202.5	220.9	240.9	262.7
Real wage	849.84	100	132.3	137.2	142.4	149.6	159.4	172.0	187.5	204.5	223.0	243.2	265.2
GDP	306.32	100	128.6	156.1	171.3	177.9	183.5	190.6	201.2	213.9	224.2	231.1	235.5

Source: The Gdansk Institute for Market Economics

These baseline projections assume no change in the benefit formula or retirement ages. Indexation of benefits is assumed at the level of 20 percent of wages and 80 percent of prices.[12] Using this scenario, the simulation results show that pension expenditures in relation to the GDP would increase by 70 percent in the next 50 years (Table 7).[13] This rise would be observed primarily in the case of old-age pension expenditures which would almost double over this period, to exceed 11 percent of the GDP in 2050 compared with six percent in 2000. Expenditures for disability and survivor pensions in the same period are projected to increase by one percent of the GDP. If contribution rates were kept constant, the resulting deficit in the pension system would reach 7.5 percent of the GDP by 2050.

---

[12] Before 1998 the regulations on indexation guaranteed only price indexation. This was changed to prices plus 20 percent of real wage growth by the 1999 pension legislation. For comparison with the results of the reform simulation, the same level of benefit indexation is assumed in the no-reform scenario.

[13] Results of the projection, including number of pensioners and replacement rates, are included in the Appendix.

Table 7
Pension system expenditures and deficit as % of GDP, 2000–2050

	2000	2005	2010	2015	2020	2025	2030	2035	2040	2045	2050
pension expenditures: made up of	10.96%	10.64%	11.16%	12.75%	14.42%	15.53%	15.61%	15.57%	15.93%	16.60%	17.32%
old-age	6.05%	6.03%	6.64%	8.10%	9.55%	10.35%	10.16%	9.96%	10.21%	10.81%	11.42%
disability and survivor	4.91%	4.62%	4.52%	4.64%	4.86%	5.19%	5.46%	5.61%	5.71%	5.78%	5.89%
pension deficit/surplus: made up of	−1.07%	−0.78%	−1.31%	−2.90%	−4.58%	−5.69%	−5.76%	−5.70%	−6.06%	−6.74%	−7.47%
old-age	−0.11%	−0.09%	−0.71%	−2.18%	−3.63%	−4.42%	−4.23%	−4.02%	−4.28%	−4.89%	−5.50%
disability and survivor	−0.96%	−0.69%	−0.60%	−0.73%	−0.95%	−1.27%	−1.53%	−1.68%	−1.78%	−1.85%	−1.96%

Source: The Gdansk Institute for Market Economics, Social Budget Model (2001)

According to the projections, the largest rise in expenditures would occur in the period 2015-2025, when most of the post-war baby boom generation retires. The second wave of increase, projected for the mid 21st century, is related to the retirement of the baby-boom generation born in the 1980s. Based on the projections, the number of pensioners would increase from the current seven million to almost 12 million in 2025 and 14.8 million in 2050. Of these, 10.5 million are old-age pensioners; 2.3 million, disability pensioners; and almost two million, survivor pensioners. The number of old-age pensioners is projected nearly to triple compared with 2000, the number of disability pensioners is predicted to remain almost constant, and the number of survivor pensioners, to increase by more than 800 thousand.

The rise in the number of pensioners would be offset to some extent by the decrease of pensions in relation to the average wage (due to the combination of wages and prices used in indexing benefits). As projections show, a dramatic reduction is in store. The ratio of the average old-age pension to the average wage would decrease from 60 percent in 2000 to 36 percent by 2050. For disability pensions, the ratio in the same period is projected to drop from 44 percent to 26 percent of the average wage, and for survivors, from 52 percent to 31 percent of wages. This decline is due primarily to the heavy reliance of the indexing method on price changes during a period when wages are expected to grow much faster than prices.

2. Substantial elements of the reform

In order to reduce the deficit due to appear in the Polish pension system, two main reform measures were relied on: an increase in the retirement age, and a reduction of pensions to a level that would allow the system to be sustainable in the long run. In April 1997, the Office of the Plenipotentiary presented the reform programme *Security through Diversity*, in which the basic principles of the proposed pension system were outlined and a framework for future legislative work was created.

This document proposed replacing the existing pay-as-you-go scheme with a multi-tier system. This would be achieved by combining a new first-tier Notional Defined Contribution (NDC) scheme with a mandatory prefunded second tier consisting of individual, privately managed savings accounts. An NDC scheme bases benefits entirely on contributions paid, so that each worker receives the benefit that he or she has paid for.[14] A voluntary third tier, operated along similar lines, would provide higher pensions for those who opt for higher levels of savings and investment during their working years.

Góra and Palmer (2001) stress that NDC systems apply a *fixed* contribution rate to earnings, which is the same for all generations. Thus, this reform curtails government's flexibility to change the contribution rate. The rate of return in the NDC scheme is set in accordance with the equation:

PV_t (Contributions) = PV_t (Benefits)

This steady state condition is in principle satisfied by accrediting individual NDC accounts with a return equalling the rate of growth of the contribution base, that is, the total wages in the economy on which contributions are paid (Palmer 1999).

In the new pension system, a minimum pension is still guaranteed by the state provided age and contribution conditions are met (age: 60 years for women, 65 for men; minimum contribution period: 20 years for women, 25 for men). This is added to the first and second tier pensions to raise benefits to a minimum threshold. The main changes from the old to the new system are highlighted in Table 8.

---

[14] Benefits are set at retirement age based on worker's lifetime contributions and an estimate of the average life expectancy of the age group to which the worker belongs at retirement age.

Table 8 Comparison of the old and new pension system		
	Old system	**New system**
Contributor	Employer	Both employer and employee
Financing	Pay-as-you-go	Combined pay-as-you-go (12.22 percent of salary) and prefunded (7.3 percent of salary)
Pension base	10-year average earnings	Lifetime earnings
Record-keeping	Documents collected on retirement	Individual accounts with ZUS for each member
Pension age	Various early retirement privileges actual retirement ages: 59 for men and 55 for women	65 for men and 60 for women for nearly all workers
First contact with ZUS	On retirement	On starting first job and receipt of annual report from ZUS
Pension formula	Defined benefit: flat-rate component (24 percent of average wage) and 1.3 percent accrual rate	Based on actuarial annuity calculation, using unisex life tables in PAYG tier

Source: Chłoń, (2000)

Insured employees were divided into three main groups according to age on 1 January 1999:
- those born after 1968 became members of both obligatory components of the new system;
- those born between 1949 and 1968 could choose if they wished to partici-pate in the new combined system, or just the reformed public system;[15] and
- those born before 1949 remained in the old, non-reformed system.

The new pension system was introduced by five acts of Parliament. The draft laws were prepared by the Office of the Plenipotentiary, discussed with the social

[15] NB: this was not a choice between the old and new systems, since the old public system is being replaced by the NDC scheme.

partners, and after being approved by the Council of Ministers, presented to Parliament. The first package was enacted in 1997, under the Democratic Left Alliance-Polish Peasant Party coalition government. This consisted of:

- the law of 25 June 1997, regarding the application of the proceeds from privatisation of a portion of state treasury assets to purposes related to reforming the social insurance system;
- the law of 28 August 1997, on the organisation and operation of pension funds; and
- the law of 22 August 1997, on employee pension plans.

The above laws established the basis for creating the new elements of the old-age pension system, including the mandatory prefunded tier and employee pension plans, which constitute the voluntary third tier of the scheme. The first law specified that the costs of reform implementation (in particular the transfer of a portion of the contribution to the prefunded tier) would be financed by the state budget from the proceeds of privatisation. Significantly, the time between the presentation of the reform programme and the adoption of the laws was rather short, as the government's aim was to complete the legislative process before the Parliamentary elections of 1997. Legislative procedures were hurried, and the manner in which some issues were resolved was not compatible with the existing Polish pension system. As a result, difficulties arose in the implementation of some of the regulations. For example, it was difficult for ZUS to identify individual private pension fund members for the purpose of allocating a portion of their contribution to the particular fund which they joined; and pension fund managers had problems ensuring their sales agents acted in accordance with the law in recruiting new members. During 1999 and 2000, the government proposed amendments to the laws on pension funds and the employee pension plan to address these problems, and these changes were approved by Parliament.

A second legislative package was passed in 1998, after the change of government to the Election Action Solidarity-Freedom Union coalition. This included:

- the law of 13 October 1998 on the social security system, and
- the law of 17 December 1998 on old-age and other pensions financed from the Social Insurance Fund.

As with the first package, the time devoted to preparation of the proposals was rather short. The new government came to power in November 1997 and the draft legislation was presented to the Tripartite Commission in the early spring of 1998. The government also decided that the legislation should be comprehensive, covering changes to the administrative structure of ZUS, as well as harmonising legislation on pensions. As a result, both drafts dealt with a broad range of issues. The 1998 law on the social security system covers the structure of social insurance including a definition of insured persons, the establishment of a wage to which the contribution rate is applied, the rights and obligations of ZUS, and the financing and management of the FUS. The 1998 law on pensions financed from the Social Insurance Fund provides rules for the assessment and payment of pensions (for both the old and new old-age pension systems as well as for disability and survivor pensions). An Extraordinary Parliamentary Committee was created to discuss the draft laws. Due to the scope of the issues covered, discussion in the committee continued until the end of the year and the laws were finally adopted by Parliament in October and December 1998 under huge time pressure, as the enactment date envisaged was January 1999. As with the first package, lack of time for discussion and preparation resulted in many imperfections in the legislation, which created the need for further amendments after implementation of the reform.

Even though implementation of the above laws is now underway, the reform is incomplete in the sense that the following additional legislation is also needed:

- the law on annuities, which will create a framework for paying benefits from the prefunded tier. In particular, the law must specify which institution or institutions will pay benefits and define the rules for benefit calculation; and

- the law on bridging pensions, which will serve as a substitute for some of the early retirement pensions provided by the old system.

The trade unions did not agree to complete abolition of early retirement, especially in industries with difficult working conditions (e.g. limited access to fresh air, extreme temperatures, difficult body posture required). The government agreed that a special system of bridging pensions should be created, which would be paid between the time of cessation of work and attainment of the legal retirement age. The introduction of such a system requires the preparation of a new law to specify the financing and organisation of this scheme.

2.1. Changes to the public tier

Changes to the public tier of the social insurance system that were introduced by the pension reform may be divided into two main categories: (i) contribution collection, and (ii) the pension formula.

2.1.a. Contribution collection

As the benefits paid by the new Notional Defined Contribution (NDC) system will be based entirely on individual contributions, it was necessary to establish mechanisms for the collection and recording of these. Under these new arrangements, all contributions are collected by ZUS, as was the case preceding the reform. Starting in 1999, however, the social security contribution had to be paid on an individual basis, rather than on a company basis as before. The contribution is divided between employers and employees, as well as among different types of social security risks (Table 9). As mentioned above, there is a ceiling on the earnings which are ensured for pension purposes corresponding to 250 percent of average earnings (both for the employer and employee portion of the contribution), although this ceiling does not apply for purposes of contributions to health or work-injury insurance. To compensate workers for the new cost of making social security contributions, wages were increased by 23 percent in January 1999 (the portion of the social security contribution paid by employees). This increase was mandated by a decree from the Minister of Labour. Beginning in January 1999, contribution rates were also re-calculated using a higher calculation base equal to 123 percent of the previous one.

All the changes required revisions to the reporting obligations of employers.

Table 9
Social security contribution rates as a percentage of gross wage

Contribution by risk type:	Percentage of gross wage: Total	Paid by employee	Paid by employer
Old age	19.52%	9.76%	9.76%
Disability & survivor	13.00%	6.50%	6.50%
Sickness & maternity	2.45%	2.45%	–
Work injury	0.4% to 8.12%	–	0.4% to 8.12%

Source:1998 law on the social security system

2.1.b. New benefit formula

The essential result of the changes to the public tier, from the point of view of benefits, is a different system for the accrual of pension rights. Under the new NDC formula, accounts are established for each worker representing the pension rights they accumulate throughout their careers.[16]

The main results are:

– increased transparency of the pension promise, in the sense that it is equal to the value of accumulated contributions (however, as will be explained later, the actual monthly benefit amount cannot be known until the time of retirement);

– stabilisation of pension system financing, as liabilities of the system grow in line with contribution revenues;

– a great reduction of income redistribution in the system; and

– a possible reduction of benefit size, which depends on contributions as well as changes in life expectancy.

As the system is based on a close link between benefits and lifetime contributions, it is assumed that it will create higher incentives to comply with the contribution requirements at an earlier stage in the working life, as well as providing a stronger incentive to postpone retirement. However, these are hypotheses which cannot be proved at this early stage in the implementation of the reforms.

The 1998 law on pensions financed from the Social Insurance Fund defines the old-age pension formula. This is based on a standard annuity formula, where the value of the benefit depends on the total amount of contributions paid by a worker during the course of his or her career, and the life expectancy upon retirement. The benefit formula can be represented as:

$$P_n = \frac{\sum_{i=k}^{n}\left(cw_i \prod_{j=i}^{n}\left(1+I_j\right)\right)}{G_{n,r,s}}, \quad \text{where:}$$

---

[16] For a detailed description and discussion of NDC, see e.g.: Cichon (1999), Palmer (2000), Góra and Palmer (2001).

P_n = old-age pension at age n
c = contribution rate
w_i = contribution base in year i
I_j = indexation of notional capital in year j
k = age on entering social security system
G_n = annuity factor

Key parameters of the pension system include:

Contribution rate – c
One key factor for stability of the NDC system is that the contribution rate remains constant in the long term, so an initial correct decision must be made in setting it. The contribution rate for the Polish NDC tier is 12.22 percent of the salary (19.52 percent for those who decided not to participate in the funded tier). This figure corresponds to the portion of social security contributions which finances current old-age pensions.

Indexation during accumulation – I_j
The indexation of notional accounts is one of the most important factors ensuring long-term stability of the pension system. In order to ensure a predictable relationship between pensions and wage levels, contributions should be adjusted to reflect growth in the total wage bill covered, that is, the total wages in the economy on which contributions are paid. Any other type of indexation could destabilise system financing and benefit levels. The decision on indexation also needs to take into account any sources of pension financing other than worker and employer contributions, e.g. subsidies from general revenues.

The method for indexing the notional contribution was specified in the 1998 law on pensions financed from the Social Insurance Fund. Initially, the government proposed that the indexation factor should range between price inflation and growth in the total wage bill, the annual value being set by the state budget law in a similar way to benefit indexation. During the parliamentary debate, however, members of the Extraordinary Committee decided that indexation should be fixed. The government argued that indexation below the full level of average growth would create fiscal space for financing the transitional period, where pensions are still high (as a result of past obligations) but a portion of the public scheme revenues have already been diverted to the mandatory private tier. Lower indexation in the future could also allow for reduction in the contribution rate for old-age pensions, which was desired by government despite the need for a stable rate under an NDC system, as described previously. Such a decision depends not only on the financial condition of the pension system, however, but also on the size and adequacy of benefits provided. Balancing these considerations, Parliament set the final level of indexation at 75 percent of wage bill growth.

Indexation of accounts is to be carried out quarterly. The indexation factor will be calculated by ZUS based on individual data on contributions paid, and the figure arrived at will be announced by the President of ZUS.

Contribution base w_i

The contribution rate applies to all wages of employees. For the self-employed it is based on declared income, but this is deemed to be no lower than 60 percent of the average wage. The 1998 law on the social security system requires subsidies from the state budget for workers during certain periods of non-contribution. This results from the public desire to reward and encourage certain unpaid activities, such as child care, and to avoid penalising those who are involuntarily unemployed. These subsidies maintain some elements of redistribution in the system, although in its pure conception it is non-redistributive. The requirement that all credits toward a pension must be paid for, either by contributions or government subsidies, increases the transparency of social transfers and reveals their actual costs. In Poland, the periods for which contributions are financed from public sources (state budget or Labour Fund) are:
   – Unemployment (during which unemployment benefits are received);
   – Maternity and parental leave;
   – Mandatory military service; and
   – Caring for a disabled family member (child, parent).

In these cases, the wage base for calculation of the contribution is either the minimum wage or the actual amount of the benefit received. The four of the above periods were borrowed from regulations under the old pension system, where these same periods were considered as non-contributory (with the exception of covered unemployment, where social security contributions were paid). Only university education has been deleted from the periods covered by the earlier regulations. When proposing exclusion of this period, the government argued that because university education is an investment in human capital resulting in higher earnings and higher pensions in the future, it should not be additionally rewarded with a pension contribution paid from public resources.

Annuity factor G

In the NDC framework, the G-value is the unisex life expectancy at retirement age. This implies redistribution within the group between men (with shorter life expectancies) and women (with longer ones). The G-value is computed by the Central Statistical Office and represents the life expectancy in months from the calendar year of retirement. As the life expectancy of groups reaching retirement age is increasing over time, the G-value used for pension computation may be slightly underestimated. As a result, pension benefits may be higher than would be the case if projected life expectancy were used, as in a standard annuity calculation. The law does not allow for differentiation of the G-value for any reasons, not only for gender differences but also health status, place of residence, profession etc.

Indexation of benefits

Under the reform, pension benefits must be indexed by at least price inflation plus 20 percent of real wage growth. This form of indexing can be viewed from two perspectives:

- in periods when wages exceed prices, it helps to reduce pension expenditures, which in turn narrows the gap between expenditures and revenues for the pension system;
- lower-than-wage indexation creates a problem of declining real wage replacement for those receiving pensions over a longer period. In the long run, this policy may cause horizontal inequities among pensioners such as those occurring at the beginning of the 1990s, which created pressure for the re-calculation of all pension benefits as described in Section 1.

2.1.c. Transition from DB to NDC

The introduction of the NDC system required transitional rules to govern the treatment of rights accrued under the old pension scheme. The pension promise under the old system, generally defined as a percentage of wages (see Section 1.2.a.), had to be converted into the new concept of notional capital in the NDC system. Under the old pension scheme, ZUS only received information on a worker's years of employment and wages upon retirement, and furthermore, most individual records for years prior to 1980 had been destroyed. Due to these difficulties, the 1998 law on pensions financed from the Social Insurance Fund set a period of five years for the initial capital of all persons insured under the new pension system to be calculated.

The formula is:

Initial Capital $(C_0) = P_0 \times G_{62}$, where:

P_0 = monthly accrued pension at the end of 1999

G_{62} = unisex life expectancy at the age of 62 in 1998 (209 months)

The monthly accrued pension is then calculated based on the old pension formula. The only adjustment to the formula is that the constant portion of the benefit (equal to 24 percent of the average wage) is multiplied by an adjustment factor equal to

$$min\left(\sqrt{\frac{A_i - 18}{A_r - 18}} \times \frac{c_i}{c_r}, 1 \right), \text{ where}$$

A_i = age of individual at the end of 1998

A_r = retirement age (60 for women and 65 for men)

c_i = actual years contributions were paid at the end of 1998

c_r = years contributions were required to be paid (20 for women and 25 for men)

The effect of the adjustment is to assign each insured person (from the youngest workers to those 50 years old) a share in the constant part of the benefit formula reflecting his or her age and work history.

It should be noted that in the previous formula, the G-value used for the calculation of initial capital is a unisex factor, calculated for a person who was 62 years old in 1998 (G = 209 months). If G-values for both 60 and 65 were used to calculate the initial capital, women with identical work histories to men would receive 30 percent higher initial capital. To avoid this, the G-value was set using the average age of 62. While this approach avoids creating an unjustified discrepancy in favour of women, it could also create another potential problem: combined with the lower retirement age for women, it would create a significant discrepancy in pension value between women retiring in the old and new systems (in 2008 and 2009, respectively). This would be the case as women retiring at age 60 would have a lower portion of their pension resulting from initial capital than men. Also, as lower paid workers, women generally lose more than men in the conversion process as a result of the absence of redistribution in the NDC system. In order to avoid such a swift drop in benefits, the first five groups in the new system will receive their pensions according to another transition rule, namely, that pensions granted in the years 2009–2013 will be calculated according to a mixed old-new pension formula. This formula will apply only to those women who do not wish to participate in the prefunded tier. Initial capital will be indexed in the same way as are all contributions registered on their notional accounts.

The introduction of notional accounts simplifies transition to the multi-tier framework with regard to the calculation of pension rights. The size of the public pension is automatically adjusted downwards for those participating in the private tier by reducing the notional capital credited on the individual account. Initial capital represents a significant part of old-age pensions for the oldest groups covered by the reform, and it strongly influences their replacement rates.

2.1.d. Demographic Reserve Fund

The 1998 law on the social security system specifies that a Demographic Reserve Fund (FRD) be established to help meet increased benefit obligations when the retired population begins to grow. The FRD will be financed from surpluses in the PAYG old-age pension system, supplemented during the years 2002-2008 by one percent of contributions paid for old-age insurance.[17] The FRD is a separate legal entity whose assets can either be managed by ZUS or contracted out to specialised asset managers. The management of FRD should be based on long-term projections of the financial situation of the PAYG old-age pension system.[18] In the event of a scheme deficit, FRD assets will be used to finance old-age pensions. The creation of a demographic reserve will make the system less dependent on state budget subsidies in the future.

2.1.e. Simulations of benefit amounts

In contrast to the old pension system, which was based on defined benefit (DB) principles and provided a specific benefit promise, the level of old-age pensions under the NDC system cannot be known precisely until a person retires. Assessment of the impact of the pension reform on benefit adequacy can therefore only be carried out on the basis of simulations. The results of a simulation of replacement rates for different groups are presented in Chart 8. In

---

[17] At the end of 2001 the government, when considering budgetary cuts, proposed · reduction of the contribution transferred to FRD to 0.1 percent in the year 2002. At the time of writing, this change had not been discussed by Parliament.

[18] Regulations on FRD were based on the experiences of the buffer fund in Sweden and the Social Security Trust Fund in the USA.

order to screen out the impact of demographic ageing, projected life expectancies from 2050 are used. The simulation presents replacement rates (as a percentage of final salary) for persons retiring at the ages of 60 (lower series) and 65 (upper series), both for the cases of individuals joining the prefunded tier and those remaining only in the pay-as-you-go system. As can be observed in Chart 8, the reform will result in replacement rates declining from approximately 50 to 30 percent in the case of retirement at age 60, and from 65 to 40 percent in case of retirement at 65.

As can also be observed in Chart 8, the decision whether to enter the prefunded tier or not has little influence on overall pension size, with the exception of the effect of the transitional rules applied in the first five years of the new system. The difference in the size of pensions can rather be attributed to lower retirement age and a shorter contribution period.[19]

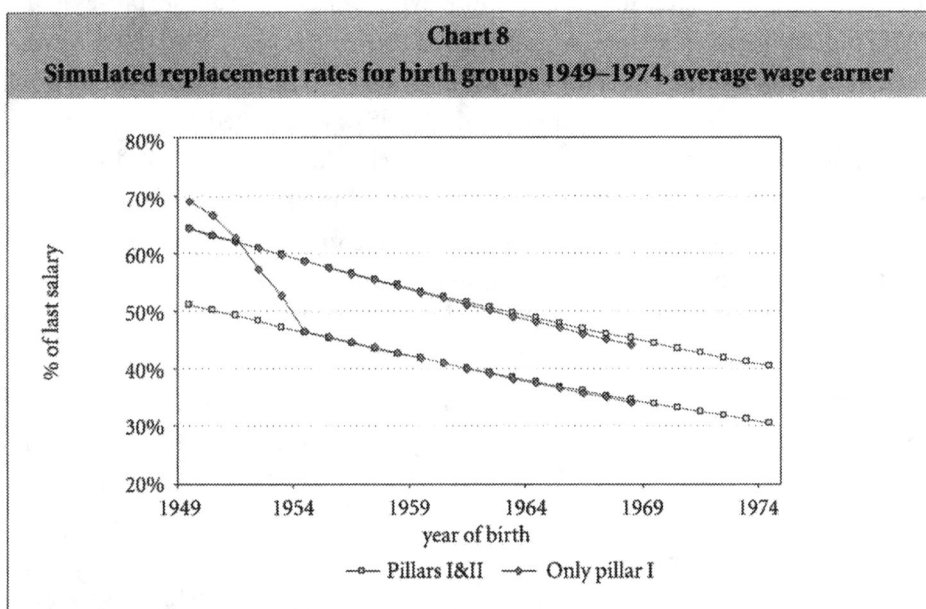

Chart 8
Simulated replacement rates for birth groups 1949–1974, average wage earner

Note: The upper two lines are for a male, the bottom two for a female. Assumptions for indexation of notional accounts and rate of return from the prefunded tier are as discussed in Section 1.3.

Source: Author's calculations

---

[19] This topic is further developed in the section of the project dealing with the reform impact on gender equality.

As the simulation shows, the reduction of the replacement rates under the new system will be quite significant. These projections are subject to considerable uncertainty, however, as the actual outcome depends heavily on the development of the labour and financial markets, as well as on demographic developments (since pension benefit amounts depend directly on group life expectancies under NDC schemes). For example, if it were assumed that the rate of return (both in the notional and prefunded tiers) were higher by one percent, benefits would increase by approximately one quarter for persons starting their working careers after the reform was implemented. Similarly, if there were no increase in life expectancies beyond 2001, benefits would also increase by one quarter. This explains the substantial differences between results of simulations depicted in Chart 8 and those presented during reform policy deliberations by the *Security through Diversity* programme. For example, a replacement rate for persons at the age of 60 was estimated to be 62 percent, and 80 percent for persons at the age of 65. However, the assumptions in those simulations included higher rates of return (in real terms 1.5 percent for NDC and 2.5 percent net for the prefunded tier) and shorter life expectancy (at the 1996 level). Consequently, the simulation results presented in the reform programme were much higher. (The subsequent change in the assumption on the rates of return was based on observations of slower growth in the economy.)

Depending on the long-term development of the actual values of the main variables influencing pension size, future policy makers may face the difficult choice of whether to allow pensions to remain at low levels, or to try to identify new ways and means of increasing pension adequacy.

2.2. Implementation of the private tier
2.2.a. The framework

The private tier covers pension savings for retirement only. Insured persons contribute to any one of a number of competing private pension funds. Their activities are regulated by the 1997 law on the organisation and operation of pension funds and modifying decrees issued subsequently. The pension funds are 'open', which means that an insured person can choose a fund from among all those operating on the market.[20] These open funds, or OFEs, are each managed

---

[20] These can be contrasted with closed pension funds, in which only selected persons can become members. This is the situation for example in employee pension funds that are established to invest voluntary contributions (paid by employers) under third tier arrangements.

separately by a pension fund society (hereafter: PTE), which is a joint-stock company. In order to establish a PTE and a pension fund, shareholders have to raise a minimum level of capital (no less than four million EURO) and be issued with a license. PTEs and pension funds are separate legal entities, and the 1997 law, designed to protect their members, stipulates that their assets cannot be commingled. PTEs are allowed to charge members two types of fees: an up-front fee deducted monthly from contributions and a management fee deducted from the member's accumulated assets (with the annual maximum specified by law at 0.6 percent of assets). Each PTE can manage only one OFE, but according to the 1997 law, a PTE will be allowed to manage two funds beginning in 2005, one of type A (with a more risky investment strategy) and one of type B (with a more conservative investment strategy).

Insured persons are allowed to participate in only one fund. Transfer between funds is permitted once a quarter in co-operation with ZUS and the National Depository of Securities, which serves as a clearing house. All transfers are reported to the National Depository, which calculates the value of net transfers between funds necessary to settle their accounts. If someone changes funds during the first 24 months of participation, a transfer fee must be paid. The maximum value of the fee is specified by a decree of the Minister of Labour, according to which this can range from five percent to 40 percent of the minimum wage (depending on the period of membership in the previous pension fund). As described already, private pension contributions are collected centrally by the ZUS, together with pay-as-you-go contributions. Workers are required to use their savings to purchase an annuity at the time that they retire, although the law regulating this part of the new system has not yet been passed by Parliament. This proposed legislation calls for annuities to be provided by specialised annuity companies (see: Chart 9).[21]

---

[21] According to the draft annuity law submitted to Parliament. After the 2001 elections, the law was not adopted. This means that the work on annuity legislation will start again with a government proposal. The final solution may differ from the initial proposal.

Chart 9
Second tier administrative structure

| Decision maker: | Worker | Investment Manager | Retiree |

(Employer → Social Security Administration → Pension Fund Manager 1 → Pension Fund 1 → Annuity 1; Pension Fund Manager 2 → Pension Fund 2 → Annuity 2; Pension Fund Manager 3 → Pension Fund 3 → Annuity 3)

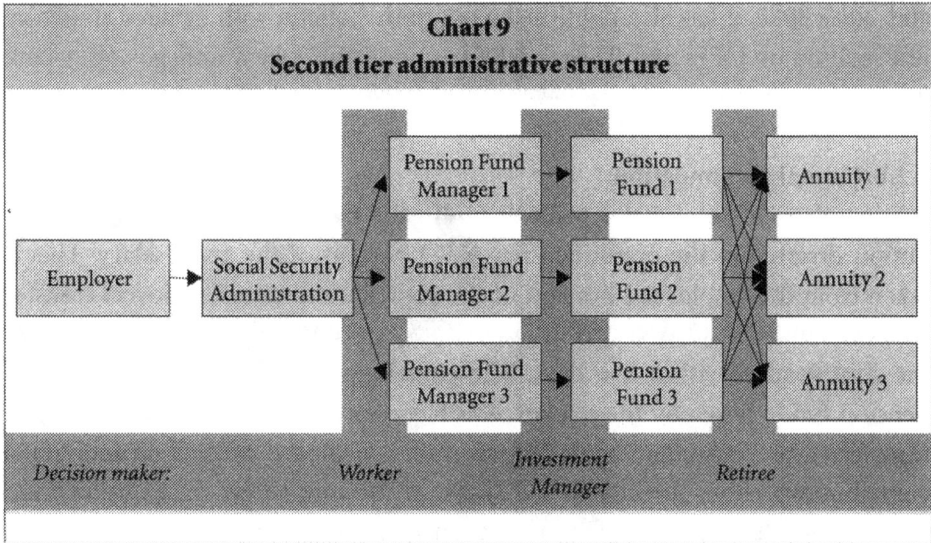

The pension funds are licensed and supervised by a special state institution, the Superintendency of Pension Funds (hereafter: UNFE), which regulates all the activities of OFEs and PTEs. It issues licenses to PTEs after reviewing documents provided by the shareholders. Among other things, UNFE analyses the articles of association of PTEs and OFEs, organisational and financial plans covering a three year period, the source and amount of capital available, and the financial situation of the shareholders. UNFE consent is required before any changes can be made to the articles of association.

As far as everyday activities are concerned, pension funds are obliged to send daily reports to UNFE, which include information on the number of members, contributions transferred to members' accounts, and the type and size of investments in particular financial assets. From these reports, UNFE obtains up to date information on the activities of pension funds, enabling it to react quickly to any mismanagement. In such cases, UNFE can penalise the PTE managing the pension fund. All regulatory functions are aimed at protecting members' interests. In carrying out its activities, UNFE co-operates closely with other governmental institutions such as the National Bank of Poland, the Social Security Administration (ZUS), and the Polish Securities and Exchange Commission, as well as employers' organisations and trade unions.

UNFE is also responsible for providing public information on pension funds. It publishes a monthly bulletin containing information on the pension fund market and, since 2000, it has also published a quarterly bulletin with detailed statistical information on OFEs and PTEs. UNFE has a web-site (www.unfe.gov.pl), where information on its activities as well as all publications can be found.

2.2.b. Capital accumulation

For members of second tier pension funds, the portion of the old-age contribution diverted to the prefunded tier is 7.3 percent of the gross salary. This is taken from the employee's portion of the contribution rate. Employers transfer the entire social security contribution to ZUS, which is obliged by law to process the contribution within five days. The contribution is then passed on to the pension fund chosen by the worker, which means that in practice the money is transferred to a custodian bank. Information is provided by ZUS on individual contributions either directly to a PTE or, in the case where the pension fund contracts out the function of record-keeping, to the transfer agent of that fund.

The custodian bank is responsible for safekeeping of the funds. It must be a Polish bank with assets exceeding EURO 100 million. The custodian monitors all transactions performed by pension fund managers, and if a transaction is made contrary to existing regulations, the custodian is financially responsible for any losses resulting from illegal practices. The bank also has a supervisory role, which is an important factor in the protection of pension fund members' interests.

According to the regulations, Polish pension funds may place their assets in selected categories of investments, including government bonds, treasury bills, equities listed on the stock exchange, bank deposits, and securities. A maximum of 40 percent of assets can be invested in equity, and up to five percent may be invested abroad. A detailed list of possible investments and limitations is presented in Appendix A.

The law has established certain guarantees for the savings of private pension fund members. This system is built on a guaranteed minimum rate of return, which is calculated quarterly by UNFE based on the average performance of the entire sector. Since June 2001, UNFE has calculated the weighted average for each calendar quarter of the rates of return of all pension funds over the preceding 24 months. The minimum is equal to half of the average rate of return, providing this average exceeds eight percent. If it is less, the minimum is set at the average achieved minus four percent. Those PTEs whose funds did not attain the minimum rate of return are obliged to supplement the accounts of their members with the difference between the rate of return actually achieved by the OFE and the minimum rate of return. This 'top-up' is financed primarily from a reserve fund, which each PTE is required to maintain, but if this is insufficient, from the PTE's capital. If neither of these sources is sufficient, the PTE must declare bankruptcy and its management is taken over by another PTE. Members' savings are then replenished from a national Guarantee Fund set up for this purpose.

According to the 1997 law on the organisation and operation of pension funds, the reserve fund must contain from one to three percent of the assets of a pension fund. A current government regulation sets this level at 1.5 percent. The reserve is financed from PTE revenue sources, as described in Section 2.2.a., and it may be invested in the same manner as OFE assets.

All PTEs must also contribute to the financing of a Guarantee Fund, as mentioned above, in order to ensure the safety of pension fund savings in the event of an individual PTE declaring bankruptcy. The Guarantee Fund is managed by the National Depository of Securities. If a PTE does not have enough resources in its reserve account or its own capital to cover a deficit, member's savings are replenished from the Guarantee Fund. According to the 1997 law on the organisation and operation of pension funds, the total assets of the Guarantee Fund should not exceed 0.1 percent of the total assets in the pension fund sector.

The savings in the prefunded tier are the legal property of each pension fund member. This involves certain rules to resolve ownership questions in the event of divorce or death of a participant. In the event of divorce, pension fund savings are divided between spouses according to a court decision. In the case of death of a participant, funds become part of his or her inheritance. Half of the accumulated amount will be transferred into the pension account of a surviving spouse, and the other half will be paid in cash to persons specified by the member, or to next of kin.

2.2.c. The 'pension promise'
While the accumulation phase of participation in the second tier is regulated in some detail by the 1997 law on organisation and operation of pension funds, a law concerning the payout phase is still to be formulated. The 1998 law on pensions financed from the Social Insurance Fund specifies basic rules by which second tier benefits are to be paid. These include the following:
- the day of retirement must be the same for the whole mandatory system (first and second tier), so that a worker must retire at the same point in time for the purposes of both portions of combined benefit;

- a second tier benefit can be received only in the form of lifetime annuity (no lump sum payments); and
- a minimum guarantee is established as a top-up to the sum of first and second tier annuities, bringing total resources for retirement to a certain prescribed level. This guarantee is financed by the state budget.

These provisions of the 1998 law create a framework for discussion on how to structure and organise the provision of second tier annuities. During discussions on this law in Parliament, two additional issues arose:

- how to minimise the costs of providing annuities, in order to provide old-age pensioners with the highest possible pensions; and
- the need to calculate annuities based on unisex life expectancies, so that women are not disadvantaged in their monthly benefit levels due to their longer average life expectancy.

Taking into account these two concerns expressed by Parliament, three possible options are under discussion: the creation of specialised private annuity companies, reliance on general insurance companies for provision of annuities, or provision by a single annuity company. A short overview of the options, along with their advantages and disadvantages, is provided in Framework 1.

Framework 1
Options for providing annuities in Poland

Option A – Specialised private annuity companies

– Advantages:
  Easy to understand, the arrangement has already been publicly announced, draft law already prepared.

– Disadvantages:
  Potential discrimination between clients due to companies' preference for shorter-living clients (men), who will automatically create profits for the company. High costs (mostly sales and marketing) to attract the desired clients, requirement to keep high reserves, related to the risk of surviving, initially bad business opportunity (few clients in the first year of operation, as only small percentage of oldest 'choice' groups are members of the prefunded tier).

The draft law for this option has been prepared and the government has submitted it to Parliament. After further consultations, however, the government had reservations about this arrangement because of relatively high costs. After Parliamentary elections of 2001, the draft was returned to the Ministry of Labour.

Option B – Life insurance companies delivering annuity products

– Advantages:
  Relatively few start-up problems, possibility of combining different types of risks.

– Disadvantages:
  Potential discrimination (similar to option A), still high marketing and costs, problem with designing a system of guarantees of safety of payouts specific only to annuity part (as the firms combine life insurance and annuity), mandatory social security old-age pension system loses part of its transparency.

This option is preferred by insurance companies for whom it would be the most natural, convenient, and profitable.

Option C – One annuity company managing pooled risk itself and contracting out management of assets, based on investment performance

– Advantages:
  Risk pooling, no discrimination, easier to provide guarantees of safety of payouts, reduction of costs due to economies of scale.

– Disadvantages:
  One institution has bad psychological connotations, there is no individual choice.

This option does not allow for insurance companies to be a part of the market. However, when asset management is contracted out to private companies, it creates potential for the development of the asset management sector.

Since the new system only covers people born after 31 December 1948 and establishes a minimum retirement age for women at 60 years and for men at 65 years, the oldest women participating in the prefunded tier can only retire after 2008 and the oldest men can only retire after 2013. Because companies providing annuities will need time to enter and develop this new business, there is a pressing need for the government and Parliament to complete the legal framework for the prefunded tier.

According to the draft annuity law, the guarantee for the second tier will apply only in the case of insolvency of an annuity provider. There is no guarantee as to the size of benefits, apart from the general minimum benefit guarantee described earlier in this section, which relates to pensions from both mandatory components of the old-age pension system.

As there is no pension reform law as yet specifying how benefits are to be calculated, for simulation purposes, the same pension formula has been used as in the case of the first tier (based on unisex life expectancies and with zero rate of real return on annuities). Given these assumptions, projected benefits are presented in Chart 10. The projection is based on gender-specific wage and participation rates.

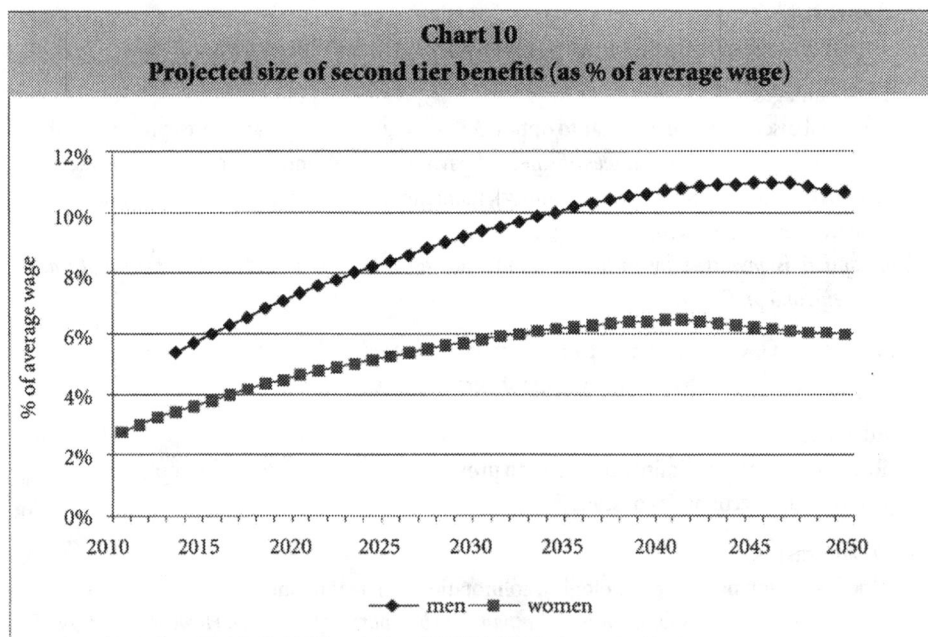

Chart 10
Projected size of second tier benefits (as % of average wage)

NB: Assumptions are as in Section 1.3.

Source: The Gdansk Institute for Market Economics

As can be observed, the size of benefits is projected to increase with time until approximately 2040. This is due to the longer period for accumulation of savings in pension funds for younger participants. After 2040, almost all pensioners will have been participating in the mixed system from the beginning of their working careers. Starting from that time, therefore, the differences in the size of pensions will be determined only by the net rates of return from savings in the prefunded tier.

2.2.d. Redistribution

The old pension system in Poland includes the following types of redistribution:

(a) Demographic redistribution from men to women, as benefits do not depend on gender.

(b) Income redistribution, including

- The constant element in the pension formula, equal to 24 percent of the average wage for all pensioners. As a result of this element, the pensions of those who earned below the average wage are relatively higher as a portion of their average earnings and pensions of those who earned above the average are comparatively lower.
- The cap on the portion of an individual's wage used for benefit calculation, at 250 percent of the average wage. This cap was not imposed on contribution payments, which were paid on the full wage.
- The minimum pension guarantee at the level of approximately 28 percent of the average salary.

(c) Recognition of pension rights for non-contributory periods, including maternity and child-care leave, caring for disabled family members, and mandatory military service. The size of benefits was increased if pension applicants could prove any of the listed periods applied to them. Since no contributions had been paid, those periods were effectively financed out of the total social security contributions.

(d) Financing of social security contributions by the state or reduced contribution rates. For covered unemployment, contributions paid from the Labour Fund, and for working disabled people, contributions partially covered by the State Fund for Rehabilitation of Disabled Persons and partially by the state budget.

Some of these elements of redistribution are preserved in the reformed public tier: in the case of the death of an insured person, his or her individual NDC account is terminated and the accumulated pension rights are treated as inheritance gain for the entire public system. (A surviving spouse and children are entitled to a survivor pension, which is paid from the disability and survivor scheme of the social security system, financed from separate contributions.) Redistribution also continues in the public tier through the calculation of benefits based on standard unisex life expectancies.[22] This creates redistribution from those participants who live shorter lives to those who live longer.

However, the new pension system reduces income redistribution as described in 'b' above in both the first and second tiers. This was also one of the goals of the reform, as the Office of the Plenipotentiary team argued that in the past system redistribution often lacked transparency or clear rationale. For example, pensions of persons working shorter periods but receiving higher wages were higher than for those who worked longer and received lower wages, even if they had paid the same total contribution when calculated for the whole working life.

Redistribution is reduced by the absence of a constant component in the new benefit formula. Moreover, the cap on the maximum earning level used for benefit calculation is now also applied to contributions, so that employees and employers do not pay contributions on earnings exceeding 250 percent of the average wage. Redistribution was only maintained with respect to the guarantee of a minimum pension, but the financing method for the minimum pension has been shifted to the state budget. Additional periods giving rise to pension rights are now financed by government contributions to the social insurance system, both in the pay-as-you-go and the prefunded tiers (see Section 2.1.b.).

While the prefunded tier is structured for individual savings, there are also elements of redistribution here, resulting from the mechanisms of guarantees. During the phase of income accumulation, the rate of return guarantee may be perceived as a redistributive component, since all participants bear the costs of creating the Guarantee Fund out of their fees. As the Fund is used to replenish the accounts of the members of pension funds with poor investment performance, all participants share in financing part of the savings of members of pension funds which function badly.

---

[22] In the case of the prefunded tier, the draft law presented to Parliament on funded pensions allowed for differentiating mortality factors, but this was strongly criticised by all political parties. As a result, it seems likely that the mortality rates will also be equalised in the second tier.

The minimum pension guarantee can also be viewed as a guarantee against bad performance of the prefunded tier, since if the size of benefit falls below the minimum, the state pays the minimum benefit thus covering the rate of return risk. If performance of the private tier is so poor that a worker's total pension falls below this level, the state will provide a subsidy from revenues collected from the general population.

Providing an explicit subsidy from the state budget for certain non-contributory periods is preferable to a cross-subsidy within the pension scheme because it improves financing transparency. This approach also removes disincentives to the creation of employment, as the financing of pensions is not only drawn from labour income. Moreover, the state budget subsidies are in keeping with government social priorities. For instance, the government's pro-family policy is reflected in the case of maternity and childcare leave. As the number of births is dropping significantly, it was felt that mothers should be protected in the social security system, so they would not lose their pension rights when deciding to stay at home to care for children. At the same time, financing of social security contributions for the unemployed and the disabled is a part of the government work rehabilitation policy, aimed at encouraging employers to hire disabled persons. Government payment of contributions for mandatory military service results from the fact that men have to leave their regular jobs in order to perform a vital public service. The government therefore felt that they should also be compensated in the social insurance system for these missing contribution periods.

A final noteworthy point is that elimination of the constant component of the pension formula has major implications for the distribution of the size of pensions. It can be expected that income inequality in the new pension system (as can be measured by the Gini coefficient) will be much higher than in the old one, reflecting the shift from social insurance to individual pension savings. As a result, the number of persons receiving the lowest benefit is expected to increase, and additional measures to protect the elderly from poverty will have to be considered by future governments.

3. Early post-reform experience

As described in Section 2, the final law on pension reform was adopted by Parliament only days before implementation was scheduled to begin, and ZUS's lack of preparation caused significant upheaval in pension administration. The drawn out legislative process in 1998 also required a three-month postponement of the introduction of the prefunded tier, as ZUS needed time to make preparations for transferring individual contributions to pension funds. Pension funds were finally able to begin operations in April 1999.

3.1. Results and problems with reform of the public tier

The experience of the first two and a half years after introduction of the reform does not allow for assessment of the actual outcome of changes to the benefit payment system legislated in the public tier, as no pensions have yet been paid. However, this period has probably been long enough to assess ZUS's administrative preparation for the tasks, as well as to learn some preliminary lessons from implementation.

ZUS has been faced with many challenges with regard to the new set of rules established by the pension reform. In spite of the partial privatisation of pensions, its role in the newly created system is even more crucial than in the old one. In addition to the functions previously performed, such as collecting contributions for the public pay-as-you-go pension scheme and paying out benefits, ZUS must now perform a long list of new tasks:

A. Administration of the pay-as-you-go system:
• Managing the Social Security Fund sub-funds
  – Old-age fund
  – Disability and Survivors fund
  – Work injury fund
  – Sickness and maternity fund
• preparing medium-term actuarial analyses for the entire social security system and long-term projections for the old-age sub-fund;[23]

---

[23] Before 1999, there was no legal requirement for the preparation of projections on the costs and revenues of the social security system. Regular planning included only one-year financial plans.

- creating and maintaining individual accounts for all those insured in the Central Register of Insured Persons;
- management of the Demographic Reserve Fund;
- calculation of the Initial Capital for notional accounts (to be completed by 2004); and
- paying social insurance contributions for persons on maternity and child-care leave, as well as other subsidised, unpaid activities.

B. Serving as a transfer agent for the second tier of the new pension system:
- collection of contributions for the second prefunded tier;
- transferring second tier contributions to the pension fund chosen by the worker;
- maintaining a central database of second tier participants;
- co-operation with National Depository in making transfers of funds and data between pension funds (quarterly); and
- preparing a lottery for assigning insured persons to pension funds in cases where they did not chose one although obliged by law to do so.

C. Collection of contributions for other elements of the social security system:
- collection of contributions for the health insurance system implemented on 1 January 1999, and transfer of these to 16 regional health care funds and professional health care fund; and
- maintaining a database for health care insurance purposes (consisting of insured persons and their dependants – some 30 million accounts).

These new duties necessitated major changes in the ZUS organisational structure, which were mandated in the 1998 law on the social security system. The institution was given formal legal status, allowing for greater independence, and a new structure that is more centralised from the management perspective. In the place of Supervisory Boards in all regional branches of ZUS, one Board has been established with members chosen on the basis of a tripartite agreement. ZUS's capacity to perform its new tasks was to be enhanced by building a complex IT system (known as KSI).

During preparation of the reform, there was little discussion about ZUS's capacity to take on the new tasks related to its implementation. Apparently it was assumed that ZUS would be able to implement all the changes starting from

January 1999. While some close observers expressed doubts about this in the period just before enactment of the law, the government decided that the reform would be launched as planned.

Throughout 1999, ZUS experienced serious operational problems, the most significant of these being:

1. Difficulties in the implementation of new regulations. As it turned out, the pension reform legislation omitted many crucial details, as well as including provisions that were impossible to implement within the short period of time specified by the law. The main problem areas were an ambiguous provision on the identification of individual contributions, a requirement for ZUS to establish individual accounts at a very early date (beginning in March 1999), and the absence of rules for assigning responsibility for errors made in the information given to, or by, ZUS, or for their correction.

2. Delays and difficulties in the implementation of the new IT system (KSI), which in turn resulted in delays in establishing individual contribution records. A contract for the development of KSI was signed in 1997, with ZUS management choosing one of the largest Polish software firms as contractor. After a change of the ZUS president in 1997 (following Parliamentary elections), the contract was re-negotiated and the terms significantly modified in order to adjust the system to the requirements of the planned pension reform of 1999. The implementation date for the new system then passed before this particular law had been approved by Parliament and, as a consequence, the new system was not ready. It also turned out that the information sent by employers to ZUS in 1999 contained numerous errors. Many of these still have to be clarified so that individual contributions can be identified.

3. Financial instability of FUS caused by a low contribution collection level. At the beginning of 1999, ZUS management decided to discontinue the old system for registering contribution payments (known as ARS) and to replace it with a new KSI module. Because KSI was not functional, however, ZUS lost its capacity to track contribution payments made by individual employers and the self-employed. When these contribution payers realised that their compliance, or lack thereof, could not be detected by ZUS, the payment rate fell precipitously, triggering a financial crisis at ZUS. Details of this problem and the recovery measures undertaken will be discussed below.

4. Inefficient organisational structure. During the 1990s, ZUS had become one of the largest institutions in Poland, employing around 40 thousand people. The structure included not only a large national headquarters but also a country-wide network of branches and offices. This giant institution had no clear vision of its mission, however, and there was little exchange of information between the branches and headquarters. The demands of the pension reform revealed the inefficiencies of the existing structures, which could not adapt to the new situation. As a result, many problems surfaced more quickly than would have been the case had ZUS continued to operate the old scheme.

The combination of these problems necessitated changes in the reform legislation. During 1999 and 2000, 17 amendments to the 1998 law on the social security system and six amendments to the 1997 law on the organisation and operation of pension funds were enacted. The amendments included:
- Revision of laws which proved difficult to implement;
- Interim solutions until such time as ZUS could develop the needed capacities; and
- Postponement of implementation dates which were impossible to meet from an administration point of view.

The various ways in which ZUS dealt with these problems are described below.

3.1.a. Implementation of new regulations

Information transfer

The most important change in the administration of the public tier was the introduction of individual reporting on all insured persons. This change was necessitated by the shift to an NDC system, as all contributions are paid on behalf of individual workers (as opposed to the previous situation, where employers had paid contributions based on the total payroll). Until 1998, ZUS received no information on individual insured persons from companies employing more than 25 people, which included most firms. Consequently, new reporting mechanisms had to be designed and implemented. Under the reform, employers are required to send the following to ZUS: **enrolment reports** (a first report, with information on new employees), **monthly reports** (contributions paid for each employee), and **monthly declarations** (of the total contribution paid by the employer). The 1998 law on the social security system allows employers to report to ZUS in one of three ways:

- in paper format, on pre-designed forms completed manually by employers and scanned by ZUS;
- in paper format, as printouts from software provided by ZUS (PLATNIK); or
- electronically, using the PLATNIK programme.

PTEs communicate with ZUS electronically, as they process information on pension fund members in-house. In addition to employers and PTEs, a third type of institution that delivers input to the KSI database are banks which process the contribution transfers. All the bank transfers are made using pre-designed formats which identify the contributors. Based on the information provided by employers, PTEs, and banks, ZUS must perform the following tasks:

- Build Central Registries of (i) insured persons, (ii) private pension fund members, and (iii) employers and self-employed individuals (these two are grouped together in a third category because they actually transmit contributions to ZUS). The central registries of (i) insured persons and (ii) employers and self-employed persons were constructed in January 1999, when employers began to send enrolment information. The central registry of pension fund members was established during 1999, as insured persons joined private pension funds.
- Assign payments to payers' accounts, and crosscheck the information on monthly declarations against the amounts actually transferred.
- Assign contributions to the accounts of the individuals on whose behalf they were made, based on the monthly reports.
- Transfer contributions to private pension funds, provided the insured person has been identified both in the central registry of insured persons and the central registry of contribution payers as a private pension fund member.
- Keep an account of FUS funds and prepare annual financial statements based on monthly declarations.
- Enforce the requirement to make contributions.

All these activities can only be performed effectively if no errors exist in the information provided to ZUS.

Both ZUS and the Ministry of Labour, as supervisor of the reform implementation, assumed that most employers would use the PLATNIK programme, which allows for direct input of data to the computer system. The software was not ready at the beginning of 1999, however, so all employers used paper forms initially, which contained many errors. It was particularly problematic that paper forms were used to register all employees with ZUS. The 1998 law on the social security system obliged employers to send enrolment reports by the end of January 1999, so since February 1999, employers have been sending this information to ZUS on a monthly basis. New reporting obligations introduced with practically no advance notice resulted in a very poor quality of data, in part because the time constraints did not allow for pretesting of the reporting format. The number of errors far exceeded expectations. Table 10 categorizes these errors by mode of communication. As can be seen, the error rate is highest in the case of forms completed manually, while it is lowest in the case of electronic transfer. For all modes of communication, the error rate has decreased over time.

Table 10
Error percentage by document type

	Percentage of errors in the documents filled in manually	Percentage of errors in printouts from PLATNIK programme	Percentage of errors in electronic transfers from PLATNIK programme
June 1999	52.78%	34.01%	13.65%
February 2000	35.62%	12.86%	9.94%
July 2000	23.05%	6.89%	6.81%

Source: ZUS

In 2000, the largest number of payers still completed forms manually (around 60 percent), while 26 percent used printouts from the PLATNIK programme, and only four percent used the electronic transfer option. The distribution was different from the perspective of the number of insured persons, however. Measured in this way, 21 percent were accounted for by paper forms completed manually, 36 percent by printouts from the PLATNIK programme, and 43 percent by electronic transfer. This indicates that the largest employers found electronic transfer the most convenient method of reporting to ZUS.

Another type of error involved reporting by banks. Many bank documents did not identify the source of payments. As a result, it was impossible to credit individual accounts with contributions; obstacles were created to contribution transfers to private pension funds; and the tasks of crediting contributions to the accounts of employers and self-employed persons and checking for compliance were complicated.

In co-operation with ZUS, the Ministry of Labour proposed an amendment to the 1998 social security law aimed at improving the quality of information. This law obliges those firms employing more than 20 people to communicate with ZUS electronically. The law came into force gradually during the first half of 2001, and since its implementation with regard to the smallest employers (with 20 to 99 employees), 80 to 90 percent of all information has been transferred to ZUS electronically. As indicated in Table 10, this is the most error-free mode of communication, so this shift has improved contribution transfer to private pension funds.

Identification of insured persons, employers, and self-employed persons
Another problem related to the introduction of the new type of reporting was the identification of insured persons and contribution depositors (i.e. employers and self-employed persons who are assigned legal responsibility for transferring their own contributions and, in the case of employers, their workers' contributions as well, to ZUS). According to the 1998 law on the social security system, two national systems can be used to identify insured persons, one based on the ID number given at birth (known as PESEL) and another, on the tax-payer number (NIP). As neither of the numbering systems is error-free, the law provided the option of using either of the two numbers. For employers and self-employed persons, one of two numbers could also be used: either the tax-payer number (NIP) or the company statistical number (REGON).

During the course of 1999, it became clear that the 1998 law on the social security system was not specific enough regarding how the ID numbers should be used. There were cases in which individuals were identified in the central registry of insured persons under one ID number (e.g. the NIP) and in the central registry of pension fund members under the other (PESEL). In such cases, the records of the two registries could not be matched and contributions could not be transferred to the individual's chosen private pension fund. The government proposed an amendment to the law on the 1998 social security system obliging employers and pension funds to use both ID numbers simultaneously. This amendment came into force at the beginning of 2000, resulting in improved identification of pension fund members and insured persons. Between the beginning of 2000 and the second half of 2001, the number of unidentified accounts (so-called 'dead-accounts' with zero contribution) was reduced from three million to 2.3 million.

In 1999, problems also arose with the identification of employers and self-employed persons. For collection purposes, ZUS had previously assigned all contribution payers internal numbers, which were used for the exchange of information between ZUS and the payers. As mentioned above, however, from 1999 ZUS had the option to use either NIP or REGON numbers. This shift caused difficulties in the identification of payers. ZUS observed that some companies used the same NIP number for all their regional branches, while in the ZUS central registry, each regional branch constituted a separate contribution payer. Thus, if the same number were entered, the computer system treated it as an error. In consequence, the contribution could neither be assigned to the employer who had made it nor to any insured person. The Ministry of Labour and ZUS therefore proposed a change to the law allowing for the creation of a Social Security Number for Contribution Payer (NUSP).[24] This change came into force in February 2001, and NUSPs are now being assigned by ZUS to all employers and self-employed persons (the timetable for the assignment has been left to ZUS).

Initial Capital

In the second half of 2000, after the relevant decree had come into force, ZUS began to collect the information necessary to calculate initial capital for the new NDC system, which will represent the accrued pension rights of all insured persons. This requires gathering historical data on past wages and employment for all persons covered by the pension reform.

The process is complex, not only requiring action by ZUS, but also co-operation from employers who must submit the necessary documentation, and from insured persons, who are obliged to obtain documents from all former places of work. The 1998 law on pensions financed from the Social Security Fund obliges ZUS to complete the calculations of initial capital by 2004.

---

[24] As explained earlier, both workers and employers pay contributions, so the term 'payer' is used here only in the sense of transferring these contributions to ZUS.

Other Changes in the Law

Other amendments to the social security law enacted in 1999–2000 include:

– Requirement for all employers to provide an annual report.

Initially, it was expected that ZUS would receive all the information needed to operate the new scheme from monthly reports. During the course of 1999, however, the combination of a large number of errors and an unfinished IT system caused extensive delays in the processing of these monthly reports. In order to complete the 1999 FUS financial statement, an additional end-of-year report was required. This report was also mandated for 2000 and 2001, but for those years the range of information required was smaller, covering only sickness benefits paid by employers.

– Changes in deadlines for contribution payments and reports.

Payment dates were shifted from the 8th, 12th and 15th days of the month to the 5th, 10th and 15th. This change was applied to budgetary institutions, the self-employed, and other employers in order to reduce 'rush hour traffic' in the arrival of reports in ZUS offices. The workload is thus evened out, and more time is available for analysing and processing the documents.

– Social security obligations for additional work contracts.

This amendment was designed to prevent misuse of the system, since many employers had resorted to paying a portion of salaries under additional work contracts that were not subject to the social security contribution requirement. Higher contribution revenues are expected as a result of this change.

– Employers to send reports monthly, even if these are identical for some months.

Originally, employers were not obliged to report in those months where no changes had occurred from the previous month. When the new IT system is up and running, it will be able to generate the necessary information from the database, but as the system was not ready at the beginning, this amendment was needed as an interim measure.

– Introduction of a penalty fee for those employers who make errors in monthly reports, declarations, or bank documents.

In the 1998 law on the social security system, there was no provision for penalising institutions which submitted erroneous information to ZUS. As information is as important as money in the new system, it was necessary to introduce penalties for those who make errors resulting in the inability to register contributions on individual accounts and thus to transfer contributions to the appropriate OFE.

– Postponement of deadlines for the treatment of individual accounts.

The 1998 law on the social security system specified that individual accounts should be indexed beginning in September 1999, and the first annual reports on individual accounts should be send to insured persons by ZUS in 2000. When it became clear that ZUS was unable to adher to these deadlines, the government proposed an amendment to extend them. Parliament agreed to delay the first indexation to 2002, at which time all past indexations will also be carried out. The first annual statements must be issued by August 2002 and include data on the account status for the period 1999-2000.

3.1.b. The IT system

During 2000 and 2001, ZUS and PROKOM (the software company preparing the system) concentrated their efforts on finalising the major component of the IT programme: the System for Registry of Accounts and Funds (SEKIF). An interim system was designed initially, since it was necessary in the short run to enable individual contributions to be transferred to private pension funds. This interim system allowed for the monthly processing of data, so that contributions could be transferred for those insured persons whose documentation did not contain any errors. However, the interim system was not capable of correcting errors or registering contributions on individual accounts.

At the end of 2000, the mainframe computer supporting the final IT system (including SEKIF) was successfully installed at ZUS. Since August 2001, all current documents send to ZUS have been processed using this system, but the backlog for 1999 and 2000 must still be transferred to SEKIF and examined for errors. Individual notional accounts can thus be created, and ZUS will be able to send remaining arrears to private pension funds.[25]

In 1999, PROKOM prepared a component of the system (known as ARS-2000) that allows for monitoring of contribution payers. Regional branches of ZUS use ARS to register the status of contribution payments and clear up any inconsistencies. The timeliness of contribution payments can also again be monitored.

---

[25] For a description of the process of contribution transfer to private pension funds, see Section 3.3.

3.1.c. The financial status of FUS

During 1999, ZUS experienced serious financial difficulties due to three factors: the collection rate decreased, the accounting principles which govern the timing of contribution payments were altered, and the introduction of the cap on insurable earnings (250 percent of the average wage) had a larger impact than estimated. Together these three factors created a large gap between projected and actual revenues totalling 5.5 billion PLN (ca. USD 1.6 bn).

The drop in the collection rate resulted from ZUS being unable to compare information from monthly declarations with actual payments. As incoming reports were supposed to be recorded on the new IT system, ZUS management had decided to stop running the old record-keeping system for employers, but the new system was not yet ready for registering contribution payments. Thus, ZUS could not verify whether payments were being made on time. As employers realised this to be the case, contribution collection dropped off significantly.[26] This was the direct opposite of the result assumed in the state budget, i.e. that due to the pension reform and implementation of the new system, the collection rate would increase.

The change in accounting principles resulted in a shift of contribution payments for those employers who pay salaries at the beginning of the month following the one in which the work was done (they paid only 11 contributions in 1999, as illustrated in Chart 11). Because of this, contribution revenues in 1999 fell short of expectations by PLN 1.2 billion.

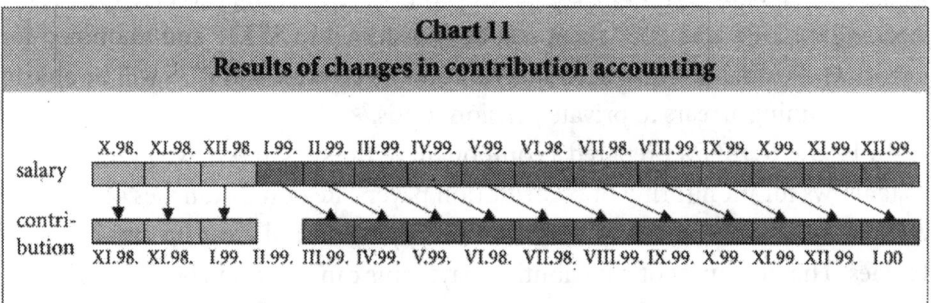

Chart 11
Results of changes in contribution accounting

salary: X.98. XI.98. XII.98. I.99. II.99. III.99. IV.99. V.99. VI.98. VII.98. VIII.99. IX.99. X.99. XI.99. XII.99.

contri-bution: XI.98. XI.98. I.99. II.99. III.99. IV.99. V.99. VI.98. VII.98. VIII.99. IX.99. X.99. XI.99. XII.99. I.00

---

[26] In order to obtain a bank loan, a company needs to receive confirmation from ZUS that it pays all contributions regularly. Prior to 1999, this was easy to obtain from ZUS. In 1999, ZUS required companies to present copies of all monthly declarations and payment transfers to confirm the payments, so this was an indication to employers that ZUS could no longer keep track of payments.

Due to lower contribution revenues, ZUS was forced to take out commercial loans, as well as a loan from the state budget, in order to meet its current liabilities. As of the end of 1999, the total debt of FUS amounted to PLN 6.38 billion or 7.4 percent of FUS expenditures. This consisted of a PLN four billion loan from the state budget and PLN 2.38 billion in commercial loans. In 2000, FUS borrowed an additional PLN two billion from the state budget.

During 2000 and 2001, ZUS was able to consolidate collection and enforcement mechanisms. The ARS-2000 system came into use in January 2000, and local ZUS offices now send requests for payments to employers and self-employed persons who do not pay on time. The requests include information on possible measures to be taken against them if they fail to pay. If contributions with interest are still not paid, local offices initiate this enforcement procedure. ZUS offices also perform on-site inspections of employers' premises, around 160 thousand inspections being performed in 2000, and almost 180 thousand during January-September 2001. As a result, significant amounts have been identified as owed to FUS. The unpaid contributions identified by ZUS inspections in 2001 alone amount to almost PLN four billion (ca. USD 1 billion). Sanctions that can be used by ZUS controllers include: informing the prosecutor's office, forcing the company to file for bankruptcy, bringing court actions against the management boards of indebted companies if they fail to send withheld worker contributions to ZUS, entering the employer's property mortgage in the land registry (which prevents its sale), placing a lien on the employer's property, or imposing additional fines. The final three measures are used most frequently.

As a result of these actions, contribution collection rates increased from 95.8 percent of the amount due in 1999 to more than 98 percent in 2000, and similar results are expected for 2001. Due to the high interest rates, the commercial debts were repaid as a first priority during 2000 and 2001, as the financial situation of FUS improved. A state budget subsidy is still required, however, not only to cover the financial shortfall created by the diversion of contribution revenues to the prefunded tier, but also to cover the gap between revenues from contributions and expenditures on benefits that would exist even without this loss of income.

3.1.d. Strategic planning

Changes in ZUS organisation and management had to be made in response to both the social security and health insurance reforms. ZUS recognised the need to develop a strategic plan to guide its actions, to enhance its institutional capacity, and to implement the most pressing business process changes effectively. The preparation of a strategic plan was financed by a PHRD Grant from the World Bank.

During preparatory sessions, management formulated a new vision for ZUS, which is presented in Framework 2.

Framework 2
Vision for ZUS

Vision for ZUS

We are a **client-oriented** institution, focused on delivering an efficient and easily accessible service to our clients in a confidential and friendly environment.

As a **public trust,** we serve Polish society within the capacity established by law, creating a feeling of stability and security for the insured.

We are to **improve public understanding of the social security system**, highlighting the role of ZUS in this system. We explain the means and financial sources of the social security programmes.

We operate efficiently, **effectively utilising public funds** in accordance with clear and constant organisational procedures. We should like to become a **benchmark** for other public institutions in Poland.

We are **based on stability and tradition,** but we foresee and will address future challenges using **advanced technology and management techniques.**

We are a **desired employer,** able to engage and retain employees with the best qualifications, to compensate them in relation to their performance, and to make them proud of belonging to ZUS.

We are **free of political influence. Professionalism and independence** are our major values in implementing national social security policies.

Our **unified and unique appearance** is recognised by our customers as a sign of top quality.

Source: ZUS strategic plan

In order to fulfil this vision, ZUS management formulated the following five strategic objectives:

1) To increase efficiency in performing the tasks required by law.
2) To focus on customer satisfaction.
3) To align ZUS organisation with the new tasks.

4) To increase internal efficiency.
5) To improve human resources management.

However, problems with the ZUS accounting and IT systems impeded the development of reliable and realistic measures for the realisation of these strategic objectives. In addition, as already noted, the pension reform required ZUS to undertake many new tasks for which there is no historical precedent and thus no baseline data against which to measure performance.

Taking into consideration these problems and weaknesses, ZUS Management decided to use quality and process-oriented measures to monitor and guide implementation of the Strategic Plan. These measures focus predominantly on:
  – clearly defined spheres of work and areas of responsibility,
  – meeting specified deadlines, and
  – completeness and quality of reports, presentations, etc.

Based on the five strategic objectives, around 60 specific tasks have been defined and a list of actions required to complete each task has been prepared by task teams. Team leaders reported directly to the strategic plan co-ordinator, located organisationally in the Presidents' office. Most elements of the Strategic Plan were implemented in 2000 and 2001, thus facilitating the process of reform.

ZUS activities in the Strategic Plan were focused on priority tasks which aimed at improving the quality of information transfer between employers and ZUS:
  – identification and reduction of errors in the documents. ZUS provided employers with a new version of the PLATNIK programme (software designed to prepare ZUS documents) with improved verification procedures;
  – analysis of errors in documents and preparation of information for employers regarding proper preparation;
  – production of a TV programme on co-operation with ZUS (broadcast on national TV in the first quarter of 2001);
  – co-operation with banks in order to improve the quality of information provided with bank transfers;
  – development of a regional IT system network and provision of access for regional branches to the central database, so that errors in the electronic files of employers can be corrected; and
  – initiating ARS-2000 usage for collection and enforcement procedures, which has improved collections (as described in Section 3.1.c.).

3.2. Transition to the mixed system

While all persons born after 1949 are affected by the pension reform, the only ones with a choice about the nature of their involvement were born between 1949-1968. They could choose whether to participate in the reformed pay-as-you-go tier alone, or in both the pay-as-you-go and the prefunded tiers. This was not a choice between the old and new systems but between the new public NDC system and the mixed system. The deadline for the choice was the end of 1999, after which the decision was final, that is, it was neither possible to join the mixed system later nor to switch back to the public system.

All those who were obliged to participate in both tiers of the pension scheme (i.e. those aged 21-30) as well as those who wished to exercise their option to do so (i.e. those aged 30-50) were required to choose a private pension fund before September 1999. After this date, the contributions made on their behalf were automatically split between the two tiers. For those who had not decided by December, a pension fund was chosen on their behalf, this group being distributed among the funds on the market. The year 1999 was therefore crucial with regard to decisions made by insured persons, as well as for the shape of the pension fund market.

3.2.a. Members of the prefunded tier

Insured persons could enrol in private pension funds beginning in March 1999, but the first payment transferred to a private pension fund was for April 1999, so all information regarding pension fund participation goes back to April. Initially it was expected that most people would join pension funds at the beginning of the open season, then activities would slow down for the holiday period and pick up again in September. These expectations were not fulfilled, however, as the increase in pension fund participation was practically linear throughout 1999, with around one million people per month joining the prefunded tier (see: Chart 12).

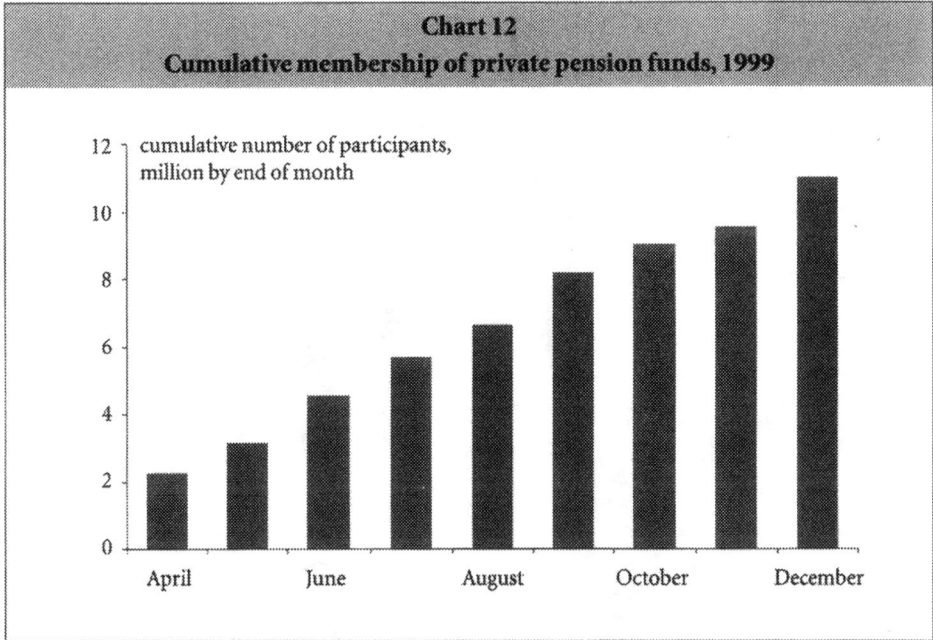

Chart 12
Cumulative membership of private pension funds, 1999

cumulative number of participants,
million by end of month

April   June   August   October   December

Source: ZUS

By the end of 1999, there was a total of 9.7 million registered members of private pension funds. Beginning in 2000, only those persons who enter the labour force for the first time can join private pension funds (although those born in the years 1949-1968 can still join if they were unemployed in 1999), so in 2000 the number of new members was a mere 0.7 million, bringing the total to 10.4 million. There were only around 50 thousand new members in the first quarter of 2001.

The age and sex distribution of pension fund members as of 31 March 2001 is presented in Chart 13. As can be seen, the largest age groups include those who were required to join the prefunded tier (aged 21–30), and as the age of participants increases, membership decreases. In terms of gender distribution, men represent 53.5 percent of all pension fund members, which is hardly surprising, as men participate to a greater extent in the labour market and consequently make up more than half of those insured.

155

Chart 13
Age and sex distribution of open pension fund membership, March 2001

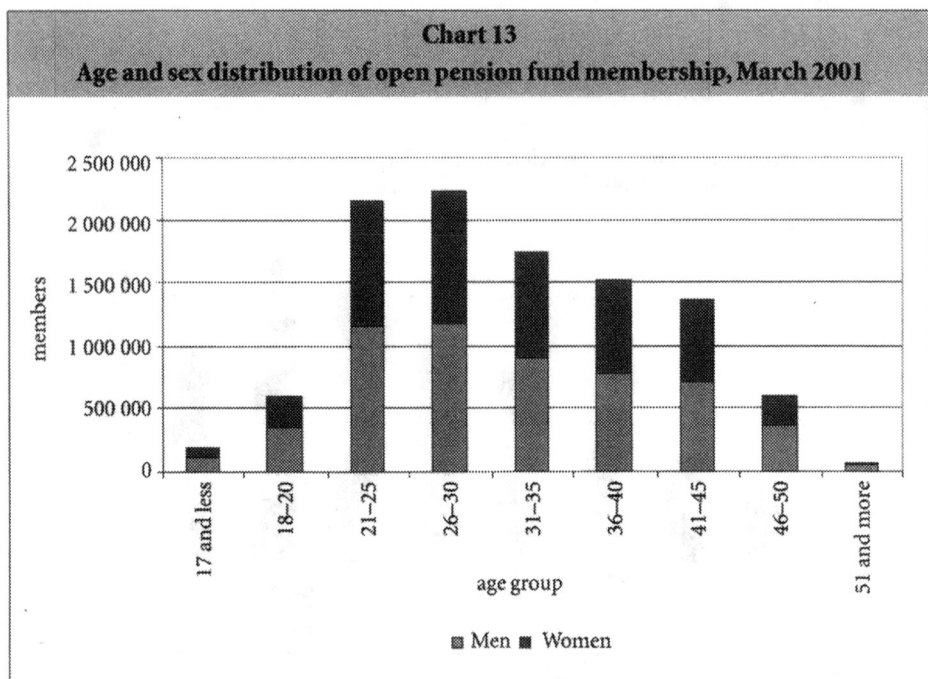

The age distribution of private pension fund membership for the 'choice' groups is presented in Chart 14. According to estimates (the ZUS database on insured persons had not been completed when this study was undertaken), more than 60 percent of the 'choice' groups decided to split their contribution between the two mandatory tiers. Chart 14 shows that age was a key factor in whether a person joined a private pension fund or not. Most 30 year-olds are OFE members, whereas only a few 50 year-olds have joined. Interesting gender differences can be observed, as there is a higher rate of participation in the prefunded tier among younger women than younger men, but for older groups the situation is reversed with women choosing less frequently to join private pension funds. This may be due to the fact that more women intend to exercise the option for early retirement, which is available to all insured persons until the end of 2006.

Chart 14

Participation of 1949–68 groups in private pension funds

membership of private pension
scheme, percent of age group

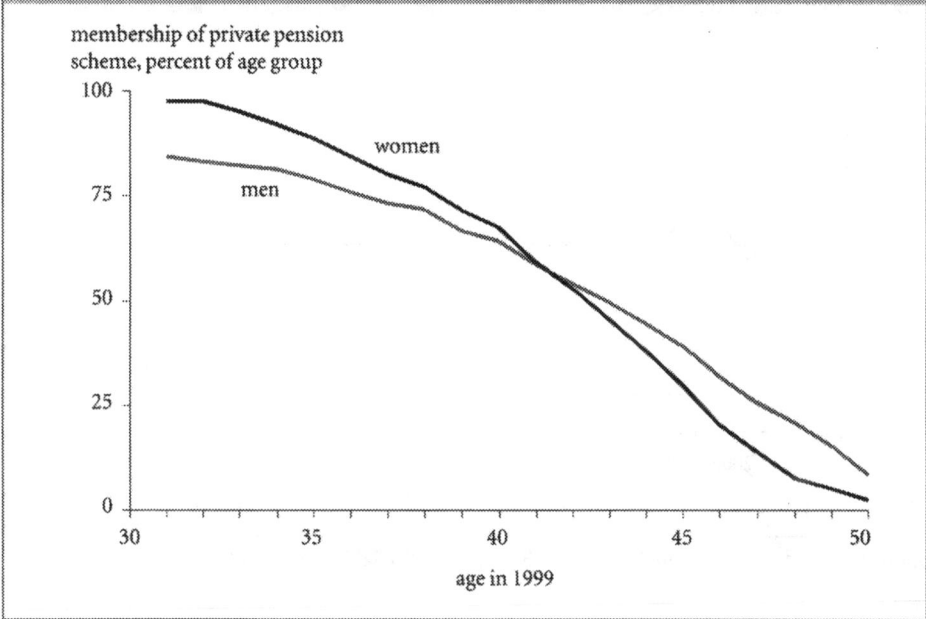

Note: based on January 2000 data

Source: The Gdansk Institute for Market Economics

In 2000, approximately 60 percent of insured people participated in the prefunded tier, but this proportion will increase in subsequent years, reaching 100 percent by 2036 (see: Chart 15).

Chart 15
Pension fund members as percentage of insured people

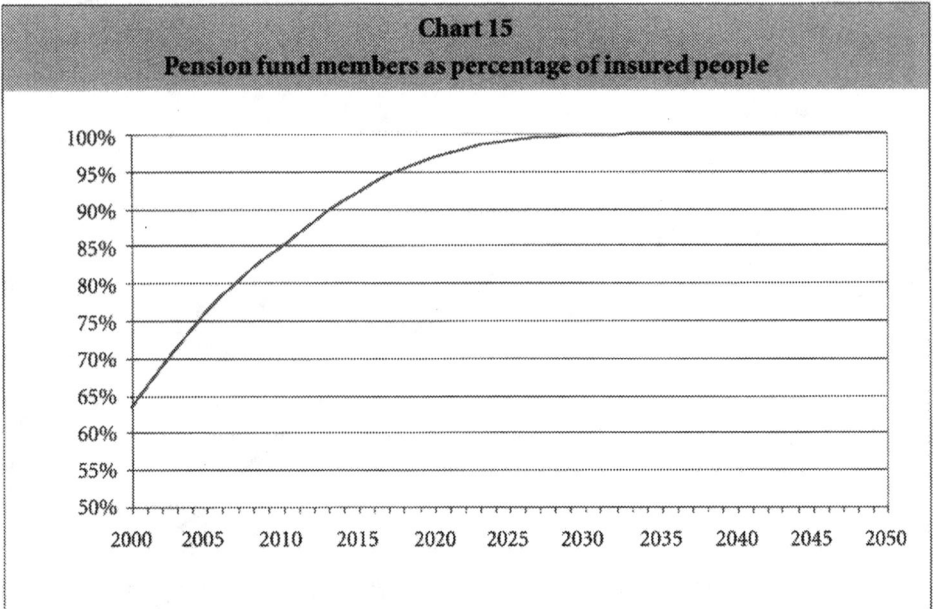

Source: The Gdansk Institute for Market Economics, Social Budget Model

The transition period may also be viewed from the perspective of contribution payments. Division of the aggregate contribution for old-age pensions will change with the progress of the transition. In 2000, the estimated effective contribution rate for the first tier was 14.96 percent and 4.56 percent for the prefunded tier (compared with 12.22 and 7.3 percent, respectively, if all insured persons were members of private pension funds). This is due to the fact that only 60 percent of insured persons have their contributions transferred, the rest remaining in the public tier. With time, these percentages will diverge until the contribution rates of 12.22 and 7.3 percent are attained. The evolution of rates until 2050 is presented in Chart 16. As can be seen, the contribution transfer will increase from year to year until it reaches a steady-state in the mid 40s.

Chart 16
Effective contribution for public old age system, 2000–2050

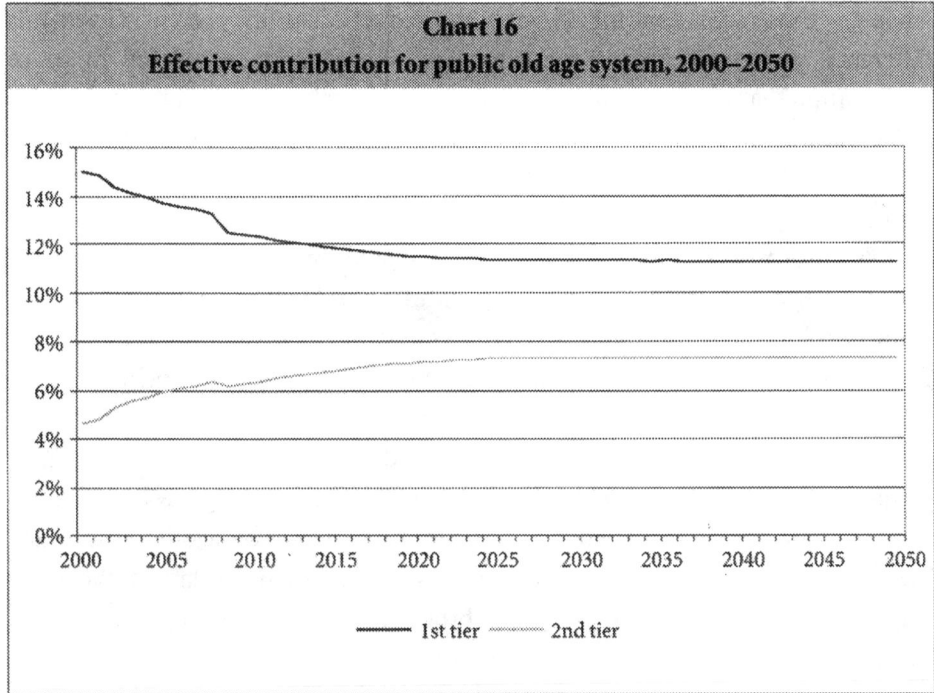

Source: The Gdansk Institute for Market Economics, Social Budget Model

3.2.b. Motivation

Participation in the second tier turned out to be significantly higher than initially predicted by the government: around 60 percent of all insured persons, compared with the original government prediction of 50 percent. It is therefore interesting to examine what motivated insured people to join private pension funds. This section analyses the choices people made and the information available to them before they came to a decision.

Implementation of the pension reform was accompanied by a government public information campaign with four main objectives: first, to inform the public about the most important elements of the new pension system, and second, to make the 'choice' groups more cautious about their decision. While there were no explicit economic disincentives in the public tier for older choice groups to join the mixed system, the fee structure of private pension funds is more disadvantageous for persons saving for shorter periods. According to the author's calculations, the rate of return for those who save for 20 years will be reduced by about 1.2 percent, while for those who save for 40 years the reduction is 0.9 percent. Given this difference, the main aim of the campaign was to provide the full range of information that would enable people to make informed choices. A third objective was to support a new image of ZUS and create a positive public attitude toward the reform. Finally, the campaign sought to eliminate fears over losing some pension rights by people not affected by the reform (those above age 50).

The information campaign was co-ordinated by the Plenipotentiary for Pension Reform, with the development stages being financed by USAID and the campaign itself, from the state budget. The cost of the latter amounted to USD five million. Initially, advertisements were broadcast on TV and printed in the press, and in later stages, the media campaign was extended to radio (the Plenipotentiary decided that money allocated to, but not used for, the ZUS campaign could finance radio advertisements). The campaign was organised around a call-centre where people could obtain answers to basic questions on the pension reform, as well as order brochures that briefly explained the most important changes to come. Sixteen brochures were prepared, focusing on various elements of the new pension system and targeted at various age groups, in order to explain the role of the old and new institutions in the pension system. Simulations of future pension benefits for several age and gender profiles were sent together with the brochures, so that each insured person could obtain the most relevant information. In both the brochures and the simulation summaries, it was stated that at least 10 to 15 years of participation in the prefunded tier was required in order to receive a pension higher than the one from the first tier alone (although the precise time depends on the performance of both financial and labour markets).

Advertising campaigns were also carried out by private pension funds, most of these being built on the theme of prosperity after retirement. All forms of media were used by the funds in their advertising campaigns. Wilczynska (2000) has calculated that total pension fund expenditures on media advertising (excluding the costs of campaign development) amounted to USD 100 million, which is 20 times the amount spent by the government. The most important influence on people's choices was not advertising campaigns, however, but the activities of sales agents. Chłoń (2000) uses regression analysis to show that the size of the agent network was the only significant factor determining the success of various private pension funds in recruiting members. Regressions on a fund's capital sum and total media spending are only significant as they are closely related to the number of agents employed. Once this variable is included, capital and media spending become insignificant.

In 1999, more than 400 thousand pension fund agents were registered at UNFE (compared with a total population of 38 million), so there were almost 40 registered agents per 1000 pension fund members, compared with around five in the Latin American countries which introduced similar reforms (for details, see Chłoń (2000)). Typically, PTEs paid an agent a fee of approximately USD 25 for each individual contract signed. Payments to agents were still made even if ZUS did not confirm that the person in question was insured (due to its uncompleted IT system). This lack of verification procedure enabled some agents to engage in fraud, such as falsifying signatures or signing up people who were not insured. While the exact magnitude of such practices is difficult to estimate, as of mid 2001 approximately a quarter of all pension fund members were 'dead accounts'. It seems likely that a significant portion of those accounts belong to persons who are either not insured or do not exist.

In order to assess people's decisions, CBOS undertook a survey at the beginning of 2000 at the request of the Plenipotentiary for Pension Reform. This survey investigated the reasons for the choices made, and the most important findings are presented in Chart 17. The most frequent reasons given for the choices made concerned the desire for higher or more secure pensions, both in the case of joining the mixed system and of remaining in the public tier alone.

Those who decided to join private pension funds also did so because they had been persuaded by someone (an agent, family member, or friend) or by an advertising campaign. Significantly, almost one fifth of people stated that they decided to join the prefunded tier due to the troubles with ZUS. Other reasons given by those who remained in the public tier in spite of having a choice reflected their intention to draw an early retirement pension or their lack of trust in private institutions. Some people also decided not to join pension funds because it was too expensive.

Chart 17

Reasons given by insured persons for differing pension choices

a. People who decided to split their pension contribution

Reason	percentage
Higher pension	49
More secure pension	48
Born after 1968	35
Inheritance	32
Persuaded by agent	20
ZUS troubles	17
Persuaded by family/friends	12
Persuaded by fund ads	8

b. People who decided to remain in the public scheme alone

Reason	percentage
Higher pension	42
Born after 1948	17
Want early retirement	13
Lack of trust in funds	9
Funds' fees too high	5

percentage of respondents

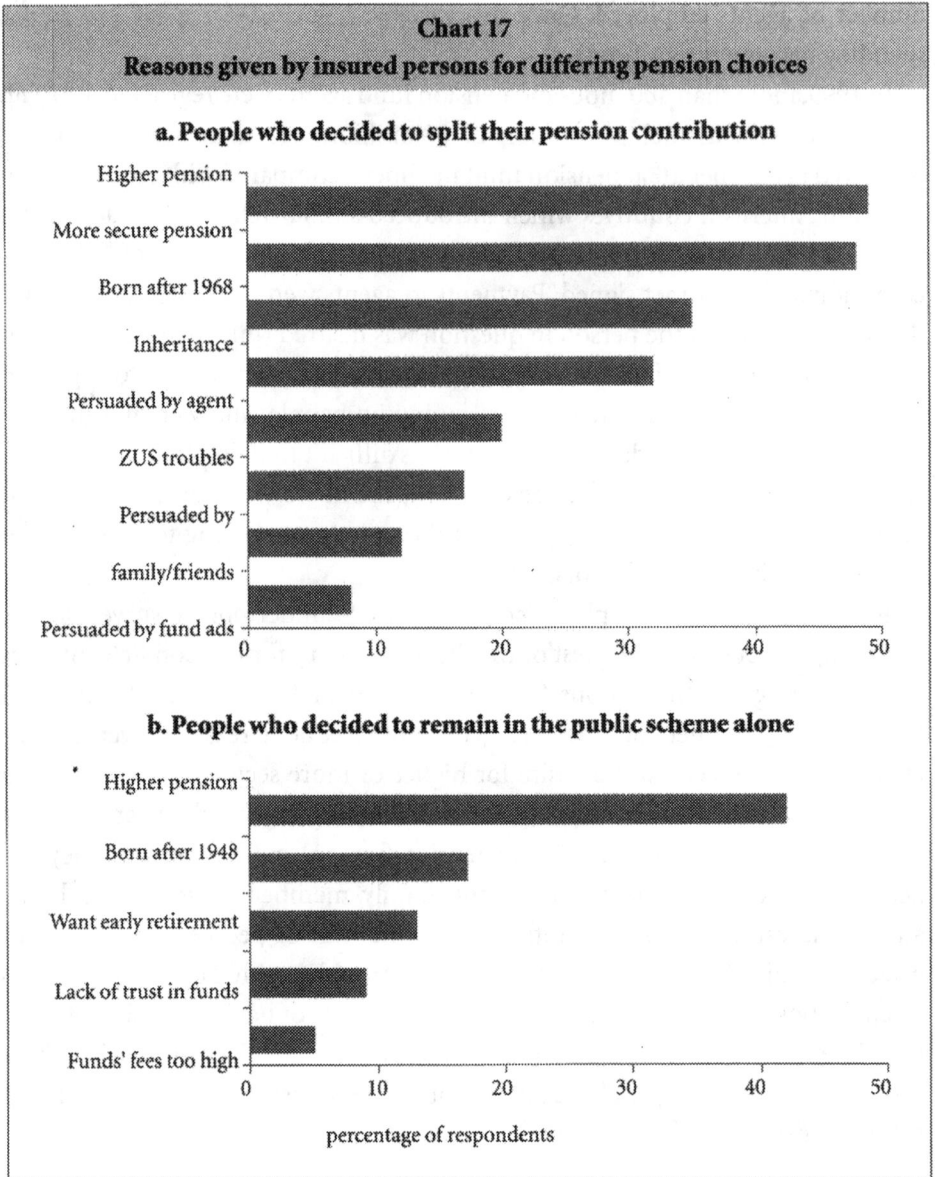

Note: Numbers do not total 100 percent, as people could chose up to three answers.

Source: CBOS, March 2000

3.3. Impact of the private scheme on the public tier

3.3.a. General observations

Creation of a multi-tier scheme can have a financial impact on a pre-existing pay-as-you-go system, since revenues are needed to build up to the prefunded tier while benefit obligations continue to be met under the public system. Depending on the exact choices made by a country, the administration of the scheme can also be affected. As far as financing is concerned, the Polish Government decided that the mandatory prefunded tier would be fully financed from existing compulsory contributions, privatisation revenues, and state budget subsidies. There will be no increase in contribution rates, which are already high by international standards. As a result of this constraint, the revenues of the public tier are reduced by the amount transferred to the private tier. The size of the transitional deficit resulting from these transfers will be assessed in the next sub-section.

In terms of administration, ZUS encountered many difficulties in the correct assignment of contributions to insured persons as described in Section 3.1. In order to transfer a portion of an insured person's contribution to a private pension fund, ZUS must first identify a payment as being from a particular employer and then assign it to the insured persons on that employer's payroll. However, these procedures cannot be followed if private pension fund members are not identified in the ZUS central registry of the insured. Moreover, when private pension fund members are identified, reports from employers (or banks) may contain errors. Both situations prevent the successful transfer of contributions.

In May 1999, when the first transfers should have been made, only about five percent of the amounts due could be successfully transferred, chiefly because of errors in the documentation provided by employers, banks, and pension funds. In the following months, ZUS took action to improve the efficiency of transfers, as described in Section 3.1. The transfer rate to private funds has since improved, and ZUS estimates that some 70 to 80 percent of contributions are now being transferred.

To view the problem in another way, contributions are currently being transferred to private pension funds on behalf of approximately six million persons, compared to 10.4 million registered members of pension funds and an estimated eight million members who are insured.[27] Contributions for the

---

[27] As mentioned above, there may be cases where pension fund members are not insured due to the over-selling by private pension sales agents.

remaining members have not been transferred, due mainly to the difficulties described above.

ZUS originally planned that all arrears to pension funds, estimated at more than PLN 3 billion, would be paid during 2001 after the IT system was complete and the database cleared of most of the errors. Further delays in the IT implementation process, however, have resulted in a further postponement of this deadline.

Table 11
Old-age contributions transferred to open pension funds (in PLN M)

In PLN m.	Planned	Realised	Arrears
1999	3 268.5	2 262.7	1 005.9
2000 total	11 073.0	7 591.0	2 783.5
From 2000	10 067.2	7 283.7	2 783.5
From 1999	1 005.9	307.3	698.6
2001 total (plan)	14 372.0	6 088.3 (until end of August)	
From 2001	10 890.0		
From 2000	2 783.5		
From 1999	698.6		

Source: ZUS

This situation indicates the depth of institutional changes needed at ZUS in order to operate the multi-tier pension system.

3.3.b. Old-age pensions vs. disability and survivor pensions

Savings in the new private pension funds are used only for old age pensions. Disability and survivor benefits are still financed purely on a pay-as-you-go basis from the public pension scheme. Two major issues arise from this situation: firstly, the application of pension savings in the case of disablement or premature death of a worker and, secondly, the need to harmonise benefit levels between the two tiers.

The question of how to deal with the private pension savings of those who become disabled was not specifically addressed in the pension legislation.

According to the general provisions of the reform law, they will receive a disability pension until they reach retirement age. If they work in spite of their disability, they will pay social security contributions and their private pension fund accounts will grow. If they do not work, no new contributions will be paid, but their existing savings will still be invested and earn returns.

According to a rule which existed prior to the reform and was not altered by it, when a disabled person reaches retirement age, he or she can choose to receive whichever benefit is higher, old-age or disability pension. Due to pension reform and the resulting changes in the reduction of pension replacement rates, the disability pension will be higher in most cases. As a result, the incentive to apply for a disability pension in the new system will be higher than in the old one.

Furthermore, a question arises as to whether the choice to continue a disability pension at retirement age involves a comparison of it with the old-age pensions from both mandatory tiers or just the public one. The 1998 law on pensions financed from the Social Insurance Fund only mentions the public tier, while the 1997 law on organisation and functioning of pension funds states that other regulations will specify the rules for withdrawal when a person becomes eligible for a disability pension. Under current legal status, disability pensioners do not have the option to withdraw prefunded tier savings. Possible solutions are deducting an amount equal to the prefunded pension from the disability pension, or alternatively, transferring the individual's prefunded tier savings to the disability insurance fund of the public system for the purpose of financing the benefits paid.

A similar dilemma exists in the case of survivors' pensions. In the public scheme, survivors are entitled to a benefit ranging from 80 to 90 percent of the amount which the deceased person would have received (a disability pension in most cases, or an old-age pension if the deceased person were entitled). At the same time, second tier pension savings are split, half being transferred to the spouse's private pension account and the other half paid in cash to specified beneficiaries. As with disability pensions, the prefunded tier is treated separately, so widows or widowers who draw a survivor's pension do not have an access to prefunded tier savings.

This situation means that survivors will receive different benefit levels depending on whether they apply for benefits before or after the retirement age of the insured person. If they apply afterward, the survivor's pension is calculated on the basis of the public old-age pension to which the insured person would have been entitled, which as a result of the old age pension reform is significantly lower than his or her disability pension. It has not yet been decided what type of private pension the survivor will receive, a single or joint annuity. According to the draft annuity legislation, such a person will receive a joint annuity (mandatory for all couples). As a result, his or her private pension should be similar to a benefit that a single person would receive.

In summary, the old-age pension reform has created inequalities in the treatment of old-age, disability, and survivors' pensioners. Some of these issues can be addressed by the draft annuities law, while others can be addressed only through closer coordination of old age, disability, and survivors benefits. If the law on annuities does not address the situation, private pension fund members will not be able to draw prefunded benefits.

3.3.c. The pension system in the future – financial projections

Long-term projections on the financial solvency of the social security system are presented in this section. The main goal is to indicate the size of transition deficit which results from moving to a multi-tier system, and the resources for financing for this deficit. Projections are made using the Social Budget Model.[28]

At the outset, an important difference between the impact of the reform on revenues and expenditures should be noted. The former is felt almost immediately after introduction of the second-tier prefunded scheme. The most important issue facing the pension system at this time is how to finance the transition deficit. According to the reform concept which was approved by government, these transition costs should be financed initially from privatisation revenues and state budget subsidies. As simulations in this section show, most of the costs in the longer term will be offset by a reduction of expenditures in the public system as a result of the reform.

For the benefit side of scheme financing, the transition starts later, since all pensions will be based on the old system formula until 2009. After this date, new system pensions will begin to be granted. The transition in the pensioners' portfolio is going to take decades.

The impact of the reform on the public, pay-as-you-go scheme is largely due to the changes which were introduced in eligibility criteria and the pension formula.

---

[28] See also: Section 1.3

First, the retirement age is increased, and this should reduce the number of pensioners compared with the non-reform scenario. Second, the replacement rate provided by pensions calculated under the new formula will be lower than that under the old pension system. Together, these changes will cause a significant reduction in old-age pension expenditures. At the same time, the revenues of the system are reduced due to the transfer of contributions to the prefunded tier.

According to our projections using baseline assumptions, public tier expenditures on old-age pensions will drop dramatically: from their current level of around six percent of the GDP to around two percent in 2050 (see Appendix B). The reduction of expenditures which began in 1995 should continue until 2040 and then stabilise. According to this simulation, the deficit in the old-age part of the system should persist until 2025, but then a surplus should appear which will reach 1.4 percent of the GDP in 2050. Within the projection period, the number of old-age pensioners increases until it exceeds four million in 2020, and then it declines to the level of 3.4 million in 2035. As a result of the retirement of the baby-boomers born in the 1980s, the number of old-age pensioners will then start to increase again and reach four million in 2050. The number of old-age pensioners in 2050 is projected to be lower by six million persons than under the no-reform scenario, but the reduction in old-age pensioners is partially offset by a rise in the projected number of disability and survivor pensioners. In the model it is assumed that the influx of disability pensioners will be higher due to the increase of minimum retirement age. The additional effect of higher incentives to apply for a disability pension due to the larger pension size is not taken into account. As the results of the simulation show, the number of disability pensioners will increase to 4.3 million (compared to 2.3 million under the no-reform scenario) and the number of survivor pensioners will exceed two million (which is slightly higher than in the no-reform scenario). The ratio of old-age pensions to wages is also projected to undergo a large decline. In the simulation, the average old-age pension from the new system will be less than one quarter of the average wage, compared to 35.7 percent for old-age pensions from the old system. Such a major reduction of replacement rates substantially reduces aggregate pension expenditures. As a result of the reform, expenditures on old-age pensions are projected to fall to one sixth of what they would be under the no-reform scenario. However, if all pension costs are taken into account (including disability and survivor pensions), pension expenditures are estimated to reach 9.65 percent of the GDP by 2050, or just less than half of what they would be with no reform. (Throughout most of the projection period, total pension expenditures from the Social Insurance Fund fluctuate between nine percent and ten percent of the GDP, compared with pension expenditures of 17.3 percent of the GDP in 2050 under the no-reform scenario). For the entire projection period, total pension expenditures (old-age, disability and survivors) will be higher than contribution revenues, resulting in an annual deficit of around two percent of the GDP. It is important to note that the partial privatisation of the pension scheme in Poland requires greater cuts in public pension benefits than would be needed to restore the financial solvency of the public pension system without privatisation. This can be observed in Chart 18. In fact, by 2005 the total deficit in the public old-age pension scheme will already be lower than the sum of contributions transferred to pension funds. This is because reforms introduced in the public system (mostly reductions in the indexation of benefits, initially) will create a 'surplus' which will be used to finance the transition to the prefunded scheme.

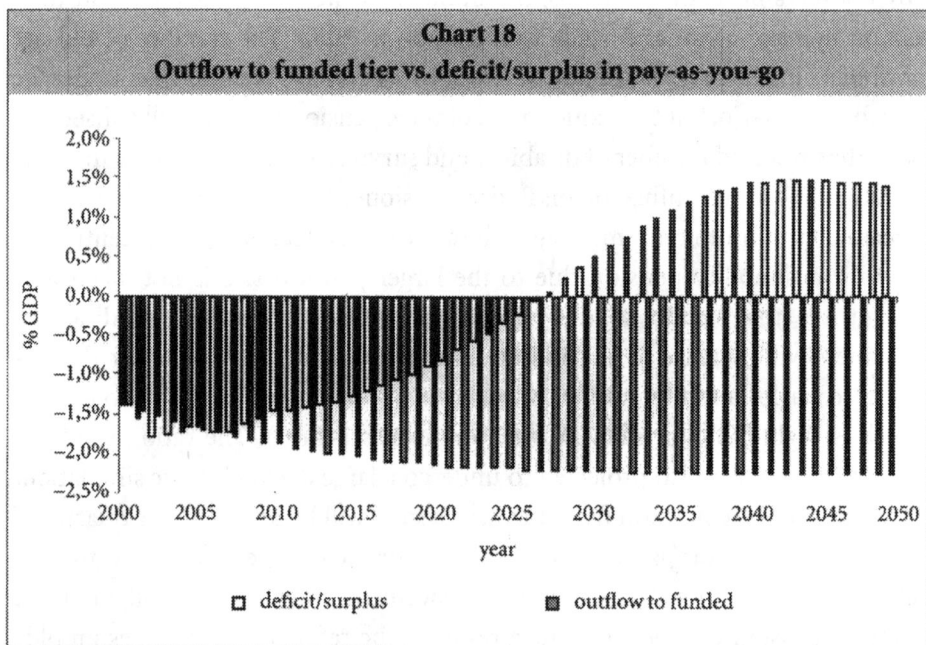

Chart 18
Outflow to funded tier vs. deficit/surplus in pay-as-you-go

Source: The Gdansk Institute for Market Economics, Social Budget Model

In the projection period, the most important factor influencing expenditures is the size of the average pension. For pensions granted under the old system (for persons born after 1948), the ratio should decrease from the current level of over 60 percent of average wages to around 35 percent by 2050. Such erosion is related mainly to the indexation of pensions. The reduction will be smaller during the early years of the projection, as newly granted pensions will be calculated according to the old rules and this will influence the average level. The drop will accelerate after 2009, when pensions are calculated according to the new rules.

Under the new system, the projected value of pensions is much lower than in the old system.[29] Reducing benefits so that people receive what they 'pay for' from an actuarial point of view was one of the goals of the reform plan. Such a policy, however, may lead to increased poverty among pensioners, and as a result, savings made in the pension system may have to be accompanied by increased expenditures on social assistance for pensioners. Moreover, transferring very large numbers of elderly to social assistance would be a controversial policy. In the future, therefore, policy makers will have to strike a difficult balance between the macroeconomic stabilisation of the pension system, broadly defined, and providing pensioners with a decent income.

A projection of the transition from the old to the new pension system is shown in Chart 19. Pensioners receiving their benefits based on the old system rules will be in the majority until the mid 2020s. After this, the ratio of 'new' old-age pensioners will become greater until by the end of the projection period, practically all old-age pensioners will be receiving new NDC benefits.

---

[29] See projections of replacement rates in Chart 8 (Section 2.1).

Chart 19

Projected number of old-age pensioners receiving benefits from the old and new system under the reform, 2001–2050

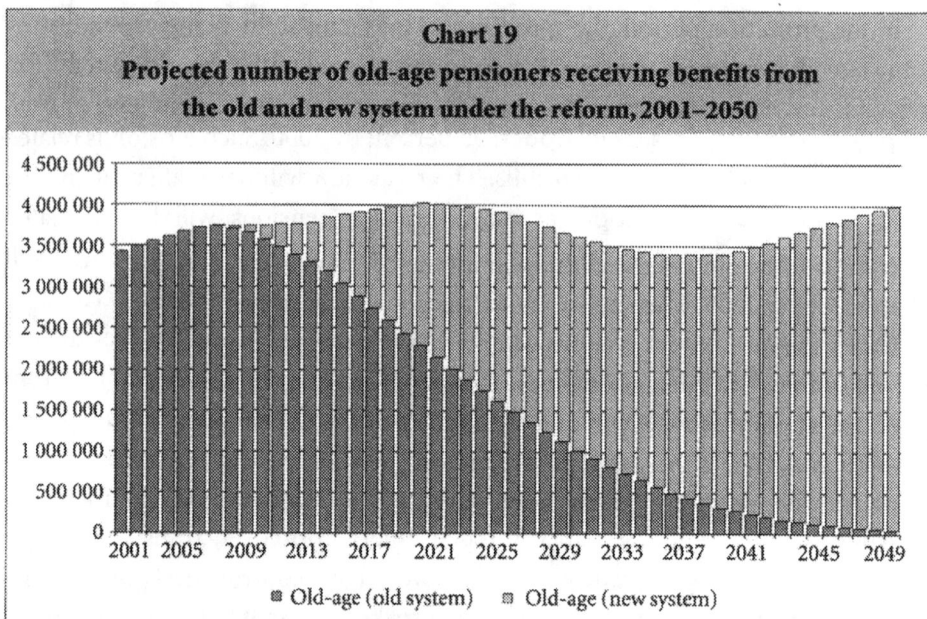

Source: The Gdansk Institute for Market Economics, Social Budget Model

Chart 20 presents a breakdown of old-age pension expenditures by source of financing. As can be seen, public pension benefits will dominate expenditures

Chart 20

Financing of pensions, 2000–2050

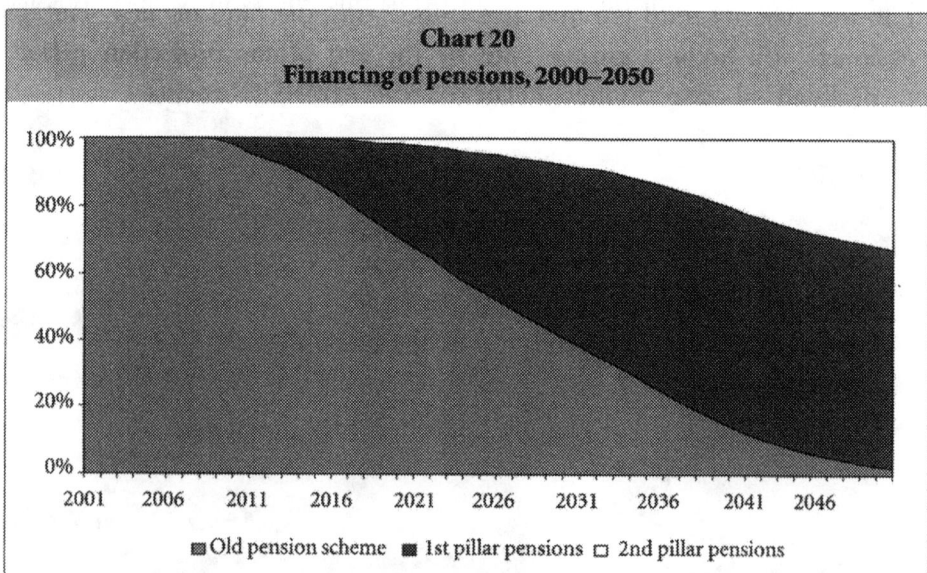

Source: The Gdansk Institute for Market Economics, Social Budget Model

throughout the projection period. By 2050, the prefunded tier will finance around one third of total pension expenditures.

As simulations have shown, changes to the public system result in a significant reduction in expenditures, but the question arises, to what extend do such savings finance creation of the prefunded tier, and to what extend does this have to be financed from increased government borrowing and privatisation revenues? **For the purpose of this analysis, transition costs are defined as the outflow to the prefunded tier, reduced by the savings achieved in the public tier due to the introduction of the prefunded tier.** Using this definition, Chart 21 shows the transition deficit for each year during the projection period. As can be seen, the deficit increases until the 2020s, reflecting the increase in contribution outflow from the first tier to the second tier. After this date, the annual deficit starts to decrease as private benefits grow and the prefunded tier assumes a greater role in the provision of old-age pensions. As noted, the sources of financing for the reform are three-fold: privatisation revenues, increased government debt, and benefit reductions in the public system. During the first years of reform implementation, the full transition costs were financed from privatisation. In 1998 the government earmarked around PLN 53 billion (approx. seven percent of the GDP) for this purpose. According to earlier estimates, this amount should have been sufficient to finance the deficit in the public tier until the pension scheme began to produce a surplus, but based on current calculations, debt financing will be required until 2025.[30] Starting in 2005, accumulation of annual surpluses in the public system is assumed, resulting from the fact that some people do not take early retirement pensions, and the transitional financing is increasingly covered by these savings. In the period 2000–2050, two thirds of the transition deficit is financed by savings in the public system, about one quarter from credit, and around ten percent from privatisation revenues.

---

[30] It must be taken into account, however, that this amount could have been used to finance other state budget expenditures if the reform had not been introduced.

Chart 21

Transition costs and sources of financing

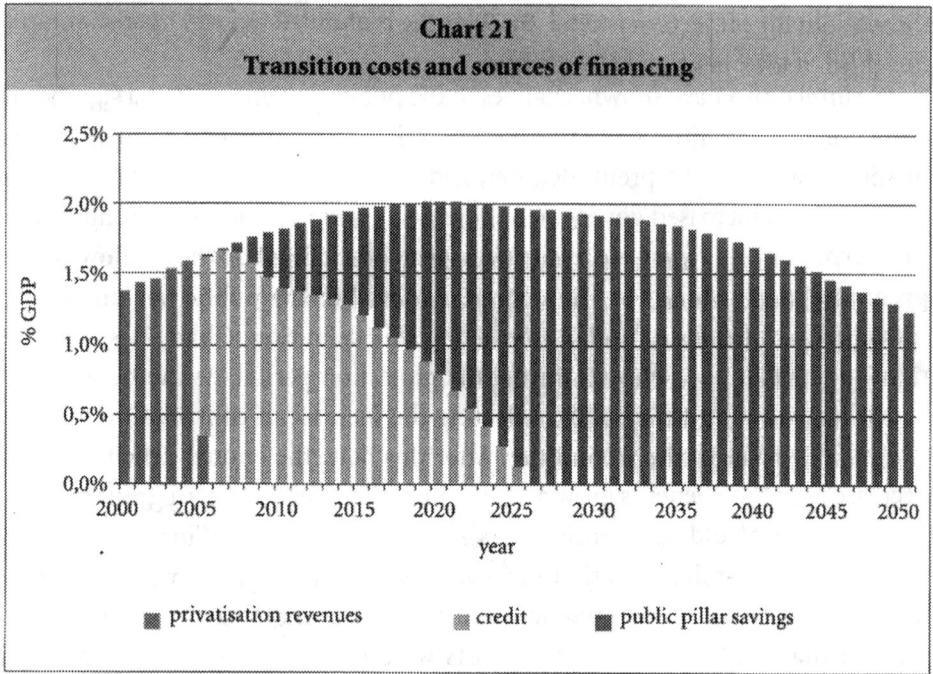

Source: The Gdansk Institute for Market Economics, Social Budget Model

According to the simulation, the cumulative transition costs reach almost 100 percent of the GDP by 2050 (see Chart 22). This simulation assumes that interest costs increase the cumulative size of the deficit and that the sole source of financing these costs is the surplus in the public system. If in the future, the transition deficit is partially financed from general budget revenues, the total size of the transition costs (including debt servicing) should be smaller.

Chart 22
Cumulative transition costs, 2000–2050

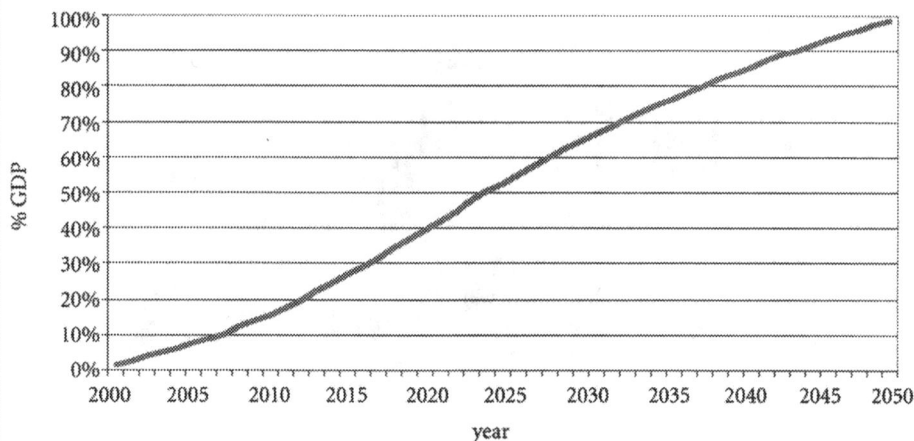

Source: The Gdansk Institute for Market Economics, Social Budget Model

Another way of looking at the costs of transition from pay-as-you-go financing to a mixed system with a mandatory pre-funded tier is to compare the size of transition costs with the projected assets accumulated by the private pension funds. In the projection period, annual revenues in this sector will range from 1.5 percent to almost two percent of GDP, but annual expenditures will be much smaller, especially in the first half of the projection period, when they should not exceed 0.5 percent of GDP. A significant increase in expenditure is projected after 2025, however, when most pensioners start to receive pensions from the prefunded private schemes.

By 2050, total assets accumulated in the prefunded tier should reach 180 percent of GDP, which is almost double the size of the cumulative transition costs at that time.

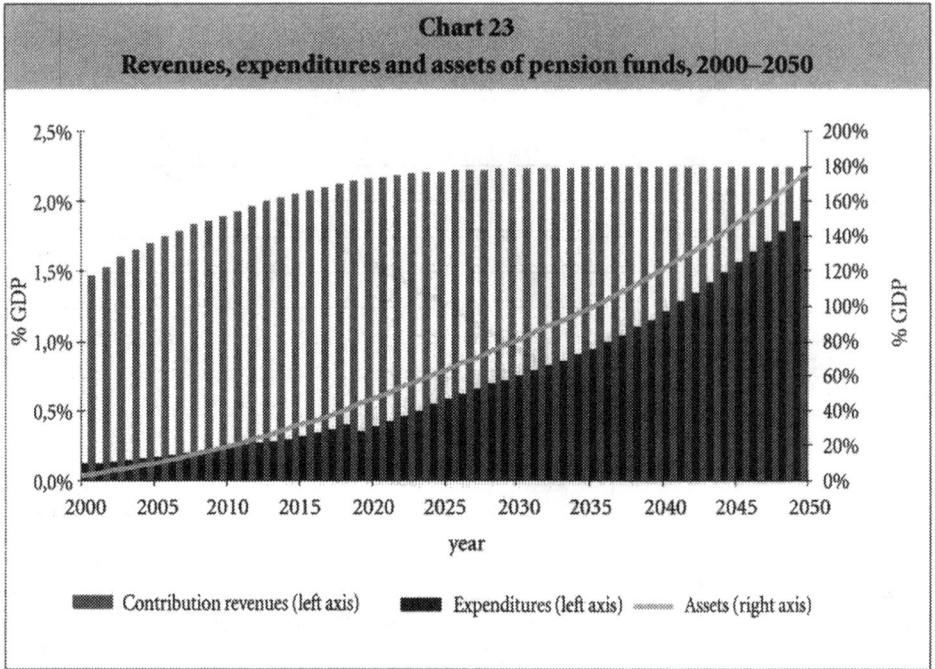

Chart 23
Revenues, expenditures and assets of pension funds, 2000–2050

Legend: Contribution revenues (left axis)   Expenditures (left axis)   Assets (right axis)

Source: The Gdansk Institute for Market Economics, Social Budget Model

Yet a third measure of the costs of pension privatisation involves comparing the financial status of the reformed system, including the transition deficit, with a hypothetical scenario in which the NDC system is introduced in the public tier but there is no prefunded tier. In this case, expenditures on pensions from the public tier would have been considerably higher. By 2050, public expenditures on pensions would be 50 percent higher than under the reform, due to the additional revenue remaining in the public system. There would also be a surplus in the old-age pension system for practically the entire projection period, as there would be no reduction in contribution revenues to support the prefunded tier. It is this surplus generated by the reform of the public tier that is used to finance the transition to the prefunded tier. If this surplus had been used instead to improve benefits in the public pension system, wage replacement rates in 2050 would exceed 40 percent, rather than falling to the level of 21.7 percent with the privatisation.

Table 12
Expenditures and deficit/surplus of public pension system
– with and without introduction of funded tier as a % of GDP

	2000	2005	2010	2015	2020	2025	2030	2035	2040	2045	2050
Reform scenario with funded tier											
Old-age pension expenditures	6.01%	5.68%	5.27%	4.93%	4.46%	3.85%	3.11%	2.47%	2.08%	2.00%	2.06%
Old-age system deficit/ surplus	–1.38%	–1.68%	–0.70%	–1.29%	–0.93%	–0.36%	0.36%	1.00%	1.39%	1.47%	1.41%
Hypothetical scenario without funded tier											
Old-age pension expenditures	6.04%	5.74%	5.34%	5.02%	4.62%	4.10%	3.44%	2.90%	2.66%	2.82%	3.11%
Old-age system deficit/ surplus	0.02%	–0.02%	0.38%	0.69%	1.09%	1.61%	2.28%	2.83%	3.07%	2.91%	2.62%

Source: The Gdansk Institute for Market Economics, Social Budget Model

In summary, introduction of the prefunded tier proves to be quite expensive in the long run. Most of the financing of the public system deficit, resulting from the creation of the prefunded tier, is covered by savings generated in the public system itself: by lower indexation of benefits, increases in retirement age, and lower replacement rates in the reformed scheme. This means that the costs of privatisation will be borne by pensioners themselves during the lengthy transition period, when they could otherwise be enjoying better pensions. Financing at the beginning of the period is from privatisation sources, which means that these revenues will not be used to finance other social needs. According to projections, around one quarter of transition costs will be financed from credit, requiring additional expenditures in the form of interest paid. This burden is placed on the shoulders of the current and future generations of workers, who will have to generate income to finance the debt.

In order to investigate the impact of macroeconomic policy and performance on the pension system if these assumptions turn out to be incorrect, projections have been made under several different scenarios.

First of all, the assumptions on labour productivity were modified. The annual growth of productivity is assumed to be lower by 0.5 percent compared with the baseline (i.e. 1.25 percent in the long run as opposed to 1.75 percent), and this leads to a drop in GDP growth. In this case, pension expenditures in relation to the GDP are higher than under baseline conditions, reaching 10.7 percent of GDP by 2050 (one percent higher than the baseline). This change results from higher pensions relative to the average wage. The difference in pension size would reach approximately seven percent by 2050 for pre-reform old-age pensions and survivor pensions, and five percent for disability pensions. For reformed pensions, the difference between the baseline projection and this one is smaller: only around two percent. In addition, the total pension deficit is higher than in the baseline scenario, fluctuating at around three percent of the GDP.

In the following three scenarios, various policies aimed at increasing the value of the old-age pensions from the new system are investigated. The *full NDC indexation* scenario assumes that notional accounts are indexed according to full wage growth, and this results in pensions from the new system being slightly higher. The average new pension under full indexation is projected at 22.4 percent of the average wage in 2050, compared with 21.7 percent under baseline conditions. Higher individual pensions are reflected in higher aggregate scheme expenditures, which would increase by approximately 0.1 percent of the GDP annually compared with the baseline. The pension system deficit would also increase by this same percentage. Such a modest increase in pension value would not change the situation of future pensioners significantly.

In order to investigate how aggregate pension expenditures would rise if all pensioners were given a more substantial increase, another policy simulation assumes *that all old-age pensioners at the time of retirement are entitled to at least 40 percent of their wages* as an old-age pension. If the combined benefit is lower that 40 percent of the final wage, then the public tier benefit is increased so that the total public and private pension equals 40 percent, but if the benefit is higher than 40 percent, then it is paid at its calculated value. After retirement, benefits are indexed as in the baseline scenario by mixed price-wage indexation (20 percent wages, 80 percent prices). In this case, the ratio between the average pension and the average wage would reach 34.8 percent by 2050 (12.4 percent higher than in the baseline), and old-age pension expenditures would rise to four percent of the GDP (compared with 2.1 percent in the baseline). In addition, the total pension deficit would rise to 3.8 percent of the GDP (compared with 2.2 percent under baseline conditions).

Yet another approach to increasing replacement rates is to improve benefit indexation. If the *Swiss indexation of benefits* is assumed (at 50 percent of wages and 50 percent of prices), all pension benefits would be higher compared to the baseline, the increase being higher for disability (6%) and survivor benefits (8%) than for old-age pensions from the new system (1.5%). As a result, total expenditures on pensions by the end of the projection period would be higher by 1.2 percent of the GDP compared with the baseline, which can be broken down into a 0.14 percent rise in expenditures for old-age pensions and a rise of 1.06 percent for disability and survivor pensions. The total pension deficit would increase by approximately one percent of the GDP. If full wage indexation is assumed, rather than a combination of wage and price indexation as provided by the Swiss method, the increase in the deficit would be so much higher that it probably could not be financed in the long run.

A fourth and final policy scenario assumes increasing the retirement age of women to 65. In this case, pension expenditures are slightly higher than the baseline: nearly 11 percent of the GDP would be devoted to pensions by 2050. This result is counterintuitive, since it is usually assumed that an increase in the retirement age results in savings for the pension system. However, these savings are only temporary: when the increase has been fully phased in and the system returns to a steady state, the expenditures return to their former level. This is due to the fact that the NDC pension formula is based on the principle of actuarial neutrality for each insured person, i.e each person receives the pension he or she has 'paid for,' so a higher retirement age will result in higher benefit payments once a person retires. While this principle explains the absence of long-term savings from increasing the retirement age, it does not explain the unexpected long-term costs under this scenario. Another factor is at work here, involving the relatively generous disability benefits in Poland which were not restructured at the time of the old age pension reform, as explained previously. Given these higher disability benefits, a later retirement age induces more older women to apply for disability pensions in their final working years, and the higher benefits they receive causes total pension spending to increase relative to the baseline.

As shown by this sensitivity analysis, various changes in macroeconomic policy and performance can exert a substantial influence on the pension system. Lower growth means relatively higher pension expenditures in relation to the GDP. Increases in wage replacement rates and retirement ages also increase expenditures, the latter being due to the lack of synchronisation between old age and disability benefits, as described previously. In all cases, including the baseline scenario, total pension expenditures are higher than projected revenues, which means that the pension system is generating deficits. If the scheme is divided, however, between old age pensions on the one hand and disability and survivor pensions on the other, it can be observed that expenditures on old-age pensions in almost all scenarios (excluding the one assuming a replacement rate of at least 40 percent) are lower than revenues, and surpluses are generated. In contrast, the simulations show persistent deficits for the case of disability and survivor pensions. The deficits under various reform scenarios are higher than if no further reforms were made, as an increase of retirement age results in an increase in the number of disability pensioners, whereas these people would otherwise be eligible only for old-age pensions. Additional expenditures on disability pensions are lower than savings generated by the reform, however, so from a macro-economic perspective a retirement age increase brings about positive effects. From a microeconomic point of view, the 1999 reform has resulted in a significant reduction in the size of old-age pensions. Significantly, this reduction is greater for women, due to the elimination of redistribution toward low-income workers and the adoption of a new pension formula that incorporates actuarial principles for the calculation of benefits. As policy simulations show, an increase in pension benefits can be achieved in several ways, but these are only significant under the assumptions that a pension that cannot fall below 40 percent of previous wages, and that the retirement age for women will be increased. Full indexation of NDC accounts and higher indexation of pension benefits using the Swiss method both increase old-age pensions granted under the new system by approximately ten percent. Higher indexation additionally implies an increase in the number of disability and survivor pensions, and a widening gap between these benefits and old-age pensions.

3.4. Initial performance of the private tier
3.4.a. Concentration and rotation

A total of 21 pension funds began operating in 1999, most launched by financial institutions (banks, insurance companies etc.) already active in Poland. This was also an opportunity for those foreign companies not yet represented to enter the Polish market.

At the end of June 2001, the total membership of pension funds amounted to almost 10.5 million. As people cannot opt out of the second tier, the number of members will steadily increase in years to come. At this time, the assets of pension funds exceed PLN 11 billion (ca. USD 2.7 billion), as shown in Chart 24. The average monthly contribution to all funds between May 1999 and June 2001 was PLN 106.1 (around USD 25).

Chart 24

OFE assets, January 2000 – June 2001

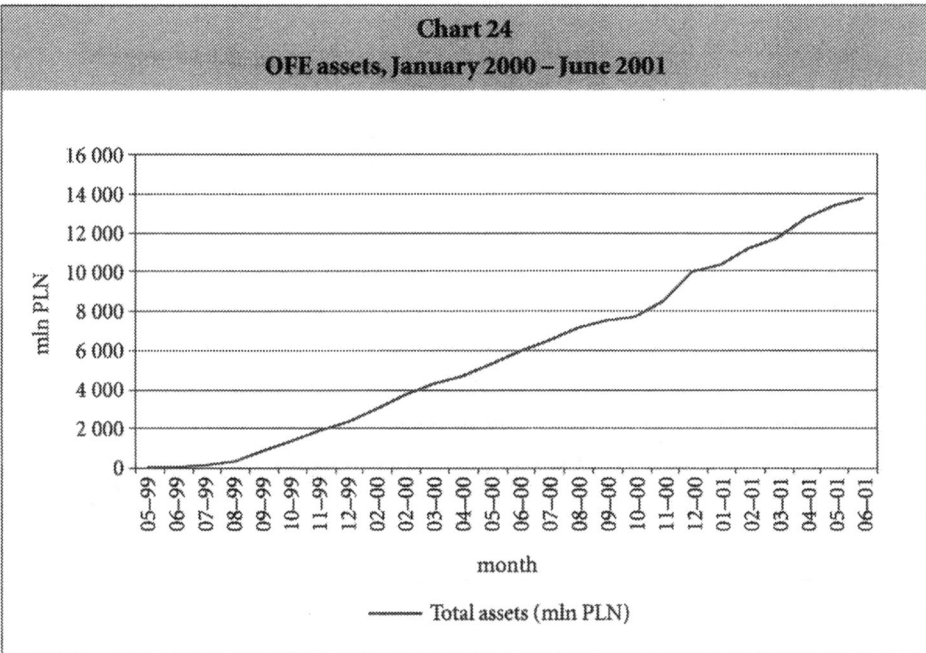

Source: UNFE

It can be observed that the market is concentrated, with the three largest funds having almost 60 percent of all members and 65 percent of the assets (see Chart 25). At the other end of the spectrum, each of the 11 smallest funds possesses less than two percent of all assets, so their total share in the sector does not exceed ten percent. The concentration appears slightly less if membership is taken into account. Smaller funds usually receive lower contributions due to the fact that persons with higher income tended to join the larger ones. Smaller funds also have a larger share of the 'dead accounts' with no contribution registered at all (due to the poorer quality of their sales agents, leading to a higher probability of fraud).

Chart 25
Cumulative membership and assets of pension funds, March 2001

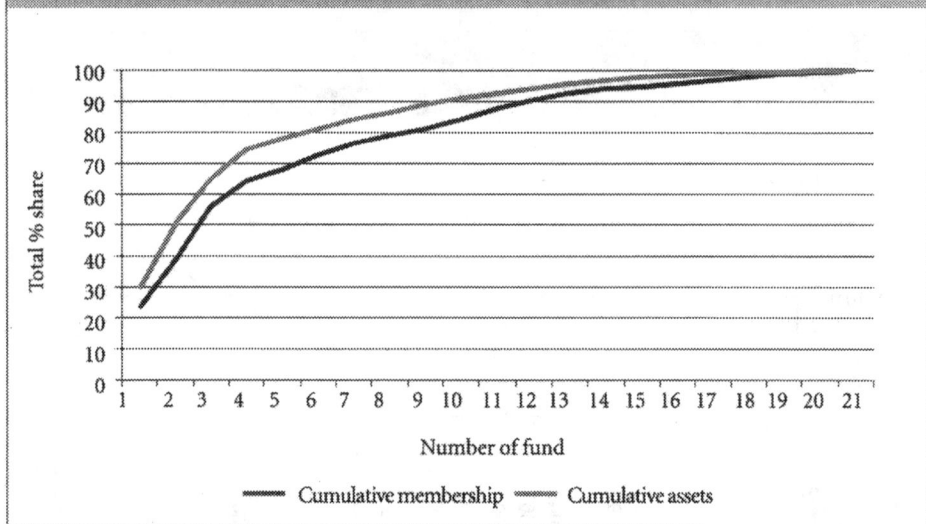

Source: Author's calculations based on UNFE data

A profile of the condition of the various pension funds in June 2001 is presented in Table 13. The list covers the 20 funds (two in liquidation) which were in operation at that time. Since 1999, one pension fund has been sold, and four mergers and acquisitions have been approved by UNFE (one has been completed and the other three are in progress).

According to the 1997 law on the organisation and operation of pension funds, no company can be a shareholder in more than one fund. This means that in the event of a merger between owners of pension funds, either those funds in which they had shares must be merged, or one must be sold. Following the merger of Commercial Union and Norwich Union (each being a shareholder in one pension fund in Poland), UNFE did not agree to a merger of these funds, but instead mandated the sale of one of them. OFE Norwich Union (as the smaller of the two funds) was therefore sold to the Finnish insurer SAMPO. No mergers of pension funds were approved in 1999 or 2000, but in 2001, UNFE agreed to the following:

- Acquisition of EPOKA pension fund by PEKAO PTE (the capital of EPOKA PTE fell below the regulatory minimum, and its shareholders did not agree to an increase, so according to the law, the management of this fund had to be taken over by another fund);

- Merger of pension funds POCZTYLION and ARKA-INVESCO;
- Acquisition of PIONEER pension fund by PEKAO PTE; and
- Acquisition of RODZINA pension fund by PEKAO PTE.

The last three mergers took place as a result of economic necessity. The merging funds had low assets and few members, so their shareholders decided to sell them, as the prospects for profitability were low.

The division of the market presented in Table 13 is not much different from the situation two years earlier.

Table 13					
Basic information on pension funds in Poland					
Name of fund	Membership on 30.06.2001		Assets managed by OFEs on 30.06.2001		Average contribution (19.05.1999– 30.06.2001)
	Total	% share	total in thou. PLN	% share	
AIG	844 632	8.04	1 168 948.2	8.83	113.8
Allianz	205 428	1.95	319 263.7	2.41	132.2
Arka-Invesco (in liquidation)	63 393	0.60	62 918.0	0.48	94.1
Bankowy	388 755	3.70	402 935.3	3.04	103.0
Commercial Union	2 429 168	23.12	2 844 116.4	21.49	113.4
DOM	190 550	1.81	187 120.8	1.41	101.9
Ego	229 969	2.19	191 441.0	1.45	90.8
Kredyt Banku	104 190	0.99	50 387.1	0.38	85.7
Nationale-Nederlanden	1 702 960	16.20	2 834 773.2	21.42	122.2
PBK Orzel	255 346	2.43	190 521.7	1.44	94.4
Pekao	112 147	1.07	120 491.7	0.91	116.4
Pioneer (in liquidation)	113 976	1.08	93 003.8	0.70	98.9
Pocztylion	374 042	3.56	215 544.6	1.63	89.3
Polsat	133 417	1.27	53 804.1	0.41	80.3
PZU Zlota Jesien	1 750 534	16.66	1 933 791.2	14.61	95.5
Rodzina	75 513	0.72	14 845.5	0.11	73.2
Sampo	463 066	4.41	402 439.9	3.04	95.2
Skarbiec-Emerytura	366 076	3.48	307 662.4	2.32	87.9
Winterthur	308 028	2.93	335 658.9	2.54	99.0
Zurich	397 675	3.78	503 970.0	3.81	103.1
Total	**10 508 865**	**100.00**	**13 233 637.5**	**100.00**	**108.1**

Source: UNFE

During the open season for fund selection, the most important factors influencing the decisions of insured persons to join a particular fund were security, potential performance, the recommendation of a friend or family member, and the first agent encountered (see Chart 26). This final factor is also a statistically significant variable in the analysis and explanation of market shares (see Chłoń (2000)).

Chart 26
Factors influencing the choice of pension fund (based on consumer survey)

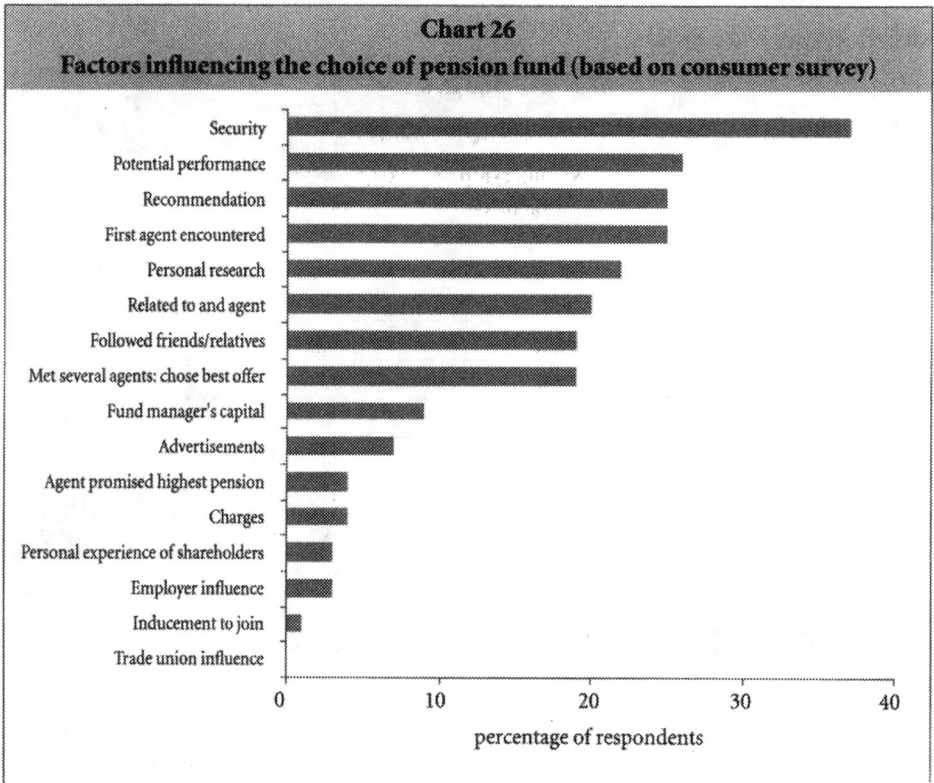

Note: Based on a sample of 1,116 adults under the age 60 in March 2000. Those surveyed could choose up to three answers.
Source: CBOS, March 2000

Before March 2001, very few people decided to change pension funds, although according to the 1997 law on the organisation and operation of pension funds, transfers are permitted quarterly. The first transfer took place in November 1999, when 32 thousand people (0.33 percent of all members) switched. In 2000, slightly more than 135 thousand people (or 1.35 percent of all members) changed their funds, this transfer activity being highest in the first quarter of 2000 and significantly lower for subsequent ones. In the first half of 2001, less than 50 thousand people transferred between funds, but in contrast to the previous year, more people switched funds in the second quarter than in the first (see Table 14).

Table 14			
Transfers of membership between open pension funds			
	Number of transfers	**Total number of members**	**% transfers**
1999–4th quarter	32 075	9 665 819	0.33%
2000–1st quarter	63 440	9 973 302	0.64%
2000–2nd quarter	31 897	10 123 229	0.32%
2000–3rd quarter	21 107	10 281 180	0.21%
2000–4th quarter	19 140	10 419 254	0.18%
2001–1st quarter	17 893	10 466 035	0.17%
2001–2nd quarter	30 100	10 508 865	0.29%

Source: UNFE, quarterly bulletins

Compared with the Latin American experience, where for example in Chile as many as 20 percent of members change their pension funds in one year, the transfers in Poland can be considered negligible.

3.4.b. Contribution compliance

As explained in Section 2, contributions for the second tier as well as for pay-as-you-go are collected by the same institution, ZUS, so compliance in the two tiers from the financial perspective is the same. Since not all contributions reached the private pension funds, however, due to ZUS's difficulties in identifying workers on whose behalf they were made, it is revealing to examine contribution compliance from the point of view of the funds themselves and the amounts they receive.

As discussed in Section 3.3., ZUS estimates that only 70 to 80 percent of contributions reach members' private pension fund accounts, so from the point of view of the funds, compliance is low. One of the most telling factors explaining low compliance is the ratio of 'dead accounts', i.e. those with zero contribution. At the end of June 2001, dead accounts constituted 21.55 percent of all members' accounts, although this ratio varied significantly among the funds. The lowest share is found in the case of Commercial Union PF (8.09 percent) and the highest for Rodzina PF (77.20 percent). One of the hypotheses put forward to explain these differences is the variation in the quality of agents and the recruitment policies of the private pension funds. For those institutions which are backed by larger insurance companies, and therefore used their sales networks, the share of dead accounts seems to be smaller; but for those funds whose sponsors had no experience with sales networks on the Polish market, the share of dead accounts is usually larger. This can be attributed chiefly to the poor quality of sales networks which were build up during 1999. Lured by the prospect of high profits, agents tended to sign contracts even with persons who were not insured. However, the ratio of dead accounts to the total number of accounts is now decreasing: from 2000 until mid 2001 the number of dead accounts fell by almost one fourth (see Table 15). Once ZUS's new IT system is fully operational and a crosscheck between the databases of insured persons and pension fund members is conducted, this ratio should be significantly reduced, as those pension fund members can be eliminated who do not exist and were registered only because agents falsified agreements. The other group to be excluded are those persons who joined pension funds even though they are not insured (e.g. students or the long-term unemployed). Agents frequently signed agreements with such persons simply to obtain their fees, sometimes even providing falsified evidence of employment for them.

	Table 15		
	Dead accounts in open pension funds		
	Number of dead accounts	Total number of accounts	% of dead accounts
2000–1st quarter*	3 069 453	10 433 680	29.42%
2000–2nd quarter	2 891 786	10 484 739	27.58%
2000–3rd quarter	2 698 652	10 614 310	25.42%
2000–4th quarter	2 548 064	10 734 246	23.74%
2001–1st quarter	2 382 117	10 783 212	22.09%
2001–2nd quarter	2 336 481	10 842 306	21.55%

* data for 30.04.2000

Source: UNFE, quarterly bulletins

3.4.c. Portfolio

The investment strategy of pension funds is restricted by regulations which set maximum limits for various types of investments, as well as by the limited development (i.e. 'shallowness') of financial markets in Poland. Before implementation of the reform, many analysts predicted that due to the investment limits and the requirement of a minimum rate of return based on performance of the entire sector, the investment strategies of pension funds would be very conservative. They also assumed that the portfolios of most pension funds would be quite similar (displaying so-called herding behaviour).

The experience of the first two years, however, showed that these predictions were not entirely correct. Average investment in equity represented approximately one quarter to one third of the sector assets (see Chart 27), which means that this was less than ten percent below the regulatory investment limit (40 percent of assets).

Chart 27
Structure of OFE investment portfolio, January 2000–June 2001

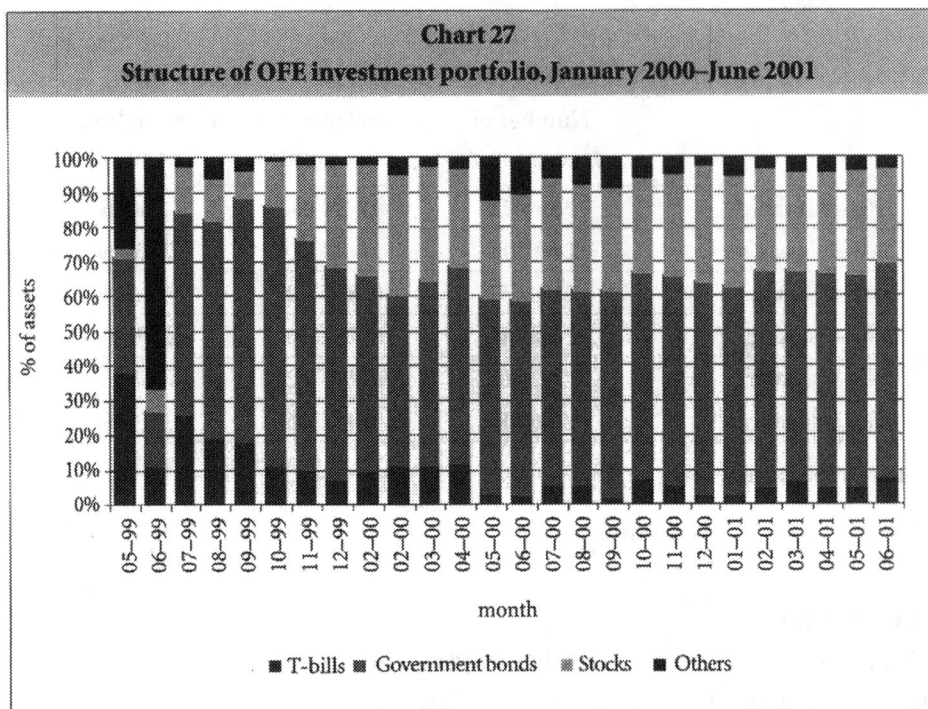

Source: UNFE

The structure of the portfolio also varies among the funds, their respective shares of equities deviating significantly from the average. In June 2001, the share of equity in the average portfolio was 27.4 percent of total assets, but among the funds this ranged from 13.2 percent to 35.6 percent.

As far as other investments are concerned, most private pension fund assets are invested in government bonds (ca. 60 percent) and treasury bills. Other investments (chiefly bank securities and deposits, shares of National Investment Funds, and investment abroad) generally do not exceed five percent of total assets.

The *Security through Diversity* programme held that private pension fund investments would enhance the development of financial markets in Poland and help to accelerate the privatisation process by creating demand for securities on the capital market. The programme also asserted that savings in private pension funds would lead to a higher level of national savings and therefore to higher economic growth. At this early stage, the only claim that can be confirmed with certainty is that private pension funds are becoming an important part of the financial market in Poland. At the end of 1999, the share of pension fund investments in the Warsaw Stock Exchange (WSE) was only around 0.5 percent, but in 2000 this percentage increased more than five times, reaching 2.6 percent of WSE capitalisation. As the assets of pension funds are growing fast, their share on the market will continue to increase in the coming years, but it is difficult to assess the impact of increased pension savings on national savings or economic growth.

On the other hand, expansion of the prefunded tier may create an imbalance on the capital market in the future, with the demand for equity by the funds becoming much higher than supply and resulting in overpricing of the market. In order to avoid this threat, pension funds should be permitted to invest more abroad than the current limit of five percent.

3.4.d. Rates of return and cost-efficiency

As of June 2001, private pension funds had been in operation for two years. At this point, the gross rates of return achieved by all funds were published for the first time by the Superintendency of Pension Funds (UNFE); and the minimum rate of return was calculated. According to many, the performance of the pension funds was unsatisfactory, as the average nominal gross rate of return achieved after two years of performance (from June 1999 to June 2001) was only 22.097 percent.[31] During the same period, the inflation rate was 16.98 percent, WIBOR (Warsaw Inter-Bank Offered Rate) 38.36 percent, and the WSE index fell by 17.12 percent. The rates of return varied among the funds, with 11 out of the 15 reaching rates higher than the average, and four falling below that level. One of the funds (Bankowy) did not achieve the minimum rate of return (50 percent of the average) and had to supplement members' assets from its reserve fund. Results obtained for the listed funds are presented in Chart 28.

---

[31] Calculated for the 15 funds operating for the full 24 months required to calculate the average rate of return.

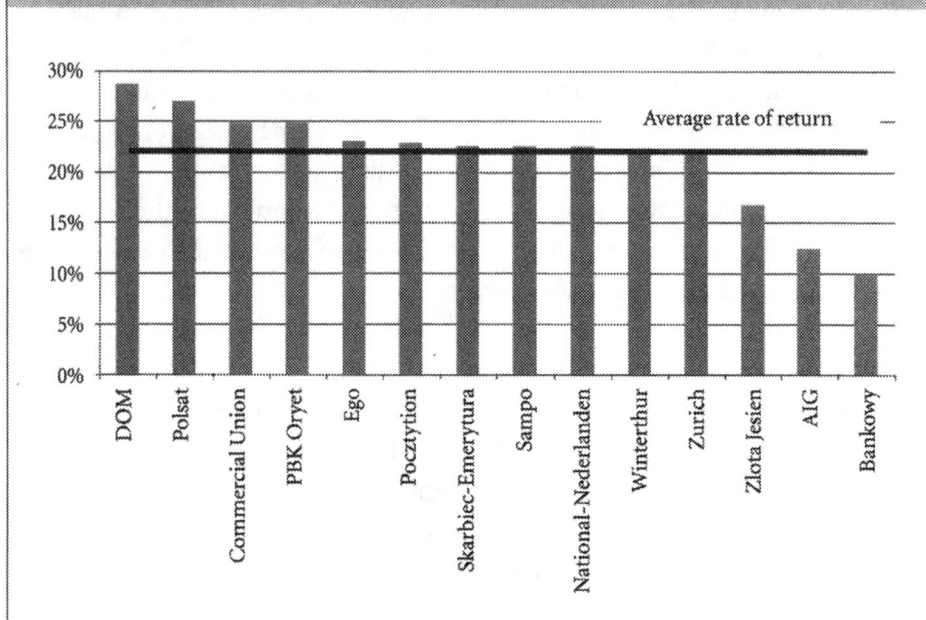

Chart 28
Nominal rates of return for funds (June 1999–May 2001)

Note: Rates of return calculated for those pension funds recording 24 months of operations.

Source: UNFE

The rates specified above show the gross returns without taking into account the fees that pension funds deduct from contributions. Table 16 presents hypothetical values of accounts assuming payment of a monthly contribution of PLN 100 for the period September 1999 to June 2001 (22 contributions in total). As can be seen, the amounts registered on accounts are lower than total payments made by members in all cases. This internal rate of return (IRR) in the period under analysis is therefore negative for all funds, the highest IRR being achieved by Polsat pension fund (–3.54 %) and the lowest by Bankowy (–13.76 %). These results differ from the gross rates of return presented earlier due to the inclusion of fees deducted by funds in the calculation.

Name of Fund	Funds on the member's account (Sep.99–Jun.01)	Internal rate of return
AIG	1982.61	−9.88%
Allianz	2113.11	-3.95%
Bankowy	1897.39	−13.76%
Commercial Union	2078.98	−5.50%
DOM	2089.69	−5.01%
Ego	2079.92	−5.46%
Kredyt Banku	2095.68	−4.74%
Nationale-Nederlanden	2092.13	−4.90%
PBK Orzel	2049.39	−6.85%
Pekao	2090.50	−4.98%
Pocztylion	2069.04	−5.95%
Polsat	2122.18	−3.54%
PZU Zlota Jesien	2055.24	−6.58%
Sampo	2107.13	−4.22%
Skarbiec-Emerytura	2076.67	−5.61%
Winterthur	2083.77	−5.28%
Zurich	2087.90	-5.10%

Table 16
Account status and internal rates of return, January 2000–June 2001

Source: Rzeczpospolita (2001), author's calculations

As the assets of private pension fund members will accumulate in the future, the internal rates of return should grow due to the decrease in the size of fees as a percentage of assets. If the fees and gross rates of return are maintained, the share of fees in total assets should decrease from around ten percent in the first year of participation to five percent in the second, and to less than two percent after five years of participation in a private pension fund.

The assumption of future stability of fees could, however, be questioned based on the funds' high initial operating deficits. That is, the fees deducted by managers are used to finance the activities of pension fund societies, but they do not cover all expenditures, as neither in 1999 nor in 2000 did any pension fund society register profits. This was due chiefly to high operating costs for this period, related mainly to marketing (sales and advertising).

As the various pension funds began operations at different points of time in 1999, the consolidated data for this year are not comparable, so the costs for 2000 will be analysed.

While marketing costs were lower than the year before, they still represented more than half the total expenditures. They are nearly four times higher than the next largest expenditure category, and they exceed the total revenues collected from fees. Table 17 presents a profit and loss account for pension fund societies in 2000. The largest cost items were: sales, costs of transfer agents (contracted-out) or individual account keeping (in house), and deductions for the Reserve Fund.[32] Overall, costs were more than twice as high as revenues from fees.

Table 17
Consolidated profit and loss account for pension fund societies in 2000

	In thou. PLN
Total revenues	726 614.36
Costs of operational activities, including:	1 646 007.34
Sales	811 375.76
Transfer agent or registry of individual accounts	213 093.36
Advertising	68 041.27
Fees for Supervision	942.21
Reserve fund	103 951.07
Guarantee fund	7 135.47
Custodian fees	1 229.91
Taxes and other payments	31 946.93
Amortisation	38 558.21
Other costs	369 735.31
Profit/loss from sales	–919 392.98*
Profit/loss on operational activity	–915 815.57*
Net profit/loss	–847 883.04*

Source: Central Statistical Office
* Include additional items not shown in the table.

[32] Sales costs in 2000 include part of the costs incurred in 1999, which were spread over several years by PTEs.

3.4.e. Public opinion on pension reform – two years later

During reform deliberations, public opinion polls indicated that the pension reform proposed by the government was supported by a majority of respondents. The question arises as to whether this opinion changed after the reform was implemented and, if so, how significantly. According to an opinion survey conducted by CBOS (Public Opinion Survey Centre) in 2001, more than one third (36 %) of Poles have no opinion on the reformed system.[33] The share of those who are not satisfied with the pension system (38 %) prevails over those who are (26 %). Public assessment of the operation of the reformed pension system was similar: 40 percent of respondents could not assess whether the pension system was operating better or worse than before introduction of the reform; 18 percent did not perceive any changes; and of the remaining 41 percent, 28 percent said that operation of the system was worse than before and 13 percent that it was better. It is not surprising that such a large number had no opinion on the new system, as the effects of the reform on pension payments will not appear until 2009.

In addition, almost two fifths of respondents are of the opinion that the pension reform has no impact on them (38 %); 18 percent believe that the reform was not beneficial for them, and 22 percent believe that it was. More than one fifth of respondents (22 %) had no opinion on this subject.

39 percent of people indicated that they would like to introduce some changes in the pension system; 19 percent believed that it does not require any changes; others (42 %) did not have a specific opinion on whether it requires changes or not. Those who wanted to change the system were asked to formulate two proposals. The following were the most frequently suggested measures:

- increase pension payments, minimum benefits and indexation — 27%
- reduce social security contributions — 11%
- improve ZUS operation (introduce individual accounts, improve transfers to pension funds, reduce costs) — 10%
- simplify regulations, distribute improved information on the new pension system, adhere to the principles of the reform — 7%
- change the way contributions are managed, improve investment of contributions — 5%
- return to the old system — 5%

---

[33] See: CBOS (2001)

4. Conclusions

During the course of the 1990s, the pension system in Poland was modified several times. The changes legislated in the second half of the 90s, but before 1999, were aimed at reducing pension expenditures and stabilising the pension system within the traditional defined benefit (DB), pay-as-you-go framework. As indicated by simulations, however, these changes would have been inadequate in the long run and the pension system would have become financially unsustainable, so further changes were required.

Discussions on how to reform the pension system continued for many years, with the debate intensifying after 1995, and a reform programme was finally prepared in 1997 by a team from the Office of the Government Plenipotentiary for pension reform. The introduction of a multi-tier system was envisaged, with a significant prefunded component. The reform programme known as *Security through Diversity* was presented in 1997.

The legislative deliberations of this programme lasted until the end of 1998, and then the final statute was drawn up in a rush resulting in many issues remaining unclear. In fact, not all sections of the legislation were prepared and approved before implementation, so that the bodies serving the pension system, especially ZUS, were not adequately prepared. Individualisation of contributions caused many problems which still have to be addressed more than two years after the launch of the new pension system. Difficulties in the identification of individuals and payments combined with a non-functioning IT system resulted not only in delays in the establishment of individual accounts in the public tier, but also in the inability to transfer contributions to the prefunded tier. In addition, the lack of information on employer payments contributed to a deterioration in the compliance rate in 1999, which in turn caused financial difficulties in the public system, and created a need to take out loans from the state budget as well as commercial banks.

The new pension laws have been amended several times during the past three years, in order to eliminate errors and add provisions which the experience of implementation has shown to be necessary. The legislative process has still not been completed, particularly as two important pieces of legislation have not been enacted: a law on annuities, setting out rules for the prefunded benefit payments, and a law on bridging pensions, which deals with the elimination of early retirement rights.

Few administrative difficulties were encountered due to the creation of the prefunded tier, but after two years of operation, the costs of running pension funds are still relatively high. The most significant expenditure item is sales and marketing, which in 2000 exceeded 50 percent of the total costs of private pension management and surpassed the total fee revenues of the second tier. As a result, despite relatively high fees, the pension fund societies sector ended both 1999 and 2000 in deficit. These early results are not particularly encouraging for pension fund members, since the internal rates of return of all funds for the period up to the end of June 2001 were also negative. In the future, however, as the assets under management increase and the impact of fees is lower, the internal rate of return should become positive.

Pension reform enjoyed significant public support before its implementation, with the majority of Poles favouring a stronger link between contributions and benefits and the introduction of a partially funded system. Two years after implementation, however, the support is not so strong. Almost two fifths of Poles would like to change the pension system again, the most important areas of proposed changes being: increase in pension benefits, reduction of social security contributions, and improvements in social security administration.

As shown by long-term simulations, the old-age pension system is financially stable and even generates a surplus, but this situation is off-set in part by high expenditures on disability and survivor pensions, although the total deficit in the pension system should remain at a level not exceeding 2.5 percent of the GDP annually. Expenditures on the old-age pension system will be reduced by increasing the retirement age and cutting pension benefits, achieved by a combination of changes to the pension formula and introduction of a more restrictive indexation of pension benefits, equal to inflation plus one fifth of real wage growth. According to projections, the relation between pension benefits and the average wage may drop by two thirds as a result of the reform, and this reduction may cause increased poverty among pensioners if unaddressed. The new pension formula also limits redistribution and increases individuality in the pension system, as a person's old-age pension will depend only on contributions paid and group life expectancy. It should be noted that more people will be receiving lower benefits in the future, and the number of pensioners falling below the minimum pension level can be expected to increase.

Savings in the public tier are to a large extent used to finance the transition to a multi-tier scheme. A breakdown of transition costs shows that in the period of

2000-2050, two thirds of the transition deficit (excluding interest paid on loans) is financed by savings in the public system and about one quarter is financed by credit. This means that the highest burden of financing is placed on the shoulders of pensioners. Current and future workers will also finance some of the cost of the reform, as increased debt will have to be paid off, and the rest is assumed to be financed from privatisation revenues. The cumulative transition deficit (including interest costs) will reach almost 100 percent of the GDP by 2050, at the same time as prefunded tier assets are projected to reach 180 percent of the GDP.

Simulations show that the entire pension system (including disability and survivor pensions) is in deficit in spite of the reform. The increase in retirement age places additional pressure on the disability pension scheme, as it leads to growth in the number of disability beneficiaries compared with the no-reform scenario. Thus, savings generated by the reform are offset to an extent by increased expenditures on disability and survivor pensions.

The pension system will need to be monitored in the future, in order to ensure the achievement of its most important task of poverty alleviation. Given the projected declining replacement rates, the factor requiring the closest attention is the size of pensions and related incomes of future pensioners.

References

BUJAK, P., JARMUZEK, M., KORDEL, S., NAWROT, W., AND SMIETANIAK, J. (2001): 'Sredniookresowa projekcja dzialalnosci inwestycyjnej Otwartych Funduszy Emerytalnych na regulowanym rynku gieldowym akcji', CASE, Warsaw

CHLON, A. (2000): 'Pension Reform and Public Information in Poland', Pension Reform Primer series, Social Protection Discussion Paper no. 0019, World Bank, Washington, D.C.

CHLON, A., GORA, M. AND RUTKOWSKI, M. (1999): 'Shaping pension reform in Poland: Security through Diversity', Pension Reform Primer series, Social Protection Discussion Paper no. 9923, World Bank, Washington, D.C.

GOLINOWSKA, S. (1995): 'Wybór reformy systemu emerytalno-rentowego dla Polski', Polityka Spoleczna, No 5/6, pp.1-8.

GOLINOWSKA, S. (1997) (ed.): 'Reforma systemu emerytalno-rentowego', CASE Reports No 6, Warsaw.

GOLINOWSKA, S. (1997): 'Eksperci Banku Swiatowego o reformach emerytalnych w Polsce i na swiecie: propozycje, wzory, kontrowersje', IPiSS, Warsaw.

GOLINOWSKA, S., AND HAUSNER, J. (1998): 'Ekonomia polityczna reformy emerytalnej', CASE Reports No 15, Warsaw.

GORA, M. (1996): 'The Labour Market in Poland: 1990-1995. Empirical and Methodological Studies', Monografie i Opracowania, No. 421, SGH, Warsaw.

GORA, M., AND RUTKOWSKI, M. (1998): 'The quest for pension reform: Poland's Security through Diversity', Office of the Government Plenipotentiary for Social Security Reform, Warsaw.

HAUSNER, J. (1998): 'Security through Diversity: Conditions for Successful Reform of the Pension System in Poland', Collegium Budapest Working Paper, March.

KOLODKO, G. W. (1996): 'Poland 2000: The New Economic Strategy', Poltext, Warsaw.

MINISTRY OF FINANCE (1995): pension reform proposal [in Polish].

MINISTRY OF LABOUR AND SOCIAL POLICY (1995): pension reform proposal [in Polish].

'Modele reformy systemu emerytalno-rentowego i sciezki dojscia. Kolejny etap dyskusji.' (1996): IPiSS quarterly, special edition.

OFFICE OF THE GOVERNMENT PLENIPOTENTIARY FOR SOCIAL SECURITY REFORM (1997): 'Security through Diversity: Reform of the Pension System in Poland', Warsaw.

ORENSTEIN, M. A., (2000): 'How Politics and Institutions Affect Pension Reform in Three Post-communist Countries', World Bank Policy Research Working Paper.

PANEK, T., PODGÓRSKI, J., AND SZULC, A. (1999): 'Ubóstwo: teoria i praktyka pomiaru', Monografie i Opracowania, SGH.

PEREK-BIALAS, J., CHLON-DOMINCZAK, A., AND RUZIK, A. (2001): 'Country Report for Poland, Public Participation and the Pension Policy Process', The Citizen and Pension Reform project, Pont Info.

RZECZPOSPOLITA (2001): 'Moje pieniądze, ranking funduszy emerytalnych', 13.07.

STEPIEN, J. (1999): 'Bilans Funduszy', Media i Marketing Polska.

THOMPSON, L. (1999): 'Administering Individual Accounts in Social Security: The Role of Values and Objectives in Shaping Options', The Retirement Project, Occasional Paper No. 1, The Urban Institute, Washington, DC.

UNFE, quarterly bulletins

UNFE (2001): 'Rynek funduszy emerytalnych w roku 2000.'

VALDES-PRIETO, S. (2000): 'The Financial Stability of Notional Account Pensions', Scandinavian Journal of Economics 102(3), 395–417.

WIKTOROW, A. (1996): 'System emerytalno-rentowy', Przesłanki i możliwości reformowania, IBnGR, Gdansk.

WILCZYNSKA, J. (2000) (ed.): 'Analiza konkurencji na rynku OFE w roku 1999', Allfinance, Warsaw.

WÓYCICKA, I. (1999a) (ed.): 'Model: Budżet polityki społecznej', Metodologia modelu symulacyjnego, IBnGR, Warsaw .

WÓYCICKA, I (1999b) (ed.): 'Strategia Polityki Społecznej 1999–2020', IBnGR, Warsaw.

Appendix A. Investment restrictions

Type of investment	Restrictions set by law			Restrictions set by decrees	
	Minimum (% of assets)	Maximum in one entity	Maximum in dependent entities	Maximum (% of assets)	
				total	One issue
Bonds, treasury bills and other papers issued by government or by Central Bank, loans to government or Central Bank					
Bonds and other credit instruments guaranteed by the State Treasury or Central Bank.		10%			
Bank deposits and papers issued by banks		5%	7.5%	20%	
Regulated stock market equities				40%	
– parallel and free market equities				10%	
– free market equities				5%	
OTC and publicly traded equities				10%	
NIF shares	95%			10%	
Investment certificates of closed-end or mixed investment funds, including				10%	60%	10%
– certificates of closed-end investment funds				5%	
Units of open-end investment funds				15%	
(1) Publicly traded bonds and other fixed-income instruments issued by local authorities				15%	
(2) Publicly traded fully guaranteed bonds and other fixed-income instruments issued by other entities than local authorities, not accepted for public trading				5%	
(3) Bonds and other fixed-income instruments issued by local authorities, not accepted for public trading				10%	
(4) Fully guaranteed bonds and other fixed-income instruments issued by other entities than local authorities, not accepted for public trading				5%	
Bonds and other fixed income instruments issued by public companies, other than those mentioned in points 3 and 4				5%	
Other instruments, allowed by decree of Council of Ministers, including					
– compensation bonds				7.5%	

Appendix B. Long-term simulation results – sensitivity analysis

1. No-reform scenario

	2000	2005	2010	2015	2020	2025	2030	2035	2040	2045	2050
Pension expenditures, of which:	10.96%	10.64%	11.16%	12.75%	14.42%	15.53%	15.61%	15.57%	15.93%	16.60%	17.32%
Old-age	6.05%	6.03%	6.64%	8.10%	9.55%	10.35%	10.16%	9.96%	10.21%	10.81%	11.42%
Disability and survivor	4.91%	4.62%	4.52%	4.64%	4.86%	5.19%	5.46%	5.61%	5.71%	5.78%	5.89%
Pension deficit/surplus, of which	-1.07%	-0.78%	-1.31%	-2.90%	-4.58%	-5.69%	-5.76%	-5.70%	-6.06%	-6.74%	-7.47%
Old-age	-0.11%	-0.09%	-0.71%	-2.18%	-3.63%	-4.42%	-4.23%	-4.02%	-4.28%	-4.89%	-5.50%
Disability and survivor	-0.96%	-0.69%	-0.60%	-0.73%	-0.95%	-1.27%	-1.53%	-1.68%	-1.78%	-1.85%	-1.96%
Number of beneficiaries, of which:	7 172 708	7 551 941	8 263 532	9 476 222	10 851 241	11 841 557	12 290 648	12 732 229	13 383 080	14 158 807	14 798 011
Old-age pension	3 388 800	3 745 037	4 422 244	5 629 264	6 931 104	7 734 860	7 975 607	8 279 206	8 914 695	9 752 110	10 452 115
Disability pension	2 629 419	2 562 198	2 523 932	2 460 924	2 441 541	2 498 832	2 568 476	2 603 968	2 567 295	2 469 207	2 353 256
Survivor pension	1 154 489	1 244 707	1 317 356	1 386 034	1 478 596	1 607 865	1 746 564	1 849 055	1 901 091	1 937 490	1 992 639
Average pension/ average wage ratios:											
Old-age pension (old)	59.9%	60.5%	58.8%	56.5%	53.7%	50.5%	47.1%	43.9%	41.0%	38.2%	35.7%
Disability pension	43.9%	44.3%	43.0%	41.4%	39.3%	37.0%	34.5%	32.2%	30.0%	28.0%	26.1%
Survivor pension	51.8%	52.4%	50.9%	48.9%	46.4%	43.7%	40.8%	38.0%	35.5%	33.1%	30.9%

Source: The Gdansk Institute for Market Economics, Social Budget Model

2. Reform scenario – baseline

	2000	2005	2010	2015	2020	2025	2030	2035	2040	2045	2050
Pension expenditures, of which	10.88%	10.11%	9.68%	9.80%	9.93%	9.91%	9.63%	9.31%	9.17%	9.33%	9.65%
Old-age	6.01%	5.68%	5.27%	4.93%	4.46%	3.85%	3.11%	2.47%	2.08%	2.00%	2.06%
Disability and survivor	4.87%	4.43%	4.41%	4.87%	5.48%	6.06%	6.52%	6.83%	7.09%	7.33%	7.59%
Pension deficit/surplus, of which	-2.30%	-2.18%	-1.19%	-2.24%	-2.49%	-2.50%	-2.23%	-1.90%	-1.76%	-1.92%	-2.24%
Old-age	-1.38%	-1.68%	-0.70%	-1.29%	-0.93%	-0.36%	0.36%	1.00%	1.39%	1.47%	1.41%
Disability and survivor	-0.92%	-0.50%	-0.49%	-0.95%	-1.56%	-2.14%	-2.60%	-2.90%	-3.15%	-3.40%	-3.65%
Number of beneficiaries, of which:	7 174 300	7 483 254	7 742 027	8 248 547	8 859 664	9 219 688	9 347 664	9 466 254	9 689 074	10 039 080	10 307 320
Old-age pension	3 390 151	3 675 109	3 758 389	3 884 533	4 028 611	3 917 212	3 613 700	3 407 450	3 455 866	3 743 150	3 998 731
Disability pension	2 629 653	2 563 416	2 666 155	2 977 388	3 350 754	3 690 476	3 979 511	4 198 465	4 318 148	4 342 155	4 296 663
Survivor pension	1 154 496	1 244 729	1 317 483	1 386 626	1 480 299	1 612 000	1 754 454	1 860 338	1 915 060	1 953 775	2 011 926
Average pension/ average wage ratios:											
Old-age pension (old)	59.9%	60.6%	58.8%	56.5%	53.7%	50.6%	47.2%	44.0%	41.0%	38.3%	35.7%
Old-age pension (new)	0.0%	0.0%	33.5%	34.7%	32.1%	30.4%	28.0%	25.5%	23.2%	22.2%	21.7%
Disability pension	43.9%	44.4%	43.1%	41.4%	39.4%	37.0%	34.6%	32.2%	30.1%	28.0%	26.2%
Survivor pension	51.8%	52.4%	50.9%	48.9%	46.5%	43.7%	40.8%	38.1%	35.5%	33.1%	30.9%

Source: The Gdansk Institute for Market Economics, Social Budget Model

3. Reform scenario – lower labour productivity

	2000	2005	2010	2015	2020	2025	2030	2035	2040	2045	2050
Pension expenditures, of which	10.88%	10.15%	9.89%	10.17%	10.45%	10.55%	10.36%	10.10%	10.03%	10.27%	10.69%
Old-age	6.01%	5.70%	5.38%	5.12%	4.69%	4.10%	3.34%	2.67%	2.25%	2.15%	2.20%
Disability and survivor	4.87%	4.45%	4.51%	5.06%	5.76%	6.45%	7.02%	7.43%	7.78%	8.12%	8.49%
Pension deficit/surplus, of which	−2.30%	−2.22%	−1.45%	−2.61%	−3.00%	−3.13%	−2.95%	−2.68%	−2.61%	−2.85%	−3.27%
Old-age	−1.38%	−1.70%	−0.87%	−1.48%	−1.16%	−0.61%	0.14%	0.81%	1.23%	1.33%	1.28%
Disability and survivor	−0.92%	−0.52%	−0.58%	−1.13%	−1.84%	−2.53%	−3.09%	−3.49%	−3.84%	−4.19%	−4.56%
Number of beneficiaries, of which:	7 174 300	7 483 254	7 742 027	8 248 547	8 859 664	9 219 688	9 347 664	9 466 254	9 689 074	10 039 080	10 307 320
Old-age pension	3 390 151	3 675 109	3 758 389	3 884 533	4 028 611	3 917 212	3 613 700	3 407 450	3 455 866	3 743 150	3 998 731
Disability pension	2 629 653	2 563 416	2 666 155	2 977 388	3 350 754	3 690 476	3 979 511	4 198 465	4 318 148	4 342 155	4 296 663
Survivor pension	1 154 496	1 244 729	1 317 483	1 386 626	1 480 299	1 612 000	1 754 454	1 860 338	1 915 060	1 953 775	2 011 926
Average pension/ average wage ratios:											
Old-age pension (old)	59.9%	60.9%	60.3%	59.1%	57.3%	55.0%	52.3%	49.8%	47.4%	45.0%	42.9%
Old-age pension (new)	0.0%	0.0%	33.8%	35.5%	33.2%	32.0%	29.9%	27.5%	25.3%	24.2%	23.8%
Disability pension	43.9%	44.6%	44.2%	43.3%	42.0%	40.3%	38.3%	36.5%	34.7%	33.0%	31.4%
Survivor pension	51.8%	52.7%	52.2%	51.1%	49.6%	47.6%	45.3%	43.1%	41.0%	39.0%	37.1%

Source: The Gdansk Institute for Market Economics, Social Budget Model

4. Reform scenario – Full NDC indexation

	2000	2005	2010	2015	2020	2025	2030	2035	2040	2045	2050
Pension expenditures, of which	10.88%	10.11%	9.68%	9.83%	10.00%	10.00%	9.72%	9.40%	9.25%	9.41%	9.73%
Old-age	6.01%	5.68%	5.27%	4.95%	4.53%	3.94%	3.20%	2.56%	2.17%	2.09%	2.14%
Disability and survivor	4.87%	4.43%	4.41%	4.87%	5.48%	6.06%	6.52%	6.83%	7.09%	7.33%	7.59%
Pension deficit/surplus, of which	-2.30%	-2.18%	-1.20%	-2.27%	-2.55%	-2.59%	-2.33%	-1.99%	-1.85%	-2.01%	-2.32%
Old-age	-1.38%	-1.68%	-0.71%	-1.32%	-0.99%	-0.45%	0.27%	0.91%	1.31%	1.39%	1.33%
Disability and survivor	-0.92%	-0.50%	-0.49%	-0.95%	-1.56%	-2.14%	-2.60%	-2.90%	-3.15%	-3.40%	-3.65%
Number of beneficiaries, of which:	7 174 300	7 483 254	7 742 027	8 248 547	8 859 664	9 219 688	9 347 664	9 466 254	9 689 074	10 039 080	10 307 320
Old-age pension	3 390 151	3 675 109	3 758 389	3 384 533	4 028 611	3 917 212	3 613 700	3 407 450	3 455 866	3 743 150	3 998 731
Disability pension	2 629 653	2 563 416	2 666 155	2 977 388	3 350 754	3 690 476	3 979 511	4 198 465	4 318 148	4 342 155	4 296 663
Survivor pension	1 154 496	1 244 729	1 317 483	1 386 626	1 480 299	1 612 000	1 754 454	1 860 338	1 915 060	1 953 775	2 011 926
Average pension/ average wage ratios:											
Old-age pension (old)	59.9%	60.6%	588%	56.5%	53.7%	50.6%	47.2%	44.0%	41.0%	38.3%	35.7%
Old-age pension (new)	0.0%	0.0%	34.9%	56.2%	33.9%	32.1%	29.5%	26.8%	24.3%	23.0%	22.4%
Disability pension	43.9%	44.4%	43.1%	41.4%	39.4%	37.0%	34.6%	32.2%	30.1%	28.0%	26.2%
Survivor pension	51.8%	52.4%	50.9%	48.9%	46.5%	43.7%	40.8%	38.1%	35.5%	33.1%	30.9%

Source: The Gdansk Institute for Market Economics, Social Budget Model

5. Reform scenario – replacement rate equal to or higher than 40%

	2000	2005	2010	2015	2020	2025	2030	2035	2040	2045	2050
Pension expenditures, of which	10.88%	10.11%	9.70%	9.90%	10.26%	10.38%	10.20%	10.03%	10.14%	10.60%	11.16%
Old-age	6.01%	5.68%	5.29%	5.02%	4.78%	4.32%	3.69%	3.20%	3.05%	3.27%	3.58%
Disability and survivor	4.87%	4.43%	4.41%	4.87%	5.48%	6.06%	6.52%	6.83%	7.09%	7.33%	7.59%
Pension deficit/surplus, of which	−2.30%	−2.18%	−1.23%	−2.34%	−2.81%	−2.97%	−2.81%	−2.62%	−2.74%	−3.19%	−3.76%
Old-age	−1.38%	−1.68%	−0.74%	−1.39%	−1.25%	−0.83%	−0.21%	0.28%	0.42%	0.20%	−0.10%
Disability and survivor	−0.92%	−0.50%	−0.49%	−0.95%	−1.56%	−2.14%	−2.60%	−2.90%	−3.15%	−3.40%	−3.65%
Number of beneficiaries, of which:	7 174 300	7 483 254	7 742 027	8 248 547	8 859 664	9 219 688	9 347 664	9 466 254	9 689 074	10 039 080	10 307 320
Old-age pension	3 390 151	3 675 109	3 758 389	3 884 533	4 028 611	3 917 212	3 613 700	3 407 450	3 455 866	3 743 150	3 998 731
Disability pension	2 629 653	2 563 416	2 666 155	2 977 388	3 350 754	3 690 476	3 979 511	4 198 465	4 318 148	4 342 155	4 296 663
Survivor pension	1 154 496	1 244 729	1 317 483	1 386 626	1 480 299	1 612 000	1 754 454	1 860 338	1 915 060	1 953 775	2 011 926
Average pension/ average wage ratios:											
Old-age pension (old)	59.9%	60.6%	58.8%	56.5%	53.7%	50.6%	47.2%	44.0%	41.0%	38.3%	35.7%
Old-age pension (new)	0.0%	0.0%	40.3%	40.4%	40.5%	39.1%	37.1%	35.7%	35.2%	35.1%	34.8%
Disability pension	43.9%	44.4%	43.1%	41.4%	39.4%	37.0%	34.6%	32.2%	30.1%	28.0%	26.2%
Survivor pension	51.8%	52.4%	50.9%	48.9%	46.5%	43.7%	40.8%	38.1%	35.5%	33.1%	30.9%

Source: The Gdansk Institute for Market Economics, Social Budget Model

6. Reform scenario – Swiss indexation of benefits (50% wages and 50% prices)

	2000	2005	2010	2015	2020	2025	2030	2035	2040	2045	2050
Pension expenditures, of which	10.88%	10.17%	9.82%	10.06%	10.33%	10.46%	10.34%	10.13%	10.10%	10.39%	10.85%
Old-age	6.01%	5.71%	5.35%	5.06%	4.64%	4.06%	3.33%	2.68%	2.26%	2.15%	2.20%
Disability and survivor	4.87%	4.46%	4.48%	5.00%	5.69%	6.40%	7.01%	7.46%	7.85%	8.23%	8.64%
Pension deficit/surplus, of which	-2.30%	-2.24%	-1.41%	-2.50%	-2.89%	-3.06%	-2.94%	-2.73%	-2.70%	-2.98%	-3.44%
Old-age	-1.38%	-1.71%	-0.85%	-1.42%	-1.11%	-0.58%	0.14%	0.80%	1.22%	1.32%	1.27%
Disability and survivor	-0.92%	-0.53%	-0.55%	-1.08%	-1.78%	-2.48%	-3.08%	-3.53%	-3.92%	-4.30%	-4.71%
Number of beneficiaries, of which:	7 174 300	7 483 254	7 742 027	8 248 547	8 859 664	9 219 688	9 347 664	9 466 254	9 689 074	10 039 080	10 307 320
Old-age pension	3 390 151	3 675 109	3 758 389	3 384 533	4 028 611	3 917 212	3 613 700	3 407 450	3 455 866	3 743 150	3 998 731
Disability pension	2 629 653	2 563 416	2 666 155	2 377 388	3 350 754	3 690 476	3 979 511	4 198 465	4 318 148	4 342 155	4 296 663
Survivor pension	1 154 496	1 244 729	1 317 483	1 386 626	1 480 299	1 612 000	1 754 454	1 860 338	1 915 060	1 953 775	2 011 926
Average pension/ average wage ratios:											
Old-age pension (old)	59.9%	61.0%	59.9%	58.3%	56.5%	54.4%	52.0%	49.8%	47.6%	45.6%	43.6%
Old-age pension (new)	0.0%	0.0%	33.8%	35.2%	33.0%	31.7%	29.7%	27.4%	25.1%	24.0%	23.3%
Disability pension	43.9%	44.7%	43.8%	42.7%	41.4%	39.8%	38.1%	36.5%	34.9%	33.4%	32.0%
Survivor pension	51.8%	52.8%	51.8%	50.5%	48.9%	47.0%	45.0%	43.1%	41.2%	39.4%	37.8%

Source: The Gdańsk Institute for Market Economics, Social Budget Model

7. Reform scenario – retirement age 65 for both men and women

	2000	2005	2010	2015	2020	2025	2030	2035	2040	2045	2050
Pension expenditures, of which	10.88%	10.13%	9.57%	9.37%	9.65%	9.90%	9.82%	9.64%	972%	10.16%	10.80%
Old-age	6.01%	5.69%	5.17%	4.47%	3.96%	3.43%	2.74%	2.14%	1.84%	1.91%	2.17%
Disability and survivor	4.87%	4.44%	4.40%	4.90%	5.69%	6.47%	7.08%	7.50%	7.88%	8.25%	8.63%
Pension deficit/surplus, of which	−2.29%	−2.19%	−1.04%	−1.81%	−2.20%	−2.49%	−2.42%	−2.24%	−2.31%	−2.76%	−3.40%
Old-age	−1.37%	−1.68%	−0.56%	−0.83%	−0.42%	0.06%	0.73%	1.33%	1.64%	1.56%	1.30%
Disability and survivor	−0.92%	−0.51%	−0.48%	−0.98%	−1.78%	−2.56%	−3.16%	−3.57%	−3.95%	−4.32%	−4.70%
Number of beneficiaries, of which:	7 175 155	7 486 270	7 634 139	7 663 971	8 153 776	8 611 673	8 736 136	8 737 670	8 765 982	9 023 044	9 365 915
Old-age pension	3 391 124	3 677 945	3 648 366	3 268 207	3 159 755	3 023 423	2 641 680	2 267 202	2 069 181	2 212 304	2 495 142
Disability pension	2 629 535	2 563 595	2 668 289	3 009 137	3 513 648	3 975 858	4 339 574	4 609 090	4 780 514	4 855 618	4 857 313
Survivor pension	1 154 496	1 244 729	1 317 483	1 386 626	1 480 373	1 612 392	1 754 882	1 861 378	1 916 288	1 955 122	2 013 460
Average pension/ average wage ratios:											
Old-age pension (old)	59.9%	60.4%	58.6%	56.3%	53.6%	50.4%	47.0%	43.8%	40.9%	38.1%	35.6%
Old-age pension (new)	0.0%	0.0%	27.7%	36.6%	38.8%	36.9%	34.5%	31.6%	29.3%	27.4%	26.0%
Disability pension	43.9%	44.2%	43.0%	41.3%	39.2%	36.9%	34.4%	32.1%	30.0%	27.9%	26.1%
Survivor pension	51.8%	52.3%	50.7%	48.7%	46.3%	43.6%	40.7%	37.9%	35.4%	33.0%	30.8%

Source: The Gdansk Institute for Market Economics, Social Budget Model

8. Hypothetical scenario – no second tier

	2000	2005	2010	2015	2020	2025	2030	2035	2040	2045	2050
Pension expenditures, of which	10.91%	10.18%	9.75%	9.89%	10.09%	10.16%	9.96%	9.73%	9.75%	10.15%	10.69%
Old-age	6.04%	5.74%	5.34%	5.02%	4.62%	4.10%	3.44%	2.90%	2.66%	2.82%	3.11%
Disability and survivor	4.87%	4.43%	4.41%	4.87%	5.48%	6.06%	6.52%	6.83%	7.09%	7.33%	7.59%
Pension deficit/surplus, of which	–0.90%	–0.53%	–0.11%	–0.26%	–0.47%	–0.53%	–0.31%	–0.07%	–0.08%	–0.48%	–1.03%
Old-age	0.02%	–0.02%	0.38%	0.69%	1.09%	1.61%	2.28%	2.83%	3.07%	2.91%	2.62%
Disability and survivor	–0.92%	–0.50%	–0.49%	–0.95%	–1.56%	–2.14%	–2.60%	–2.90%	–3.15%	–3.40%	–3.65%
Number of beneficiaries, of which:	7 174 300	7 483 254	7 742 027	8 248 547	8 859 664	9 219 688	9 347 664	9 466 254	9 689 074	10 039 080	10 307 320
Old-age pension	3 390 151	3 675 109	3 758 389	3 884 533	4 028 611	3 917 212	3 613 700	3 407 450	3 455 866	3 743 150	3 998 731
Disability pension	2 629 653	2 563 416	2 666 155	2 977 388	3 350 754	3 690 476	3 979 511	4 198 465	4 318 148	4 342 155	4 296 663
Survivor pension	1 154 496	1 244 729	1 317 483	1 386 626	1 480 299	1 612 000	1 754 454	1 860 338	1 915 060	1 953 775	2 011 926
Average pension/ average wage ratios:											
Old-age pension (old)	59.9%	60.6%	58.8%	56.5%	53.7%	50.6%	47.2%	44.0%	41.0%	38.3%	35.7%
Old-age pension (new)	0.0%	0.0%	33.7%	34.9%	32.4%	30.8%	28.4%	25.8%	23.6%	22.6%	22.0%
Disability pension	43.9%	44.4%	43.1%	41.4%	39.4%	37.0%	34.6%	32.2%	30.1%	28.0%	26.2%
Survivor pension	51.8%	52.4%	50.9%	48.9%	46.5%	43.7%	40.8%	38.1%	35.5%	33.1%	30.9%

Source: The Gdansk Institute for Market Economics, Social Budget Model

www.ingramcontent.com/pod-product-compliance
Lightning Source LLC
Chambersburg PA
CBHW061734270326
41928CB00011B/2231